THE DEVIL'S GARDEN

THE DEVIL'S GARDEN

ROMMEL'S DESPERATE DEFENSE
OF OMAHA BEACH ON D-DAY

Steven Zaloga

STACKPOLE
BOOKS

Published by
STACKPOLE BOOKS
5067 Ritter Road
Mechanicsburg, PA 17055
www.stackpolebooks.com

10 9 8 7 6 5 4 3 2 1

Library of Congress Cataloging-in-Publication Data

Zaloga, Steve, 1952–
    The devil's garden : Rommel's desperate defense of Omaha Beach on D-Day / Steven Zaloga.
        pages cm
    Includes bibliographical references and index.
    ISBN 978-0-8117-1228-6
    1. World War, 1939–1945—Campaigns—France—Normandy.   2. Rommel, Erwin, 1891–1944—
Military leadership.   3. Normandy (France)—History, Military—20th century.   I. Title.
    D756.5.N6Z374 2013
    940.54'21421—dc23
                                                                            2013010197

This book is dedicated to the memory of my father, Sgt. John Zaloga,
who served in the 2nd Battalion, 393rd Engineer Special Service Regiment,
and landed on Omaha Beach on D+15, 21 June 1944.
Also to my grandfather, Sgt. Frank Zaloga, also a U.S. Army engineer,
who landed on Omaha Beach on D-Day.

Contents

Introduction ix

Technical Notes xi

Chapter 1   The Controversy 1

Chapter 2   The Iron Coast 19

Chapter 3   The Rommel Factor 37

Chapter 4   Opposing Forces 53

Chapter 5   Fire and Brimstone 73

Chapter 6   The Devil's Garden 101

Chapter 7   Deadly Geography 125

Chapter 8   The Pigeon Patrol 157

Chapter 9   Day of Reckoning 185

Chapter 10   D-Day Postmortem 229

Appendices 247

Glossary 253

Notes 255

Bibliography 263

Index 269

Introduction

WHY ANOTHER BOOK ABOUT Omaha Beach? D-Day has been the subject of countless books over the years, and Omaha Beach has been the focus of many. I have written two previous books on the subject: one a short campaign history of Omaha Beach and the other a study of German fortifications on the D-Day beaches. The latter project, in 2004, made me realize that the German perspective of D-Day is usually missing, especially in English-language accounts. Some years ago, I read a book entitled *Facing East from Indian Country: A Native History of Early America*. It made me realize that a similar perspective of Omaha Beach would be a valuable addition to our understanding of D-Day.

Most of the recent books on D-Day have been first-person perspectives of the heroism and sacrifice of U.S. soldiers of "the Greatest Generation." This book avoids this approach since it already has been so amply documented. Instead, my focus in this book is battlefield forensics—not so much *what* happened, but *why* it happened. My intention is to explore some of the most neglected aspects of the Omaha Beach fighting and, most especially, the overlooked German side of the battle.

In this book, I have followed three threads to explore this subject. The severe casualties suffered by American forces have led to the nickname "Bloody Omaha." Why were the casualties so high on Omaha compared to the other four D-Day beaches? Not to spoil any surprise, but my conclusion is that the nature of German defenses at Omaha Beach explains much of the casualty disparity. Furthermore, many of the dangerous innovations of the Omaha defenses can be traced back to the actions of Erwin Rommel, the "Desert Fox," who was appointed by Hitler to oversee the anti-invasion efforts in late 1943. This provides the second thread of the book. Rommel was not present at Omaha Beach on D-Day, but his actions in the preceding months strongly shaped the German defenses there on D-Day.[*] Finally, I have been struck by the poor visual record of Omaha Beach available in the published accounts. To help illuminate the description of the German defenses on Omaha Beach, I have attempted to present as complete a picture as possible of the numerous fortifications and weapons present on D-Day. Original German photos of Omaha Beach on D-Day are non-existent, but an ample photographic record of the defenses is scattered through many archives, much of the material previously unpublished. To further amplify these images, I have added my own photos of Omaha Beach that I have taken during the course of several visits starting in the 1980s. I also have compiled numerous maps, architectural models, and computer diagrams to illustrate various historical issues raised in the book.

---

[*]Due to the Channel storm on 4–5 June 1944, Rommel assumed a landing was unlikely and took the opportunity for a short trip back to Germany.

Technical Notes

A few technical notes are worth clarifying at the start of this book. I have left most German unit designations in their original German form since they are easy for an English-reading audience to understand, and they help to distinguish between German and American units. For example, I have used *352.Infanterie-Division* rather than 352nd Infantry Division. I have made a few exceptions for the sake of clarity, using the alternative form *84.Korps* instead of the cumbersome *LXXXIV.Korps*, and using Army Group B instead of *Heeresgruppe B*. I have used English spelling for the German ranks even if they are not entirely equivalent—so lieutenant colonel rather than *Oberstleutnant*. Likewise, I have used the more familiar contemporary style of "mm" (millimeters) for gun calibers rather than the German "cm" (centimeters)—so 50mm gun rather than 5cm gun.

For brevity, the traditional conventions have been used when referring to units. In the case of U.S. units, 2/16th Infantry refers to the 2nd Battalion, 16th Infantry Regiment. The U.S. Army traditionally uses Arabic numerals for divisions and smaller independent formations (29th Division, 741st Tank Battalion), Roman numerals for corps (V Corps), and spelled numbers for field armies (First Army).

In the case of German regiments, an Arabic numeral is used for the smaller formation (com-

pany or battery) and a Roman numeral for the battalion. So *2./Artillerie Regiment.352* refers to the 2nd Battery, 352nd Artillery Regiment; *II./Artillerie-Regiment.352* indicates the 2nd Battalion, 352nd Artillery Regiment. German field armies are contracted in the usual fashion (*7.Armee* for Seventh Army).

Regarding the times presented in this account, on D-Day, the Allies were on British Summer Time (A Time). This was Greenwich mean time (GMT) plus one hour. The *Wehrmacht* operated on the equivalent of British Double Summer Time (B Time), which was GMT+2. So an Allied report of a landing at 0630 hours would be reported by the Germans as 0730 hours. However, some German units in France used the local time, which was the equivalent of British Summer Time. For clarity, the times in this book are British Summer Time as used by the Allies.

The author would like to thank several people for their exceptional help on this project. Andrew E. Woods, research historian at the Col. Robert McCormick Research Center of the First Division Museum at Cantigny, was most helpful in providing material from the museum's collection. Simon Trew of the Royal Military Academy at Sandhurst was most generous with his help on research material and helpful comments. Thanks also to Richard Anderson, Alain Chazette, Emmanuel Ferey, and David Isby for their generous help on this book.

CHAPTER 1

The Controversy

ON 29 JANUARY 1944, FIELD MARSHAL Erwin Rommel conducted a tour along the lower Normandy coast to inspect the progress of anti-invasion efforts. This section of the coast was locally known to the French as Côte de Nacre—the Pearl Coast—because of its white sand beaches. His command car stopped on the bluffs between the small towns of Colleville-sur-Mer and Vierville-sur-Mer, where he looked out over a flat length of beach.* This particular beach was called the Plage d'Or—the Golden Beach—by the local inhabitants. It stretched for about five miles, bounded by high cliffs on either side. It was a popular summer resort for Parisians, and there were numerous cottages along the coast. He was accompanied by the staff of the unit defending this sector, Maj. Gen. Wilhelm Richter's *716.Infanterie-Division*. Rommel noticed the distinct similarity of this beach to the one at Salerno in Italy, where the Allies had staged their amphibious invasion the previous September.

Rommel had begun to question the conviction in Berlin that the Allies would stage their anticipated landings on the Pas-de-Calais. He began to wonder whether Normandy might be a more likely invasion point. His intuitive connection between Salerno and this Normandy beach prompted him to proclaim to the accompanying officers: "This bay must be quickly protected against a possible Allied landing because here will decide the fate of Europe."[1] The Plage d'Or is better known by its later Allied code name, Omaha Beach.

---

*The French suffix "-sur-Mer" means "on the sea." It was added to the names of many coastal villages to distinguish them from similarly named towns elsewhere in France. For example, there are no fewer than three Collevilles, ninety-two Saint Laurents, and three Viervilles in France.

The view that Rommel had of Omaha Beach in 1944 would have been similar to this. This is a view from defense nest WN62 overlooking Fox Red and Fox Green Beaches, as well as the E-3 Colleville draw, with the Plateau du Calvados in the background. The area in the valley is more built-up today than in 1944. AUTHOR

The fighting on "Bloody Omaha" on D-Day, 6 June 1944, was the single costliest day of combat for U.S. forces in World War II. Casualties on Omaha Beach alone were 4,720 men. The horrible price for this small bit of French coastline has been burned into the popular consciousness by the graphic depiction of the slaughter in the film *Saving Private Ryan*. Omaha was one of five landings conducted by the Allies on D-Day. Casualties there totaled nearly as many as the other four beaches combined.

Why were the casualties on Omaha Beach so high? This historical mystery has been the subject of debate for decades. This book will argue that the root cause of the disparity in casualties can be explained by German preparations at Omaha Beach and by the actions of Erwin Rommel in particular.

It is foolish to suggest that a single cause explains a complex historical event. This chapter will begin to explain some of the plausible reasons for the high casualties on Omaha in order to clarify the German role in this battle.

While the German role in "Bloody Omaha" might seem blatantly obvious, details of German actions on Omaha Beach have been shrouded in mystery for decades. The German garrison on Omaha suffered high casualties, and there are only a handful of memoirs by junior soldiers. There were only a few prisoner-of-war interrogations of captured German troops, and they reveal little about German actions on D-Day. Records for the German unit defending Omaha Beach, the *352.Infanterie-Division*, were lost during the war, and the U.S. Army captured very few divisional records later in the war. As a result, most existing accounts of D-Day provide little detail on the German side of the battle.[2]

Although there are scant records of German actions at Omaha Beach on D-Day, there is a surprisingly rich assortment of accounts for the months preceding D-Day. Many of these accounts are little known to American military historians since they have been published in Europe, often in obscure magazines or by small publishers. Besides these accounts, there are extensive documentary records for the higher levels of command above the *352.Infanterie-Division*. They help to illuminate the German preparations for D-Day and to explain why the defenses on Omaha Beach proved to be so much more formidable than on the neighboring D-Day beaches.

Two GIs on board transport ships in the Channel in the days preceding D-Day. NARA

D-DAY AT OMAHA BEACH: A THUMBNAIL SURVEY

It is not the intention of this book to provide a detailed account of the fighting on Omaha Beach. The American side of this story has been told many times, and there are several outstanding studies for readers interested in more detail.[3] Nevertheless, it is necessary to briefly outline the main details of the battle to serve as a framework for later discussions in this book.

The D-Day landings on Omaha Beach were preceded by a naval bombardment from 0545 to 0625 hours. This was far from overwhelming. Some weapons, such as the bombardment rockets, failed to hit their intended targets. The naval gunfire was not sustained enough to damage many of the bunkers or other German defenses. This inadequacy is one plausible explanation for the later problems on Omaha Beach.

The naval bombardment was supplemented by a heavy bomber attack around 0620 hours. The Allies had refrained from bombing the German defenses on the Normandy beaches prior to D-Day, fearing that heavy attacks would reveal the intended location of the landing. Surprise was essential to the landings. The pre-landing bombardment at Omaha Beach in the early morning hours was a complete flop. Cloud cover obscured the beach, and rather than risk hitting Allied forces in the vessels below, the bombers waited about thirty seconds after crossing the beach to drop their loads. As a result, the bomb carpet fell well inland, and the German defenses remained unscathed by air attack—another plausible explanation for the Omaha Beach disaster.

The landing on Omaha Beach was conducted by elements of two American infantry divisions—the

LCVP landing craft head to shore on D-Day under the protective gaze of the USS *Augusta*, the flagship of the Western Task Force. The navy censor has partly obscured the cruiser's radar masts in this photo. NARA

The preliminary naval bombardment of Omaha Beach was of too short a duration to seriously undermine the German defenses. This is the battleship USS *Nevada* , which saw action mainly off the Cotentin Peninsula on D-Day. NARA

1st Infantry Division on the eastern side of the beach and the 29th Division on the western side. The initial landings began with regimental combat teams consisting of an infantry regiment from each division, supported by tanks and engineers. The 16th Infantry Regiment of the 1st Infantry Division landed on the eastern side near Colleville-sur-Mer, and the 116th Infantry Regiment of the 29th landed to the west near Vierville-sur-Mer.

Each of these regimental combat teams was supported by a tank battalion, the 741st Tank Battalion supporting the 16th Infantry and the 743rd supporting the 116th Infantry. These tank battalions were equipped with specialized versions of the Sherman tank designed for amphibious operations. Two of the three companies in each battalion had DD (Duplex Drive) swimming tanks, while the third had Sherman tanks fitted with deep-wading gear.[4] The DD tanks were designed to be launched from off shore and swim into the beach in advance of the infantry. They were instructed to sit in the water, up to the depth of their turrets, and fire at German strongpoints. The companies with deep-wading gear were landed directly near the beach from their landing craft after the DD tanks. This initial tank landing was a small-scale disaster. The two DD tank companies of the 741st Tank Battalion on the eastern side followed procedure and were launched from 5,000 yards off shore; most of these tanks sank on the way into the beach. The DD tanks from the 743rd Tank Battalion were landed directly on the beach from their landing craft, and so most survived. The loss of nearly two entire companies of DD tanks has been frequently exaggerated in many accounts, which suggest that most or all of the supporting tanks sank; in fact, only two of six tank companies were lost. Nevertheless, the weakened tank force has often been proposed as a reason for the subsequent failures on Omaha Beach.

One of the firepower innovations for D-Day was the conversion of LCT landing craft to carry hundreds of 5-inch bombardment rockets. These proved to be a major disappointment on Omaha Beach, where most missed their intended targets. This photo shows LCT(R)-125 on a practice mission before D-Day. NARA

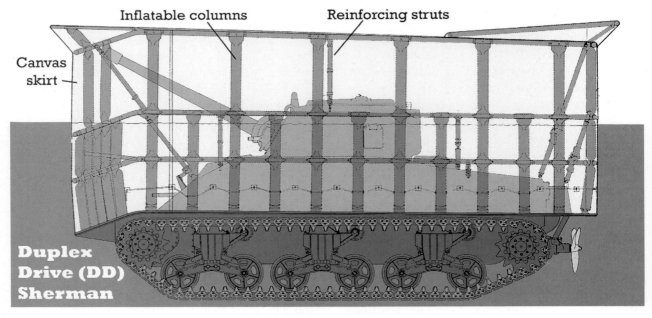

The DD (Duplex Drive) amphibious tanks were derisively referred to as "thirty tons of steel in a canvas bucket" by their crews because of their dubious floating qualities in rough water. They consisted of an M4A1 Sherman medium tank with a canvas screen erected by pneumatic tubes and a propeller driven off the main drive train. AUTHOR

Only five DD tanks of the 741st Tank Battalion reached shore, and most were knocked out in the subsequent fighting. This is a rare view of one of them, stuck in the shingle on the beach near the Colleville draw. NARA

Besides the DD tanks, the two tank battalions at Omaha Beach also had a company of M4 tanks fitted with deep-wading trunks to permit them to wade ashore from the landing craft. Above are an M4 dozer tank and M4A1 with M8 ammo trailer (named *Aide de Camp*) of Company A, 741st Tank Battalion, on board their LCT(A) prior to departure for Omaha Beach in June 1944. NARA

LCT(A)-2273 is seen carrying tanks of Company A, 743rd Tank Battalion, to the Vierville draw area of Omaha Beach on the morning of D-Day. This shows the standard load on D-Day, with two M4 tanks on elevated platforms in front and an M4 dozer tank behind them. This craft was damaged by German shore fire and split in half; it sank later in the day after delivering the tanks. NARA

Shortly after the tanks landed, the first waves of infantry disembarked from their landing craft, starting around 0630 hours. The first two regiments ashore suffered the worst casualties. During the course of the day, the 16th Infantry Regiment suffered 971 casualties and the 116th suffered 1,007—about a third of their men.

The other units to suffer horrendous losses were the Gap Assault Teams, specialized detachments of navy and army engineers assigned to destroy the German obstacles near the beach. The D-Day landings took place at low tide so that the landing craft could avoid the obstacles. But with the tide rising after dawn, the obstacles had to be removed to clear the way for later waves of landing craft. These engineer troops attempted to plant demolition charges on the obstacles to clear paths, but the process proved far more difficult than anticipated. The Gap Assault Teams suffered 41 percent casualties, the highest casualties of any single element of the D-Day force.

Landing the first Regimental Combat Teams was scheduled to take three hours, from 0630 to 0930 hours. By the time the second wave was

An LCVP carrying elements of the 16th Regimental Combat Team approaches Omaha Beach near the E-3 Colleville exit. NARA

scheduled to arrive, the tide had risen. The undamaged German beach obstacles blocked their path to shore and the beachmasters shut down further traffic to the beach around 0830 hours. In this critical interlude during midmorning, the two infantry regiments ashore were trapped on the beach and subjected to continual fire from the German defenders with no reinforcement. Finally, the young navy and coast guard craft commanders decided to ignore the obstacle threat and simply plow through to the beach. Landing craft losses were high, but the second wave began to arrive on Omaha Beach after 1000 hours. The flotilla bring-

ing the 18th Infantry ashore on the eastern side lost twenty-two LCVP, two LCI, and four LCT craft because German defenses were still relatively intact.

The tide began to turn in favor of U.S. forces in late morning. Small penetrations had been made through German defenses by midmorning, and the arrival of the second wave from 1000 to 1130 hours added to the momentum. Several of the most dangerous German defenses were abandoned or overrun from noon to early afternoon. The battle for Omaha Beach was not over, but the American forces were firmly ashore.

An LCVP from the USS *Samuel Chase* was hit by German fire as it approached the beach; the fire detonated explosives carried by the infantry and started a fire. The craft landed safely and later returned to the transport. NARA

The final approach to the beach by LCVPs carrying the 16th RCT from the USS *Samuel Chase* during the second wave on D-Day around 0730 hours. There are already troops on the beach ahead. NARA

An iconic image of D-Day at Omaha Beach as seen by a U.S. Coast Guard photographer on an LCVP landing troops of 1/16th Infantry on Easy Red Beach. The tank visible in the foreground is A-9, one of the few M4A1 tanks from the ill-fated 741st Tank Battalion to make it ashore. NARA

COMPARING THE CASUALTIES

As mentioned earlier, casualties on Omaha Beach represented the single most intense bloodletting suffered by American forces in any single day of fighting during World War II. One official account put casualties at 2,476, but a more recent study places the total at 4,720.[5] Total American D-Day losses, including Utah Beach and the extensive airborne operation, brought the total casualties to over 6,600 men. The next closest casualty counts were Pearl Harbor with about 3,585 casualties in a single day of fighting and the landings on Tarawa on 20 November 1943, when the U.S. Marines and U.S. Navy suffered 3,407 casualties in three days of fighting.

What was especially shocking about the intensity of casualties on Omaha Beach was the comparison between the casualties there and on the other four D-Day beaches. As can be seen from the table below, casualties on Omaha Beach were comparable to total Allied casualties on the other four beaches *combined*, even if the lower V Corps casualty reports are used. Total casualties on D-Day remain controversial, in part because different accounts use different parameters. For example, some count only the casualties suffered in the immediate beach landings, while others include all casualties suffered on D-Day. The table below shows the estimates in the 1945 AORG study compared to a contemporary assessment of overall D-Day casualties by historian Richard Anderson based on more recent research.

Why were casualties at Omaha Beach so much higher than at the other beaches? This question has baffled historians for more than half a century. Part of the problem has been the lack of data. Although casualty figures are relatively well known, the cause of the casualties has never been accurately explained. Were the U.S. troops killed by small-arms fire? Machine guns? Mortars? Artillery? If figures were available for the cause of casualties, it might be easier to pinpoint the answer to the casualty question. However, such a tally was not compiled at the time, nor is it likely that such a tally can ever be made with any degree of accuracy.

The other way to tally the source of the bloodshed is from the German side. How much firepower was available to the Germans defending the Normandy beaches? In this respect, more data is available, though it is far from complete.

The first attempt to analyze the Omaha Beach casualties was conducted by the British Army Operational Research Group (AORG) in August 1945.[6] This secret report was not declassified in the U.S. until 1984, forty years after D-Day, and so is not particularly well known. This study examined five possible tactical reasons for the casualty discrepancy:

- Strength of beach defenses
- Strength of beach obstacles
- Weight of fire preparation
- Use of DD tanks
- Quality and number of defending troops

The study began by assessing the casualty disparity. These differ from the numbers presented earlier here, but this discrepancy results in part from more recent research, as well as the issue of which casualties are counted and which are omitted. The report summary, though, is still useful in showing the scale of the disparity (Table 2).

TABLE 1: D-DAY ARMY CASUALTIES BY BEACH					
	Omaha *U.S.*	Utah *U.S.*	Gold *British*	Juno *Canadian*	Sword *British*
AORG estimate	2,476	315	460	1,140	630
Contemporary assessment	3,686	589	1,023	1,242	1,304

TABLE 2: SUMMARY OF AORG REPORT					
Beaches	Utah	Omaha	Gold	Juno	Sword
Forces Employed	U.S.	U.S.	British	Canadian	British
Approx. troops landed on D-Day	21,300	34,200	25,000	24,000	28,800
Approx. casualties on D-Day	300	3,000	413	805	630
% casualties	1.4	8.8	1.7	3.4	2.2

TABLE 2a: GERMAN FIREPOWER ON D-DAY BEACHES					
Beaches	Utah	Omaha	Gold	Juno	Sword
Antitank guns (37–88mm)	14	18	9	9	7
Mortars	0	6	1	5	7
Machine guns	65	85	18	33	14
Length of beach (yards)	9,600	7,500	7,000	4,500	2,000

TABLE 2b: GERMAN FIREPOWER DENSITY PER 1,000 YARDS					
Beaches	Utah	Omaha	Gold	Juno	Sword
Guns	1.46	2.4	1.3	2.0	3.5
Mortars	0	0.8	0.14	1.2	3.5
Machine Guns	6.8	11.3	2.6	7.3	7.0

The study then began its assessment by calculating the numbers of major weapons defending the beaches to determine whether there was a major discrepancy in firepower (Table 2a).

Using these numbers, the British research teams then assessed how much firepower was available per 1,000 yards of landing beach to see if there was a major difference in density of firepower (Table 2b).

The study concluded that there was indeed a noticeable difference in German firepower on Omaha Beach. Furthermore, the report noted that the survey did not include other sources of firepower available to the German forces. For example, Omaha was subjected to fire from *Werfer* artillery rockets not common on the other beaches.

However, this study had notable flaws. The figures on Utah Beach are misleading since they cover a much wider section of beach than the actual area assaulted on D-Day. In fact, Utah Beach was much narrower and had much less firepower than these figures would suggest. Also, some of the figures for German defensive firepower are not particularly accurate compared to more recent research. Finally, and most importantly, the study did not examine the role of German field artillery in the battle. Field artillery was the primary cause of battlefield casualties in World War I and World War II, often

The strong eastward tide pushed many units away from their intended landing zones, sometimes to the benefit of the troops. These troops are landing on Fox Red Beach at the eastern end under resistance nest WN60. The cliffs in this sector shielded the troops from the German forces above. NARA

After the first waves, the larger LCI landing craft were used based on the expectation that German resistance would have subsided. LCI-83 first tried landing at 0830 hours but was unable to do so, transferring some of the troops of the 20th Engineer Battalion to shore via LCVPs. Another attempt around 1115 hours (as seen here) was more successful, but the craft was struck by an artillery round, killing seven and damaging a ramp. Two of the M4A1 tanks of Company A, 741st Tank Battalion, are visible farther down the beach. NARA

Infantry go ashore in an LCVP in one of the later waves. Equipment and vehicles can already be seen on the beach ahead. NARA

accounting for 70–80 percent of casualties. This issue will be discussed in more detail later in the book. As a hint of later discussions, the amount of field artillery directed against Omaha Beach was significantly higher than the other Allied beaches, further reinforcing the study's conclusions.

Although no detailed casualty statistics were gathered for Omaha Beach, the British found that each German 81mm mortar caused three times as many casualties as every machine gun or 50mm light mortar on the British/Canadian beaches. Therefore, they attempted to assess whether the number of crew-served heavy weapons could help

explain the number of casualties on the D-Day beaches. The German firepower was summarized as "MG equivalents," with 81mm mortars valued as three and machine guns and 50mm mortars as one. The results from this survey were inconclusive (Table 2c). Utah showed an unusually high ratio of crew-served weapons per casualty, but as mentioned earlier, the British study used a particularly excessive beach frontage for Utah Beach, which helps accounts for this numerical outlier. In the end, the British study discounted crew-served weapons as a satisfactory explanation for the casualty discrepancy.

TABLE 2c: GERMAN CREW-SERVED WEAPONS DENSITY ON D-DAY BEACHES					
Beaches	**Utah**	**Omaha**	**Gold**	**Juno**	**Sword**
MG equivalents	65	103	21.5	45	35.5
Casualties	300	3,000	413	805	630
Casualties per MG equivalent	0.26	0.08	0.09	0.07	0.11

TABLE 2d: GERMAN TROOP DENSITY PER 1,000 YARDS					
Beaches	**Utah**	**Omaha**	**Gold**	**Juno**	**Sword**
MG equivalents	6.4	14.0	3.0	10.0	17.7

TABLE 2e: ALLIED NAVAL GUNFIRE DENSITY ON D-DAY BEACHES					
Beaches	**Utah**	**Omaha**	**Gold**	**Juno**	**Sword**
Density	0.22–0.26	0.04–0.08	0.09	0.07	0.11

TABLE 2f: OBSTACLE DENSITY ON D-DAY BEACHES					
Beaches	**Utah**	**Omaha**	**Gold**	**Juno**	**Sword**
Obstacles per yard	0.41	0.49	0.43	0.47	0.30
Weight of obstacles per yard (pounds)	250	401	394	340	217

The AORG report also studied the number of German troops facing the beaches and calculated their firepower in "MG equivalents" per 1,000 yards (Table 2d). The report found that Omaha Beach was defended by more troops than most, but not all, of the British/Canadian beaches. It concluded that this factor alone offered no predictive value for the casualty-gap question since Sword Beach had greater troop density than Omaha yet markedly lower casualties. As will be detailed later, this analysis can be questioned since it underestimated the actual German troop density on Omaha.

The AORG study then examined the amount of naval gunfire directed against German beaches to determine whether the amount of naval bombardment was significantly different (Table 2e). The study did conclude that there was some difference, but that data made it difficult to be precise how great the difference was on D-Day. The values on the chart are expressed in terms of pounds per square yard equivalent to the standard British 25-pdr. field gun.

Omaha Beach received a lower density of naval bombardment than the other beaches, but the number was not so far removed from the other beaches as to offer a satisfactory explanation for the casualty discrepancy. This issue has not been thoroughly examined since but will be detailed later in this book.[7]

Heavy construction equipment goes ashore later in the day after the tide changed. This appears to be in front of the D-3 Les Moulins draw. There are a number of drowned trucks in the foreground. NARA

The AORG study then examined the density of beach obstacles as a possible causative factor (Table 2f). The idea behind this consideration was to calculate the delaying factor that the obstacles might have had in reinforcing the beach assault. The study could find no correlation between the obstacle density and the casualty discrepancy. Indeed, it was pointed out that the Gap Assault Teams on Omaha had between thirty minutes and an hour extra to work on the obstacles than was the case on some of the British beaches. What this calculation did not assess was the actual progress of the teams. As mentioned earlier, the heavy losses of the Omaha Beach Gap Assault Teams precluded a successful clearance of much of the beach. In more clinical terms, German firepower enhanced the value of the obstacles on Omaha Beach since it prevented the Gap Assault Teams from conducting their clearance work.

The AORG study then turned to tank support as a possible means to explain the casualty gap. The study had reasonably accurate figures for the British beaches but lacked accurate figures for Omaha Beach. The study concluded that the U.S. landed twenty-six tanks on D-Day out of fifty-three launched. As a result, the study concluded that the tank shortage was one plausible explanation for the Omaha Beach casualties. The report noted: "Conditions on Omaha resemble in some respects those at Dieppe during the Canadian raid of Aug. 19, 1942." In both cases, troops on the beach were enfiladed by fire from strong natural positions, and in both cases there were few tanks available to support the infantry in the early stages of the assault. However, these numbers were considerably mistaken since they failed to consider the deep-wading tanks used on the American beaches. This issue also will be detailed later in this book.

The British AORG study concluded that the casualty gap was best explained by the German defenses, most notably the heavy weapons available on Omaha Beach, as well as by the shortage of tanks. In the following chapters, we will examine how this analysis has held up when compared to more recent research.

CHAPTER 2

The Iron Coast

TAKING A STROLL ALONG THE FRENCH COAST, the casual tourist is greeted by a succession of megalithic concrete blocks. At times, they seem like evidence of a lost world. Many lie partially buried in the sand or sit lopsided on the beach, victims of the sea's erosion. Others sit like massive concrete sentinels on the cliffs overlooking the English Channel. These are the remnants of the Atlantic Wall, erected by Nazi Germany as the outer protective barrier of Fortress Europe. They constitute the largest military fortification program in modern history, dwarfing the much smaller French Maginot Line in length, volume, and cost. To better understand how the Germans planned to defeat the Allied invasion, it is necessary to understand how they planned to defend the Atlantic coast.

The focus of German activity on the French coast in 1940–41 was primarily offensive, not defensive. The major French ports on the English Channel and the Atlantic coast were an essential ingredient in the *Kriegsmarine* effort to strangle Great Britain by means of a U-boat campaign against its vital shipping. As an architectural adjunct to this effort, Germany poured most of its construction resources into modernizing and fortifying the ports, especially the U-boat facilities. This initial focus on ports and harbors shifted the center of gravity of German fortification in France toward port defense.

As the war dragged on into 1942 and 1943, the probability of an Allied invasion of France continued to increase. Germany faced a classic dilemma when planning its anti-invasion strategy. Should the coast be fortified and the invasion crushed on the beach? Or should the defense be based on mobile reserves that would wait for the Allies to

The French coast remains an elephant's graveyard of concrete bunkers from the Atlantic Wall program. This is a jumble of bunkers from Strongpoint 120 Pommern, located on the beach south of Wissant. AUTHOR

Hitler's ideas for the Atlantic Wall were strongly influenced by the success of the heavily fortified U-boat bunkers built in the French Atlantic ports to ward off British heavy bomber attacks. These massive structures consumed most of the military construction resources in France in 1941–42. LIBRARY OF CONGRESS

land and then mass a counterattack force to crush the beachhead? Traditional German doctrine favored the latter approach. Frederick the Great once said: "Who defends everything, defends nothing." His point was that any defensive scheme that spread out the defensive assets equally, in a linear fashion, was bound to fail since the enemy could mass its forces against a single segment of the defenses and overwhelm them. Yet Germany's anti-invasion strategy became based on a linear defense scheme—the Atlantic Wall.

The reason for the disharmony between traditional German anti-invasion doctrine and the actual Atlantic Wall scheme was that this coastal fortification program was the brainchild of Adolf Hitler, not the German General Staff. Hitler was an avid architecture buff, intent on creating a permanent reminder of the Thousand-Year Reich. He viewed Nazi Germany as the natural successor to the Roman Empire and was determined to create an architectural legacy of imposing structures to rival Rome's. This obsession with military fortification was no doubt reinforced by his own experiences as a young soldier in the trenches in World War I, where deep bunkers provided the only relief from the hellish onslaught of modern firepower.

Hitler's first military fortification program was the *Westwall*, built in 1936–39 as a linear defense of Germany's western border opposite the French Maginot Line. The *Westwall* was not as elaborate as the Maginot Line, and its intent was more political and psychological than military. In contrast to the secrecy that enveloped most fortification efforts, Hitler proudly proclaimed the power of the *Westwall* in speeches and the media with numerous photos and publicly released film of the fortification line. This propaganda was intended to create the image of an impregnable barrier as strong as the Maginot Line. It was a bluff. The *Westwall* was intended to discourage the French and British from striking western Germany when the *Wehrmacht* began its conquests in central Europe. The *Wehrmacht* was still weak during the Czech crisis of 1938. During the invasion of Poland in 1939, the *Westwall* shielded Germany's western frontiers while the bulk of the army crushed Poland in a lightning blow.

The appointment of Field Marshal Gerd von Rundstedt to head the OB-West in 1943 was the first sign of Hitler's effort to reinvigorate the anti-invasion front in France. NARA

The success of the *Westwall* encouraged Hitler's later fortification schemes. There was very little effort made to fortify the French coast through the summer of 1941. Indeed, in the spring and summer of 1941, there were explicit instructions against fortification efforts since it might hint that the *Wehrmacht*'s intention had shifted from the invasion of Britain to the invasion of Russia. Construction efforts in 1940–1941 focused on the fortification of U-boat bunkers and the reinforcement of major ports. This attitude slowly began to change following the invasion of the Soviet Union in June 1941. The Russian campaign inevitably drained troops from occupation duty in France and Western Europe, and British commando raids on the northern Norwegian coast in March and December 1941 created anxieties about the vulnerabilities of the long stretches of undefended coastline. This prompted a Führer directive on 14 December 1941 ordering the construction of a "new *Westwall*." The directive recognized that the Western Front was seriously short of troops because of the war in Russia and planned to substitute fortification for manpower.

British commando raids continued in early 1942, including a daring raid on Bruneval on the French coast to steal a top-secret radar. Another directive on 23 March 1942 began to refine the idea of a major fortification scheme for the Atlantic coast. These early plans were mainly intended to deal with the threat of commando raids, not a full-blown invasion, so first priority was given to Nor-

The propaganda image of the Atlantic Wall focused on the massive gun bunkers erected on the Pas-de-Calais opposite the English coast. This is *Batterie Todt*, named after Fritz Todt, the head of Germany's paramilitary construction industry, *Organisation Todt*. He was killed in a plane crash in 1942 and his place taken by Albert Speer. This battery consisted of four massive 380mm guns and was located at Cap Gris Nez. LIBRARY OF CONGRESS

way and the Channel Islands rather than the French coast. The ink was hardly dry on the new directive when the British staged a spectacular seaborne raid on the port of St. Nazaire on the French coast, severely damaging the vital dry docks used to repair German warships operating in the Atlantic. This forced Hitler to place a new emphasis on port defense to prevent a repeat of the St. Nazaire raid.

The first major planning meeting for the Atlantic Wall followed in May 1942. Hitler assigned the construction of the Atlantic Wall to *Organisation Todt*, the paramilitary construction organization created in the 1930s to undertake major state projects, including the *Autobahn* and the *Westwall* defensive fortifications.

On 13 August 1942, Hitler held a meeting with the senior leadership of the construction industry to outline the strategic aim of the Atlantic Wall:

> There is only one battle front [the Russian Front]. The other fronts can only be defended with modest forces. . . . During the winter, with fanatical zeal, a fortress must be built which will hold in all circumstances . . . except by an attack lasting for weeks.

Hitler planned to defend the 3,800 kilometers (2,400 miles) of Atlantic coastline from Spain to Norway with 15,000 bunkers and 300,000 troops. The Atlantic Wall was to be completed by May 1943, the earliest time an Allied invasion was likely. Hitler emphasized the defense of ports that were viewed as the most likely Allied objectives. The open beaches between ports were assigned a lower priority and punctuated by a modest string of gun batteries and earthworks.

Days after the meeting, on 17 August 1942, the British and Canadians struck with their largest raid yet at the port of Dieppe on the French coast in Upper Normandy. The Dieppe raid was an embarrassing and costly fiasco and demonstrated that even a modestly fortified port could be defended. For Hitler, the Dieppe raid reaffirmed the value of coastal defenses to enable weak and badly overex-

tended *Wehrmacht* units in France to defeat amphibious attacks. It also reinforced his conviction that the main Allied invasion would be directed against a port. Some German officers felt the success in repelling the Dieppe raid was exaggerated, warping later plans for the defense of France. Gen. Freiherr Leo Geyr von Schweppenburg, who later led the *panzer* forces in France during the Normandy campaign, argued:

> The basic misconception of the anti-invasion defense stemmed from the opinions based on the Dieppe raid. The personal ambition of a certain military personality[*] in the west, and above all, the subsequent propaganda nonsense, had changed the story of the Anglo-Saxon experimental raid on Dieppe into a fairy tale of defensive success against a major landing attempt. This was all the more irresponsible, as captured orders clearly indicated a time limit for the operation. The self-satisfied interpretation could never be dislodged from the minds of high command. Together with Rommel's fallacious theories of defense, it was responsible for the grotesque German situation (in France).

Construction of the Atlantic Wall began in earnest in June 1942 and accelerated through 1942–43. The portions in France alone consumed more than 17 million cubic meters of concrete and 1.2 million tons of steel, and cost some 3.7 billion Reichsmark. The steel consumption was about 5 percent of German annual production—roughly equivalent to the annual amount used in German tank production.

German construction resources were not limitless, and the Atlantic Wall could not be equally strong all along the coast. German intelligence believed that the Pas-de-Calais was the most likely invasion site since it was the closest to Britain and offered a prompt route to Germany's industrial heartland in the Ruhr. The Belgian and Dutch coasts were also of special concern to German

---

[*]The "certain personality" referred to Gen. Maj. Kurt Zeitzler, who was chief of staff of Rundstedt's OB-West headquarters and who frequently quarreled with Schweppenburg over defense doctrine.

planners. Over the centuries, these had been traditional invasion routes between England and the Continent. These coastal areas had major ports such as Antwerp, Rotterdam, and Amsterdam, which would be essential for supplying the invading Allied armies. Not surprisingly, most of the construction work in 1942–43 occurred in these areas.

The Pas-de-Calais was dubbed "the Iron Coast" for the sheer volume of artillery batteries dotting the beaches. In contrast, landings in Normandy were considered unlikely, and very little construction took place there except for major ports, such as Cherbourg and Le Havre. For example, the *84.Korps* in Lower Normandy in 1943 was allotted only 20,000 metric tons of concrete for fortification efforts; the neighboring *81.Korps* on the Seine estuary—closer to the Pas-de-Calais—was allotted four times as much.[1]

The areas between the ports were much less heavily defended than the major ports. This was in part because of the early favoritism shown to the *Kriegsmarine* during the construction programs of 1940–42, and also because of the assumption that ports would be the main Allied objectives. The *Kriegsmarine* built massive and sophisticated coastal artillery batteries around the key ports as part of the Atlantic Wall program. The areas in between were gradually defended by new army coastal artillery batteries spaced along the coast like "a string of pearls." Coastal artillery was viewed as a cheaper expedient than manpower since a single battery could cover about ten kilometers (six miles) of coastline to either side. In contrast, using infantry units to defend the areas between the ports would consume an enormous amount of manpower that was simply not available because of the demands of the Russian front.

The army's coastal batteries were most heavily deployed in the *15.Armee* sector, starting in upper Normandy and extending along the Pas-de-Calais toward the Belgian coast. There was an average of one battery every twenty-eight kilometers (seventeen miles) along the Iron Coast. In the *7.Armee* sector from Lower Normandy along the Cotentin

The priority in the early construction of the Atlantic Wall went to the heavy gun batteries on the English Channel. This is one of the three massive 406mm guns of the famous *Kriegsmarine Batterie Lindemann* in Sangatte after its capture by Canadian troops of the North Shore Regiment in 1944. In recent years, this battery was submerged under earth as part of the construction of the Channel tunnel. NAC PA-133142

Away from the Pas-de-Calais, the strongest Atlantic Wall defenses could be found in the major ports. This is a 280mm SKL/40 naval gun of the *Kéringer "Graf Spee"* battery during the U.S. Army's siege of Brest in September 1944. NARA

The heaviest gun batteries in Lower Normandy were deployed to protect the harbor of Cherbourg on the northern tip of the Cotentin Peninsula. This 150mm naval gun in a M272 bunker was part of *MKB Landemer* of *6./MAA.260* in Strongpoint 230 near Castel-Vendon to the west of Cherbourg. NARA

Peninsula—the future D-Day beaches—there was only one battery every eighty-seven kilometers (fifty-four miles).

Inevitably, some infantry defense of the coast was necessary, if only to provide minimal protection against commando raids. The Channel coast was divided into coast defense sectors (KVA: *Küsten Verteidigung Abschnitt*), with one infantry division per KVA. For most of the war, the coastal sectors were defended by a special type of static infantry division (*Infanterie-Division bodenständige*). These reduced-strength divisions had little or no transport and were usually manned by overage or medically disabled troops. Each divisional KVA was further broken down into regimental coast defense groups (KVG: *Küsten Verteidigung Gruppe*), and then into smaller and smaller sectors: battalion-strength strongpoint groups (*Stützpunktgruppe*), company-size strongpoints (StP: *Stützpunkt*),

and finally platoon-size defense nests (WN: *Widerstandsnest*). Except for the Pas-de-Calais, there was little concrete fortification of these infantry coastal defenses until 1944.

German doctrine recommended that an infantry division be allotted no more than six to ten kilometers (four to six miles) of front to defend. Because of a lack of manpower, the occupation divisions in France were frequently allotted fifty to one hundred kilometers (thirty-one to sixty-two miles) of coastline to defend. In remote locations of Brittany or the Atlantic coast, they were assigned even longer stretches.

In 1943, the *Wehrmacht* was deployed in three major formations in France and the Low Countries: the *15.Armee* from Antwerp westward along the Channel coast to the Seine estuary near Le Havre; the *7.Armee* from Lower Normandy to Brittany; and the *1.Armee* on the Atlantic coast from the Loire

During 1943, the emphasis in Atlantic Wall construction shifted to the defensive strongpoints away from the Pas-de-Calais. This is a fortified 50mm pedestal gun photographed in the *716.Infanterie-Division* sector in WN38 in St. Côme in February 1944 during a winter storm. This particular style of *Ringstand* with overhead cover was a special design found in Lower Normandy, most notably around St. Aubin-sur-Mer, better known on D-Day as Juno Beach. LIBRARY OF CONGRESS

estuary near Nantes to the Spanish coast near Bayonne. The *15.Armee* on the Channel coast received the disproportionate share of the fortification, and the *7.Armee* most of the remainder. Of the 15,000

bunkers envisioned under Hitler's 1942 plan, 11,000 were allocated to the *15.Armee* and the *7.Armee*, and the remainder to the Atlantic coast of France, the Netherlands, Norway, and Denmark.

GERMAN FORTIFICATION TECHNOLOGY

The army fortification engineers established protection standards during the *Westwall* program based on steel-reinforced concrete. Most Atlantic Wall fortifications were built to the B standard, which was two meters of steel-reinforced concrete. This was proof against artillery up to 210mm (8-inch) and bombs weighing up to 500kg (1,000lb). Many minor bunkers, such as the ubiquitous Tobruks, were built to the slightly lower B1 standard of 1 to 1.2 meters since these structures

were mostly buried and protected by soil. The designers attempted to minimize the amount of steel necessary in construction, so aside from the cheap steel reinforcing bars (rebar), steel plate and especially expensive steel armor plate were kept to a minimum.

Atlantic Wall bunkers were based on standard designs that were developed by the fortification command in Berlin. These were given numbers—for example, "677" for the type of

The most common type of fortification in Normandy was the small Tobruk, most often used as a machine-gun position, as seen here with this example armed with an MG 34 light machine gun in Franceville to the east of the Sword Beach area in February 1944. When completed, all that was evident was the circular gun mount, but in fact there is a substantial concrete structure underneath. LIBRARY OF CONGRESS

Access to the Tobruk was usually through a side or rear entrance. The Tobruk was supposed to have the side facing the enemy completely buried since the concrete was only B1 standard and not resistant to heavy artillery fire. AUTHOR

88mm gun bunkers seen on Omaha Beach. This designation is usually listed as "R677," the "R" indicating *Regelbau* (Construction Standard). Sometimes, the bunkers are listed by their service—for example, "H677," the "H" indicating *Heer* (Army). Navy and air force bunkers were, respectively, "M" (*Marine*) and "L" (*Luftwaffe*).

Nonstandard bunkers were often indentified as "SK" (*Sonder Konstruktion*: Special Design).

Individual bunkers were often assigned a project number by the *Pionier-Stab*—for example, "BW Nr. 882" (*Bau Werk* No: Construction Work Number) for the "R677" 88mm bunker in WN72 in the Vierville draw on Omaha Beach.

TABLE 3: ATLANTIC WALL CONSTRUCTION IN *7.ARMEE* SECTOR, 1 JANUARY 1944[2]

Type	Planned	Completed	In Construction	Not Started
Tobruk	4,411	3,430	384	597
Open MG nest	7,751	7,316	248	187
MG bunker	92	79	13	0
MG turreted bunker	22	17	3	2
Panzer turret (MG)	173	146	20	7
Panzer turret (47mm + MG)	36	24	7	5
Panzer turret (37mm + MG)	70	59	7	4
Panzer turret (37mm)	66	57	5	4
Open AT gun pit	520	424	45	51
AT gun bunker	69	46	12	11
AT gun garage	36	29	7	0
Infantry gun bunker	67	52	8	7
50mm pedestal gun pit	609	505	67	37
Mortar pit	1,330	1,110	165	55
Open gun pit	1,050	980	45	25
Gun ammo bunker	6	6	0	0
Gun bunker	29	22	6	1
Flak gun pit	1,530	1,460	45	25
Searchlight stand	620	590	14	16
Flamethrower stand	1,384	1,145	108	131
Munitions bunker	5,245	4,880	208	157
Supply bunker	2,225	1,948	160	117
Kitchen bunker	516	408	78	30
Water reservoir	595	524	38	33
Medical bunker	66	50	6	10
Decontamination bunker	148	127	12	7
Communications bunker	222	215	7	0
Machinery bunker	94	76	7	11
Command bunker	149	128	12	9
Observation bunker	348	318	24	6
Obstacles (km)	1,945	1,810	103	32
Tank obstacles (km)	334	298	20	16

The completion of the Atlantic Wall became more urgent in the spring and summer of 1943 as the likelihood of the Allied landings increased. The first sign of this was the appointment of one of Germany's premier commanders, Field Marshal Gerd von Rundstedt, as the head of the Supreme Command-West (OB-West: *Oberbefehlshaber-West*) headquarters in the spring. Rundstedt was best known for his leadership of Nazi Germany's greatest victory, the astonishing defeat of France in 1940. He began by ordering a comprehensive inspection of the Atlantic Wall defenses from May to October 1943. The survey revealed that the Atlantic Wall was far from its propaganda image and suffered from numerous shortcomings. Some sections, especially the Pas-de-Calais and the Belgian-Dutch coast, had an impressive array of fortified strongpoints. But other sectors, such as Lower Normandy, were very weakly protected except at a few ports. Defenses in other sectors, including the Bay of Biscay and Brittany, were meager. A later report from 1 January 1944 listed the progress in the *7.Armee* sector that covered Normandy (Table 3); although 89 percent of the field positions had been completed by early 1944, in many sectors the defenses were extremely thin and brittle.

CHANGE OF COURSE: FÜHRER DIRECTIVE 51

Rundstedt's main mission was to convince Berlin to stop draining resources out of France and the Low Countries and to reverse the flow of men and weapons in favor of the "Invasion Front." Berlin finally recognized the need for a major shift with Hitler's Directive No. 51, issued on 3 November 1943. It began by stating:

> For the last two and one-half years the bitter and costly struggle against Bolshevism has made the utmost demands upon most of our military resources and energies. This commitment was in keeping with the seriousness of the threat, and the over-all situation. The situation has since changed. The threat from the East remains, but an even greater danger looms in the West: the Anglo-American landing! In the East, as a last resort, the vastness of the space will permit the loss of territory even on a major scale, without suffering a mortal blow to Germany's chance for survival.

> Not so in the West! If the enemy here succeeds in penetrating our defenses on a wide front, consequences of staggering proportions will follow immediately. All signs point to an offensive against the Western Front of Europe no later than spring, and perhaps earlier. For that reason, I can no longer justify the further weakening of the West in favor of other theaters of war. I have therefore decided to strengthen the defenses in the West.

The winter 1943 construction plan intended to fortify the divisional artillery of static divisions along the coast. This is the rear of a R669 bunker being built in February 1944 for the *1./Artillerie-Regiment.716* in WN01, the easternmost artillery position of the *716.Infanterie-Division.* This battery is better known as the Merville Battery and was the subject of a British airborne attack in the predawn hours of D-Day because of the threat it posed to Sword Beach. LIBRARY OF CONGRESS

THE GERMAN INTELLIGENCE DILEMMA

The central problem faced by Rundstedt was the lack of any convincing evidence as to where the Allies would land; to understand Rundstedt's dilemma, it is worthwhile to take a quick look at German intelligence efforts. There were three principal means to determine the date and location of the Allied invasion: human intelligence, signals intelligence, and photo reconnaissance. Of these, human intelligence was by far the most valuable. However, the Germans utterly failed at establishing any reliable human intelligence sources in Britain. The agents planted in Britain ended up being turned by British counterintelligence by the highly successful "Operation Doublecross." They fed false information back to Berlin, where some of these agents were believed to be highly reliable. The false intelligence supported the idea that the Allies would land on the Pas-de-Calais.

Signals intelligence was also of limited use. Unlike the Allies' highly successful "Ultra" decryption program, German code breakers did not succeed in cracking major Allied codes and failed to provide any reliable information on the time or location of the Allied landings. Even if they failed to break key codes, signals-intelligence monitoring of Allied radio chatter could be useful in identifying the identity and location of major Allied units. However, Allied counterintelligence forces exploited this technique by creating false radio networks that confused the Germans with false units. These false units were deployed in areas that reinforced the idea that the Pas-de-Calais was the main Allied invasion target. This Allied deception program was code-named "Operation Fortitude."[3]

While it is not widely known, the *Luftwaffe* had a very active aerial reconnaissance program over

Some of the new bunkers in the seafront villages were cleverly camouflaged like this machine-gun casemate, completed in February 1944 and located in Strongpoint 20 in Hermanville-Le Brèche, in the center of Sword Beach on D-Day.
LIBRARY OF CONGRESS

Britain through 1943–44. Although many aircraft were lost in the process, the *Luftwaffe* secured numerous photos of the build-up in areas along the British coast, including all the major coasts. They even photographed the secret Mulberry floating harbors, though they were misunderstood as flak barges. Operation Fortitude attempted to confuse the *Luftwaffe* reconnaissance analysts by creating false encampments full of decoy buildings and decoy weapons. Nevertheless, the photographic missions were helpful in establishing when the Allies were likely to invade, since there was a substantial increase in the number of landing ships in British harbors in the spring of 1944. However, these aerial missions provided no positive information on where the Allies would land. Allied naval superiority presented the *Wehrmacht* with an insoluble problem, since sea power and the narrowness of the English Channel gave the Allies the strategic mobility to strike quickly at nearly any point along the French, Belgian, and Dutch coasts.

The shortcomings of the German intelligence services forced German commanders to make assessments based on the suitability of landing areas and assumptions about Allied intentions. There was no consensus. In 1943, the commander of *7.Armee*, Gen. Friedrich Dollmann, began to have second thoughts about the center of gravity of his defense effort. With the U-boat campaign suffering serious setbacks in 1943, Dollmann began to move the bulk of his forces from Brittany, where they had been defending the *Kriegsmarine* ports, into Lower Normandy, which he viewed as a more probable Allied landing target. The *Kriegsmarine* and *15.Armee* continued to view the Lower Normandy coast between the Vire and Orne Rivers—the future D-Day beaches—as unsuitable for amphibious landing operations by the Allies. Various commanders agreed that the east coast of the Contentin Peninsula below Cherbourg was a more attractive invasion objective. The presumption was that Cherbourg would be the main objective and, as

Tobruks were often used as the basis for tank turret bunkers in Normandy. The camouflaged Tobruk to the right is fitted with a *Berliet-Girod* turret from a World War I Renault FT tank, a common arrangement in this sector. To the left, the crew has created an alarm signal by hanging two spent shell casings from a beam. This Tobruk was located in Strongpoint 18 on the coast at Hermanville-Le Brèche (Sword Beach). LIBRARY OF CONGRESS

such, the Carentan-Caen sector from the Vire River to the Orne River was not especially attractive. OB-West's Inspector of Fortifications, Lt. Gen. Rudolf Schmetzer later wrote that:

> In the opinion of the *Kriegsmarine*, however, the area east of the mouth of the Vire river was not suitable for this purpose [large-scale landing]. Although the coast northwest and north of Caen offered favorable landing conditions, it was too far away for close cooperation with any forces landed on the east coast of the Cotentin [Peninsula]. It appeared out of the question that the center of gravity of a large scale landing would be placed from the beginning in the Caen area.[4]

Following its 1943 review of anti-invasion defenses, Rundstedt's OB-West headquarters conducted a fresh study in January 1944 to identify the most likely landing sites based on their suitability for landing and unloading large cargo ships.[5] The probabilities were characterized at three levels—high, medium, and low—and the forty-two most likely landing sites were identified. The map below summarizes the results of this study. Given the criteria, it is not surprising that the eleven landing sites with a high probability were all major port areas, starting with Antwerp and the Scheldt estuary in the east, and continuing to St. Nazaire and the Loire estuary in the west. Only two ports in Normandy were identified as "high" probability—the port of Le Havre in Upper Normandy and Cherbourg in Lower Normandy. In the actual D-Day invasion zone, the Orne estuary on the coast near Caen was rated "medium" due to the numerous small ports, while the actual D-Day beaches near Bayeux were rated "low." The January 1944 study did little to clarify where the Allies were likely to land and, if anything, merely muddied the waters by offering too many potential landing points.

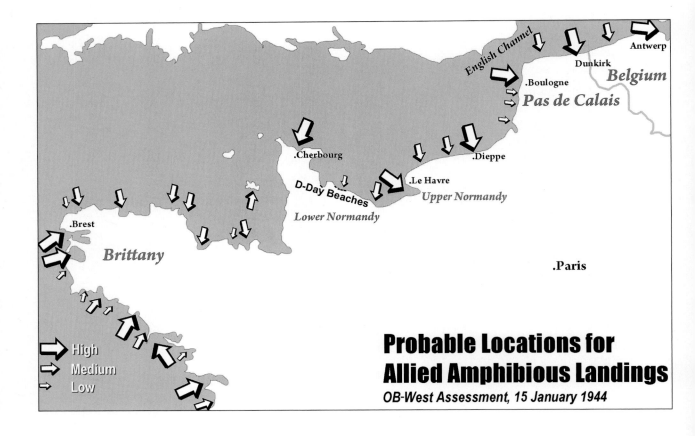

Probable Locations for Allied Amphibious Landings
OB-West Assessment, 15 January 1944

One of the densest concentrations of tactical fortifications in lower Normandy was the small port village of Riva-Bella, site of the future Sword Beach landings on D-Day. Besides its modest port facilities, Riva-Bella guarded access to the Orne River estuary. This is an observation bunker located on the coast on a stormy day in February 1944. LIBRARY OF CONGRESS

As a result of the lack of firm evidence about the location of the planned Allied invasion, Berlin continued to disperse the Atlantic Wall fortifications along the entire French coast, though heavily favoring the Pas-de-Calais. Toward the end of 1943, the pace of the program had slackened considerably due to dwindling supplies of concrete and manpower and the onset of winter weather. Of the 15,000 concrete fortifications planned for completion, only about 8,500 were ready by year's end. The British aerial bombing campaign against the Ruhr industrial region in the autumn of 1943 diverted many of the construction resources back to Germany in late 1943. Adding to the dispersion problem was Hitler's latest fanciful scheme, a plan to deploy fortified mis-sile launch sites along the French coast to bombard England, which consumed much of the limited concrete supply in France.[6] In the *7.Armee* area, Hitler gave five ports the *Festung* (Fortress) designation, meaning that they were to be defended to the last: Cherbourg, St. Malo, Brest, Lorient, and St. Nazaire.[7] This further diverted the limited concrete supplies to the already well-protected ports and left the defenses between the ports, such as Omaha Beach, very weak.

As part of Directive No. 51 to activate the anti-invasion front, Hitler assigned his favorite general, Erwin Rommel, to invigorate the program. Rommel's initiatives would fundamentally change the defenses in Normandy, especially at Omaha Beach.

CHAPTER 3

The Rommel Factor

ROMMEL IS A DEMIGOD IN MOST English accounts of the war. Indeed, he is probably the only German general who can be identified by most English-speaking readers. Rommel's prominence results from his victories against the British Army in North Africa in 1941–42. Usually outnumbered by a considerable margin, his *Afrika Korps* inflicted numerous defeats on the British 8th Army through the autumn of 1942. There has been an inclination on the part of many British historians to attribute these setbacks to Rommel's military genius rather than to shortcomings of the British Army. He was dubbed the "Desert Fox" in the British press. After the war, a movie was produced with the distinguished actor James Mason playing the role of Rommel. It is hard to imagine any other German or Japanese commander being portrayed in such a reverential fashion. British admiration for Rommel is widespread in American circles as well, since so much of the historical literature on American bookshelves consists of British histories reprinted in the United States. But from the German perspective, Rommel was a fairly minor figure among *Wehrmacht* commanders, especially when compared to the giants who had led the *Wehrmacht* in the brutal war in Russia.[1]

Erwin Rommel stood out from much of the senior *Wehrmacht* leadership in several ways. He was not a member of the Prussian military aristocracy—he was a schoolmaster's son from the Swabian region. He served on several fronts during World War I, and he was decorated with the Iron Cross for his exemplary leadership in the mountain fighting in Italy. Unlike most German officers of the Great War, he had few

Rommel's fame in the English-speaking world is undoubtedly based on his reputation as the "Desert Fox" from the successful campaigns of his *Afrika Korps* in 1941–42. MHI

experiences in the brutal trench warfare that so strongly shaped *Wehrmacht* tactical doctrine after the war. His meteoric rise in Nazi Germany was largely because of a personal association with Hitler. The *Führer* had read Rommel's memoirs of the Great War, *Infantry Attacks!*, and found them in tune with his own views. Hitler greatly resented the Prussian dominance of the army, almost as intensely as he despised staff officers. He sought out young officers like Rommel who had displayed exceptional military talent without the Prussian aristocratic taint. In early 1938, Rommel was assigned to lead the *Führer*'s escort battalion. He returned to regular army duties as the head of the war college at Wiener Neustadt, but was recalled by Hitler prior to the start of the war to head the special *Führer* headquarters (*Führerbegleithauptquartier*).

Rommel was not content in such a staff role and wished to see combat. Hitler acceded to his request, generously promoting him from colonel to major general and authorizing his transfer to the command of the *7.Panzer-Division* in time to see action in the Battle of France in 1940. Rommel's outstanding leadership in France helped to quell complaints within the army about his self-promotion and political scheming, but he retained the reputation of a "political general" whose advancement was tied directly to his association with Hitler.

Rommel escaped the cauldron of the Russian Front by a new appointment from Hitler in February 1941. He was assigned to lead a special force to rescue Germany's hapless Italian ally in its failed campaign in North Africa. Rommel's success in halting the British drive in North Africa became the stuff of legend and a major propaganda coup in Berlin. His *Afrika Korps* outfought a much larger British contingent for the better part of a year. In June 1942, Hitler elevated "his favorite general" to the rank of field marshal, a meteoric rise for an officer who had been a mere colonel three years before. German historians have taken a more

Rommel was not content to sit out the war in Hitler's headquarters and requested a combat posting. He was assigned to lead the *7.Panzer-Division* during the Battle of France in May–June 1940, where his superb performance bolstered his reputation with Hitler. NARA

Rommel's official portrait after his appointment as General Field Marshal on 22 June 1942. MHI

jaundiced view of Rommel's performance in recent years. In particular, there have been disclosures about the secret role of German signals intelligence. It now would appear that much of Rommel's supposed genius in North Africa resulted in no small measure from his astute use of intercepted British communications. The codes being used by the American military *attaché* in Cairo were broken, and Rommel was able to learn Britain's most secret plans in a very timely fashion. This intelligence bonanza was finally cut off by the summer of 1942. Along with the capture of his key tactical intelligence unit, Rommel's successes began to fade.[2] Following the victory of Montgomery's 8th Army at El Alamein in October 1942, Rommel suffered a string of defeats. In March 1943, with his health broken from hard desert service, Rommel was evacuated from North Africa for medical atten-

Field Marshal Rundstedt inspects a 50mm PaK 38 during one of his periodic visits to the Atlantic Wall. NARA

tion and rest. This spared him the ignominy of capture when the remnants of his *Afrika Korps* surrendered in Tunisia in May 1943.

After medical recuperation in Germany, Rommel returned to service in the spring of 1943, spending much of his time at Hitler's headquarters. His reputation as Hitler's "favorite general" had been diminished by the North Africa defeats, but Hitler still regarded him as a loyal and talented leader and planned to use him as a special commander for sensitive and important missions. In August 1943, he was appointed to lead Army Group B, stationed in northern Italy. Mussolini had been deposed by the king, and it appeared that Italy would soon withdraw from the Axis alliance. Rommel's new Army Group B headquarters was assigned the task of preventing the valuable industrialized provinces of northern Italy from falling into Allied hands.

Hitler's appointment of Rommel at the end of 1943 to head a special anti-invasion command stepped on the toes of the theater commander, Field Marshal Rundstedt. They are seen here in Paris in December 1943 at the Hotel George V. NARA

Rommel is shown a new type of obstacle during his 8 March 1944 inspection tour of *KVA* in Brittany. MHI

Rommel's brief Italian command gave him an intimate understanding of the three most recent Allied amphibious landings—the invasion of Sicily in July 1943, the British Operation Baytown landings in southern Italy in August 1943, and the Salerno amphibious landings in September 1943. He was not in command of any of these three sectors, but he learned in detail about new Allied amphibious landing tactics. As energetic and inquisitive as always, Rommel studied the lessons of these recent Axis defeats. German tactics during the Sicily and Salerno campaigns had followed predictable German doctrine. There was no serious attempt to defend the landing beaches, and instead the emphasis was placed on creating a mobile

panzer reserve that was launched on a violent counterattack a few days after the landings. Both *panzer* counterattacks were smothered by intense naval gunfire and the attacks failed. Rommel's study of the Sicily and Salerno failures undermined his confidence in existing German tactical doctrine for dealing with Allied amphibious landings. He began to consider other approaches.

As Rommel pondered the changing tactics of modern warfare, Hitler decided to send him on his most sensitive and difficult mission. On 21 November 1943, his headquarters was transferred from northern Italy to northern France as part of *Führer* Directive No. 51 to reinforce the invasion front as the "Army Group for Special Employment." Rommel's new command was awkward since Rundstedt's OB-West headquarters had already been focused on rejuvenating the Invasion Front. Both officers attempted to make the best of a confused and delicate situation. Rommel's headquarters returned to its old name of Army Group B in early 1944 and was assigned a more conventional role in the German command structure.

As soon as Rommel arrived in France, he embarked on a whirlwind tour of the Atlantic Wall defenses. He was not content to read the reports already collected by Rundstedt's command and wanted to see the anti-invasion defenses firsthand. He started in Denmark and made his way down the coast through the Netherlands and Belgium to the French coast.[3]

Rommel quickly realized that the depictions of Fortress Europe as an impregnable bastion against invasion were an elaborate propaganda bluff. The Atlantic Wall was far from complete, except for the Iron Coast along the Pas-de-Calais in northern France and the Low Countries. More alarmingly, the coast was defended by third-rate static divisions that had been culled of their better troops to satisfy the insatiable manpower demands of the Russian Front. Whole sections of the coast were being defended by utterly unreliable Soviet "volunteer" units.[*] The German Army in France had become a backwater where the *Wehrmacht* sent its shattered units for reconstitution after their decimation in Russia. Very few of the defense sectors were ready for combat.

*There were about 33,000 *Ost-Truppen*, former Red Army prisoners of war, in German army service on the Normandy Front.[4]

Rommel made frequent tours of the "Iron Coast" on the Pas-de-Calais in northern France. He is seen here in mid-April 1944 with Gen. Johann Sinnhuber (*82.Korps*); his chief of staff, Lt. Gen. Hans Spiedel; and his aide, Captain Lang (behind). NARA

A pungent view of the state of the Atlantic Wall at this time was provided to Berlin from the *15.Armee* commander, Gen. Hans von Salmuth. He commanded the best section of the Atlantic Wall, from the Pas-de-Calais to the Dutch coast. The other sectors were in far worse condition:

> The Atlantic Wall is no wall!! Rather it is like a thin and fragile cord which has a few small knots at isolated places such as Dieppe and Dunkirk. The strengthening of this cord was no doubt underway during the past spring and summer. Since August the effort has been getting steadily weaker . . . and any considerable increase in bunker construction will not take place til spring [since] material and labor are lacking. When I visit a position, I invariably receive the report ". . . workers have been transferred to Todt construction work for the Luftwaffe" . . . usually of course "on the Fuhrer's orders." Hell! Are we army soldiers just dirt?? We are supposed to stand to the last man and to the last bullet. And we do it. Then they should treat us accordingly.

Rommel attempted to reinvigorate the defense efforts along the coast by frequent visits to each division. To emphasize the urgency of anti-invasion preparation, he insisted that infantry units no longer depend on engineer units or conscripted labor to build defenses. Many of the tactical defenses could be built by the infantry units themselves, even if it meant cutting back on training time. At the same time, he pleaded with Berlin to dispatch more divisions to France, especially badly needed *panzer* divisions. There was a constant stream of dispatches back to the Armed Forces High Command (OKW) reporting the dismaying lack of preparation on the Invasion Front.

THE TACTICS OF DESPERATION

Any reinvigoration of the anti-invasion defenses had to be based on some common set of assumptions about the tactics that would be employed to defeat the Allied amphibious landings. Rommel was not convinced that the existing German anti-invasion tactics could succeed, and he came up with his own ideas about defensive approaches. The ensuing debate over tactics would drag on for the six months from December 1943 to D-Day itself.

Rommel's experiences in Italy convinced him that the established German tactical doctrine had no chance of success. As had been shown at Sicily and Salerno, if the Allies managed to establish a beachhead, they could not be pushed back into the sea by a *panzer* counterattack. The counterattack inevitably would fall victim to Allied naval gunfire. Furthermore, Rommel argued that Allied air power

was becoming a greater and greater threat and that by the summer of 1944 it would smother any attempt to maneuver *panzer* counterattack forces against the beachhead. Rommel's views were further reinforced in January 1944 when the Allies staged another amphibious landing at Anzio near Rome. A large-scale *panzer* counterattack was launched against the beachhead but failed to push it back into the sea.[5]

Rommel proposed that the principal tactic for anti-invasion operations was the need to stop the Allied amphibious attacks immediately on the beaches. To accomplish this, infantry divisions had to be moved forward as closely as possible to the beaches and as many weapons as possible positioned to fire directly on the beaches.

To many German commanders, Rommel's new tactics were too reminiscent of discredited

Rundstedt convened a meeting of his top commanders in Paris to discuss anti-invasion planning on 8 May 1944. Seen here from left to right are Gen. Geyr von Schweppenburg (*Panzergruppe West*), Gen. Johannes Blaskowitz (Army Group G), Field Marshal Hugo Sperrle (*Luftflotte.3*), Field Marshal Rundstedt (OB-West), Rommel (Army Group B), and Admiral Krancke (Navy Group West). NARA

pre–World War I doctrine. They ran completely counter to current 1943–44 *Wehrmacht* tactics that were based on the lessons of the Great War. By 1917–18, German defensive tactics had evolved into "elastic defense." The massive increase in firepower of modern field artillery made it impossible to base the defense along the forward edge of battle. If concentrated along the front, the defense was simply demolished by enemy artillery. The linear defense tactics of prewar doctrine gave way to defense-in-depth with successive defensive lines. Instead of basing the main line of resistance forward, the Germans created a weakly held forward line of advanced positions and outposts, only sufficient to stop enemy patrols. Behind these forward barriers was the main combat line (HKL: *Hauptkampflinie*), fortified with small machine-gun bunkers and earthworks. The destructive effect of

enemy artillery was diminished by compelling it to fire on widely dispersed targets. Reserves were stationed in the rear in deep bunkers that provided shelter from artillery. Once the direction of the enemy attack was determined, these reserve forces from the rear staged violent counterattacks to staunch any penetration of the German defensive line.

While the *Wehrmacht* of World War II is remembered for its offensive tactics such as *blitzkrieg*, it often is forgotten that when the *Wehrmacht* was resurrected in the 1930s, Germany was encircled by more powerful enemies.[6] The interwar German Army's principal focus was on defensive tactics to protect the Reich. The lessons of World War I were a sacred text to German World War II combat leaders, but commanders were not inflexible and were happy to incorporate innova-

Rommel visited the *716.Infanterie-Division* at Riva-Bella on 30 May 1944. From left to right: Gen. Hans von Sallmuth (*15.Armee*), Rommel, Gen. Friedrich Dollmann (*7.Armee*), Gen. Walter Buhle (OKW), Gen. Erich Marcks (*84.Korps*), and Gen. Alfred Jakob (OKW Inspector of Fortifications). NARA

Rommel was a "hands on" commander and spent most of the spring of 1944 on the road in his Mercedes staff car, visiting his units along the Atlantic Wall. He is seen here in late May 1944 near Paris. NARA

tions. One of the most important innovations in German defensive doctrine was the advent of *panzer* forces that could serve as a powerful counterattack force.

Most German commanders had spent the years of 1941–44 on the Russian Front, where the defensive lessons of 1918 still remained valid. The campaign on the Russian Front was fought by overextended infantry divisions with only a thin reinforcement of tank units. Although the German Army gradually deployed more and more *panzer* units in Russia than in France in 1940, the length of the front meant that they were at a much lower density than during the great *blitzkrieg* victories of 1939–41. Air power was spread even thinner, and the Soviet air force did not pose a serious threat to the German Army until well into 1944. There was

some improvement in weapons technology between 1941 and 1944, but the German Army in Russia in 1943 was suffering from technical and tactical stagnation compared to the United States and Britain. The technical stagnation was worsened by equipment shortages and an emaciated manpower reserve. The *Wehrmacht* still relied on horses for transport at a time when the British and American armies were fully motorized. The *Luftwaffe* might have been working on jet fighters and rockets, but the army operated second-rate radios and poor communication equipment.

In North Africa and Italy, Rommel had seen firsthand the effects of the Allies' advantages in army motorization, tactical air power, and modern command-and-control. He was especially fearful that air power would invalidate traditional

German defensive doctrine, since it would prevent the movement of the counterattack force. Rommel was not as deeply wedded to the 1930s defensive doctrine as many other German commanders. He had not experienced trench warfare firsthand, as had many commanders, but had seen most of his combat in the mountains of Italy where the tactics were quite different. Consequently, he was more open to questioning army doctrine.

Rommel's plan to place as much firepower as possible on the beaches was a tactic of desperation. He feared that any reserves kept more than a few miles from the beaches would be immobile and useless once Allied air power intervened. He was fully aware that the concentration of his infantry forces on the beaches would expose them to the full might of Allied naval gunfire, but the existing tactics had failed time and time again in Italy, and he was convinced that something new had to be tried. He hoped that the Atlantic Wall, for all its faults, would provide the coastal units with some measure of protection against naval gunfire.

More Russian Front commanders arrived in France in late 1943 and early 1944 as part of the *Wehrmacht* reinforcement of the anti-invasion front. The debate over anti-invasion tactics grew increasingly bitter.[7] Rommel laid out his new tactical vision at meetings with Rundstedt on 19 December 1943 at OB-West headquarters. Rundstedt, a very traditional officer, was not convinced by Rommel's arguments. Even so, Rommel was not alone in his viewpoint. General Hans von Salmuth, of the *15.Armee* in the critical Pas-de-Calais sector, also felt that more emphasis had to be placed on reinforcing the forward edge of battle.[8]

Rommel's most bitter critic in 1944 was General of Panzer Troops Leo Freiherr Geyr von Schweppenburg, the commander of *Panzergruppe West*, the main strategic reserve on the western front. Schweppenburg was a decorated veteran of the great *panzer* battles on the Russian Front and felt that Rommel's proposed tactics were fundamentally misguided. MHI

The most vivid controversy was over the deployment of *panzer* divisions. The Russian Front commanders expected to place the *panzer* divisions in a strategic reserve, back in the Paris area away from the coast. They argued that there was no certainty about where the Allies would land, and so it was more prudent to keep the *panzer* divisions uncommitted until the landings took place. Once the location of the invasion was clear, the *panzer* divisions could be launched in an overwhelming counterattack. The most vigorous spokesman for this viewpoint was the commander of *Panzergruppe West*, Gen. Leo Freiherr Geyr von Schweppenburg. He had commanded a *panzer* corps in the battle of France in 1940, and again during the attack on Moscow in 1941. He stayed on the Russian Front through 1943, and from this experience he remained convinced that a reserve of *panzer* divisions kept deep behind the main line of battle was the most potent tactic to counterattack the invasion beaches.

The debate over the deployment of the *panzer* divisions remained intense through the early months of 1944. Hitler finally intervened with a compromise that satisfied no one. He gave Rommel direct control over a small number of *panzer* divi-sions near the beaches, but left much of Schweppenburg's force in strategic reserve under his direct control.

Under these contentious circumstances, OB-West attempted to meld accepted tactical doctrine with Rommel's tactical changes. The resulting tactical compromise was dubbed "crust-cushion-hammer." The Atlantic Wall was the crust, which would stop or delay the initial Allied invasion and give the army time to move its mobile reserves into action. The cushion was the coastal region immediately behind the Atlantic Wall, which would be reinforced by a proposed second line of defense. The hammer was Schweppenburg's *Panzergruppe West*.

Rommel was indefatigable and continued to press his case. In early May, at a meeting of senior commanders in Paris, Rommel continued to push for the forward deployment of Schweppenburg's *panzers* closer to the coast. In particular, he wanted the *I.SS-Panzer-Korps* deployed to Lower Normandy. This would have put the *Panzer-Lehr-Division* behind Omaha Beach and the *12.SS-Panzer-Division* closer to the British invasion beaches. Rundstedt refused Rommel's request, knowing that Hitler would not permit it.

WHERE WILL THEY LAND?

Rommel's iconoclastic views extended to other aspects of the defensive plans. German planning since 1942 assumed that the Pas-de-Calais was the most likely location for the Allied invasion. This was the narrowest point of the English Channel, and the invasion force could be supported by fighter aircraft based in southern England. It also offered a direct approach into Germany on terrain better-suited to mobile operations than the soggy lowlands of Holland or the wooded hills of the Belgian-German frontier. As a result, the Atlantic Wall defenses were far denser on the Pas-de-Calais than on any other stretch of the French coast. The concrete defenses were bolstered by the best-equipped units—the *15.Armee*. German intelligence seemed to confirm that this was the main Allied target.

Yet the Pas-de-Calais was such an obvious target that Rommel began to consider whether another location might be more likely. Rundstedt and the senior commanders remained convinced that the Allies would strike at or near a port. They had done so at Salerno and Anzio. But the landings at Sicily made it clear that they could conduct an amphibious landing without a major port. As mentioned earlier in this book, Rommel's visit to the Grandcamp sector of Lower Normandy in late January 1944 opened his eyes to the threat in this area. His intuitive association of this sector with the Salerno beachhead led him to believe that this site was a more likely invasion location than Berlin believed.

It can certainly be argued that his admonition to the officers that "the fate of Europe will be decided

Another of Rommel's defensive improvements in Lower Normandy was to bolster the base of the Cotentin Peninsula with the *91.Luftlande-Division*. This forced the U.S. Army to make major changes in its airborne landing plans. Rommel is seen here visiting the division commander, Lieutenant General Falley, at his headquarters in May 1944.

here" might simply be the usual sort of pep talk he gave to all gatherings of officers to encourage their work. Yet Rommel repeated this viewpoint on several occasions to several officers. Maj. Werner Pluskat, who commanded one of the artillery battalions at Omaha Beach, recalled a conversation with Rommel during one of his inspection visits to the future Omaha area: "Pluskat, in my opinion it is in this very area that the Allies will land. If they do, you're going to have to fight one of the toughest battles of your life." When Pluskat asked him why he thought so, Rommel replied: "Because this is exactly the type of place that the Allies will choose. They did so in Italy."[9]

It is doubtful that Rommel thought the Grandcamp sector was the only—or most likely—invasion site. Overall, Rommel agreed with Berlin's assessment that the Pas-de-Calais was the most likely objective.[10] At the same time, he was unwilling to gamble all of his resources on the Pas-de-Calais, and he fully realized that the Allies might strike in the less likely *7.Armee* area of Lower Normandy. The *7.Armee* did not have lavish resources, so Rommel decided to concentrate these modest assets along the sectors of the beach he thought most vulnerable. The Grandcamp sector was one of those he chose for special attention.

Further evidence of Rommel's concern about this sector can be determined from his later actions. In early 1944, his Army Group B had only one first-class infantry division in lower Normandy, the *352.Infanterie-Division*, which was in the process of reconstruction in the St. Lô area. He could have deployed it to other "high probability" invasion sites in this area, such as Cherbourg or Le Havre, which were defended by badly overstretched, second-rate static divisions. Instead, in February 1944 after his visit, he began his efforts to move it to the beaches in the Grandcamp sector.

Besides his transfer of the *352.Infanterie-Division* to the future Omaha Beach sector, Rommel also attempted to reinvigorate the Atlantic Wall effort in Lower Normandy. The program had largely run out of steam at the end of 1943 because of the diversion of construction assets to the reconstruction of the Ruhr industrial region and Hitler's new enthusiasm, the V-weapon launch sites. Locations away from the major ports, such as the Grandcamp sector, had seen virtually no fortification work. The army coastal battery at Pointe-du-Hoc was deployed in open concrete gun pits. The field guns deployed on the future Omaha Beach did not even enjoy the benefit of gun pits, but instead simply were deployed in open field entrenchments with a primitive concrete base. Another surge of building was planned in the winter of 1943, with a special effort directed at putting major artillery pieces in bunkers. Under Rommel's prodding, a major construction program began in March and April 1944 in the Grandcamp sector to reinforce the infantry defenses with additional concrete fortifications. By the time of the invasion, about 12,250 of the Atlantic Wall's planned 15,000 fortifications had been completed.

CHAPTER 4

Opposing Forces

ONE OF THE ENDURING MYTHS ABOUT OMAHA BEACH was that the U.S. Army had the misfortune to land there days after the Germans had moved an attack division to the beach on a training exercise. Instead of facing a handful of poor troops, they were confronted by a force they did not expect to encounter until a day or more after D-Day, when an initial German counterattack could be expected. In fact, the division had been moved to Omaha Beach three months before D-Day as part of Rommel's scheme to defeat the invasion on the beaches.

The popular impression of the *Wehrmacht* in 1944 has often focused its impressive Panther and Tiger tanks, its elite *Waffen-SS* divisions, and its jet and rocket wonder weapons. In reality, the German Army in the early summer of 1944 was in a slow death spiral to inevitable defeat. The fighting on the Russian Front had left it threadbare. Manpower was in short supply, many of the best troops and most experienced combat leaders were dead or wounded, and fuel supplies were evaporating. The fuel shortages not only restricted the mobility of the army, but also caused the gradual collapse of training standards for *panzer* crews and other specialized troops. Ammunition also was in short supply, especially compared to the British and American armies.

While the Lower Normandy coast did not have a particularly impressive array of Atlantic Wall fortifications, Rommel's real defense problem was the shortage of troops, not a shortage of bunkers. The Russian Front received the priority for troops until 1943, and the occupation units in France received the dregs. The *Wehrmacht*'s personnel problems became far more acute in September 1943, when Italy's withdrawal from the Axis forced Germany to divert more divisions to

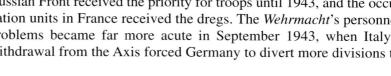

53

Alarm! A German infantry section on tactical exercise on the Atlantic Wall emerges from an underground bunker. These large underground shelters were more common in the more heavily fortified "Iron Coast" in the *15.Armee* sector, such as the Pas-de-Calais, than in the more sparsely fortified Lower Normandy sector of the *7.Armee*. NARA

replace Italian occupation divisions in the Balkans. This could not have come at a worse time, since it coincided with the *Wehrmacht*'s attempts to rejuvenate its defense force in France in anticipation of the Allied invasion. Hitler's Directive No. 51 from November 1943 was intended to shift priority back to the invasion front, but the *Wehrmacht* in France remained woefully undermanned up to D-Day.

The number of divisions assigned to OB-West reached its nadir in March 1942, with only twenty-five divisions. More divisions arrived in late 1942 and early 1943, though many of these were units temporarily in France for training and re-equipment, not for anti-invasion duties. Strength in 1943 peaked in April at fifty-six divisions but fell to forty-nine divisions by year's end because of the diversion of units to the Mediterranean after Italy's defection in September. The recognition that an Allied invasion was likely in the spring of 1944 finally reversed the flow out of France, and OB-West strength increased to fifty-three divisions in February 1944 and sixty in May–June.

An anti-invasion drill on the Atlantic Wall in 1944. The gunner in the foreground is armed with a *Rheinmetall* 7.92mm IMG 15, an alternative to the more common MG 34, which was commonly seen in *Luftwaffe* field divisions. This may be one of the *Luftwaffe* infantry units stationed in the Atlantic Wall's *15.Armee* sector in 1944. MHI

INITIAL GARRISONS AT OMAHA BEACH

The first unit deployed along the future D-Day beaches on the Normandy coast was the *323.Infanterie-Division*. It was raised in late 1940 and first posted to the Abbeville sector. It remained in northeastern France until February 1942, when it was sent into combat in Russia.

The unit most closely associated with the D-Day beaches was the *716.Infanterie-Division*.[1] It was raised in May 1941, mostly from overage draftees. Like many new units, it was dispatched to France for training and first posted in the Rouen area and later in Normandy. With training complete, on 20 March 1942 it was deployed under the *84.Korps* in Normandy, taking over the defense of the coast from the *323.Infanterie-Division* in the Carentan-Caen sector.[2] During the summer of 1942, the division was still understrength with 6,000 troops and 1,500 horses. In late October

1942, the *716.Infanterie-Division* was reclassified as a *Bodenständig* (Static) division. These divisions were intended for static coastal defense and had a limited table of organization and equipment, with few of the usual horses and trucks for tactical maneuver. The *Wehrmacht* categorized the combat value of divisions on a sliding scale from one to four—a one indicated the division was suitable for offensive missions; a two meant it had limited suitability for offensive operations; a three indicated the division was suitable only for defensive operations; and a four meant it had limited readiness for defensive duty. The static divisions were rated at three or four. On the positive side, the static divisions were deployed in fortified positions with a special authorization for additional heavy weapons for coastal defense. These firepower additions are detailed in the following chapter.

A German infantry patrol in Normandy after D-Day. LIBRARY OF CONGRESS

For most of the spring, German infantry units on the Atlantic Wall were involved in the construction of the Devil's Garden at the expense of tactical training. MHI

Rommel's push to improve the Atlantic Wall defenses in Lower Normandy meant that in the spring of 1944, many German riflemen spent more time digging entrenchments and planting coastal obstacles than performing tactical exercises. MHI

Besides their limited mobility, these static divisions were granted a lower priority for personnel. The division's troops included many soldiers with medical issues or overage draftees—the average age was around thirty-five years old, with some soldiers as old as forty-five. Most of these divisions had one or more *Schlagsahne* (Whipped Cream) battalions, so named since they contained troops with intestinal problems who were allotted a special diet. To make matters worse, these divisions were subjected to periodic "combings" to pull out any younger troops suitable to deploy to combat units in Russia or the Mediterranean theater. The manpower situation became so bad in 1943 that many German troops were replaced by *Volksdeutsch*.

The *Volksdeutsch* label had originally been applied to ethnic Germans who resided outside of Germany in the Balkans and other regions of Europe. As the *Wehrmacht* became more and more desperate for manpower, *Volksdeutsch* eventually came to encompass many non-Germans.* Regions in central Europe that had been absorbed into the Reich after the conquests of 1938–41 were subjected to the military draft, even if much of the local populace was not ethnic German. Likewise, areas of France absorbed into the Reich, such as Alsace, were also subjected to the draft. Many of the young Poles and Czechs drafted into the *Wehrmacht* could not understand German instructions. By 1944, about 40 percent of the personnel of the *716.Infanterie-Division* were *Volksdeutsch*, mostly Poles. The language barrier was not the only issue—German officers also had little confidence that such troops would remain loyal in the face of combat. The Poles were mostly from the border regions of Silesia and Pomerania, a hotbed of ethnic tension and the scene of a bitter ethnic civil war in 1918–21 between the local Polish and German

villages. Many of the young Poles had served in the Polish Army in 1939 and had been subjected to German discrimination during the years of occupation. Not surprisingly, German officers considered their loyalty to be suspect. American accounts from D-Day confirm the tendency of these troops to surrender as soon as it was safe to do so. A prisoner-of-war interrogation on D-Day provides a glimpse of the problem: "*Obergefreiter* Niemitz . . . is a Pole [*Volksliste* III] who was conscripted into the Army in December 1940. . . . He is intelligent and very co-operative . . . and deserted at the first opportunity."**

By August 1943, the division numbered 8,421 troops and reached a peak strength of 9,343 that December. Even at this late date, the division was combed for troops to send to the Russian Front, and its strength fell to 7,197 troops by February 1944.[3] To make up for the decline in strength, the division was reinforced with three *Ost-Bataillons* (Eastern Battalions) in January–February 1944: *Ost-Bataillon.642* (Ukrainian) to *Grenadier-Regiment.736*, and *Ost-Bataillon.439* (Cossack) and *Ost-Bataillon.441* (Ukrainian) to *Grenadier-Regiment.726*.***

The *Ost-Bataillons* were recruited from Soviet army prisoners of war. Young Russians, Ukrainians, Georgians, and others "volunteered" to serve in German units rather than starve to death in the horrific German prisoner-of-war camps where millions of Soviet POWs had already died. To encourage separatism in the Soviet Union, the units were often organized by region, with Ukrainian, Georgian, Turkoman, and Cossack battalions some of the more common types in Normandy. It should come as no surprise that local German commanders in France were deeply suspicious of the combat value of such troops. Some units put them to work as construction troops on the coastal fortifications.

Volksdeutsch included subcategories for draftees from the former Poland, with Category One and Category Two being ethnic Germans and Category Three being "partially Polonized" non-German ethnic groups still considered suitable for the draft, unlike Category Four Poles, who were regarded as anti-German. Out of desperation for manpower, the Poles from Silesia and Pomerania were categorized as *Volksliste* Category Three and still suitable for the draft.

**Niemitz is the Germanized version of the Polish name Niemiec, which, ironically, is the Polish word for a German. He served in the *1.Schwadron./Füsilier-Bataillon.352* and was a veteran of the Russian Front.[4]

***Ost-Bataillon.439* was assigned to coastal defense duty on 6 February 1944; *Ost-Bataillon.642* was assigned to *Grenadier-Regiment.736* on 8 February 1944; *Ost-Bataillon.441* on 9 March 1944.[5]

The *Wehrmacht*'s chronic manpower shortages led to dangerous expedients, such as the excessive use of Soviet "volunteer" units in the defense of France. In mid-January 1944, Rommel inspected the *North Caucasus Bataillon.781*, a unit composed of Turkoman prisoners of war from the Red Army serving in the *711.Infanterie-Division* near Barneville, France. NARA

Germany's desperate scrounging for manpower had some exotic results. This photo of a prisoner taken at Utah Beach from an *Ost-Bataillon* of the *709.Infanterie-Division* has been identified in some sources as Yang Kyoungjong, a Korean who had been drafted into the Japanese army, taken prisoner by the Red Army during the 1939 border battles in Manchuria, forcibly drafted by the Red Army in 1942–43, captured by the *Wehrmacht*, and recruited again for an *Ost-Bataillon*. It's equally possible that this photo shows one of the innumerable Turkoman or other Soviet Asian troops who ended up in the *Wehrmacht* in Normandy. NARA

There were some odd results to the desperate manpower effort. One of the more extreme examples was Yang Kyoungjong, a member of an *Ost-Bataillon* in the *709.Infanterie-Division*, who was captured by U.S. troops near Utah Beach on D-Day. Born in Korea, he had been conscripted in Manchuria by the Imperial Japanese Army in 1938, captured by the Red Army during the border battles near Khalkin-Gol in 1939, sent to a Soviet labor camp, drafted into the Red Army in 1942, captured by the *Wehrmacht* in 1943 during the battle for Kharkov, and recruited for an *Ost-Bataillon* that was destined for Normandy later in 1943.* The large number of Asian "volunteers" from Turkmenistan and other Soviet eastern provinces led to occasional reports of Japanese troops in German service in Normandy.

The *716.Infanterie-Division* was the principal German unit on the future D-Day beaches, covering a ninety-kilometer (fifty-six-mile) sector from Carentan in the west to Ouistreham in the east. This sector included all three British/Canadian beaches—Juno, Gold, and Sword—as well as Omaha Beach. Utah Beach was farther west in the sector of the *709.Infanterie-Division*, another static division. The *709.Infanterie-Division* was assigned to cover 220 kilometers (137 miles) of coastline, including the critical port of Cherbourg, a gross overextension even by 1943 standards.

---

*Unlike most *Ost-Bataillon* prisoners, Yang Kyoungjong was not forcibly repatriated to the Soviet Union in 1945–46, but instead ended up becoming a U.S. citizen. Korean historians have concluded that about 500 Koreans ended up in *Ost-Bataillons* in France. Research by the Korean TV network SBS found evidence not only of Korean "volunteers," but also of a few from Iraq, Iran, Java (Indonesia), and even Guatemala. This tale is so well known in Korea that a film, *My Way*, was produced in 2011 by the popular director Kang Je-gyu and was the most expensive movie production in Korea to date. (The film is called *Far Away* in Europe.)[6]

TABLE 4: *716.INFANTERIE-DIVISION* STRENGTH IN STRONGPOINTS ON D-DAY BEACHES, JUNE 1943[7]

	Utah	Omaha	Gold	Juno	Sword
Troops	90	243	174	305	370
Rifles	48	212	170	250	298
Sub-machine guns	14	31	16	26	28
Light MG	6	22	14	27	33
Heavy MG	3	14	9	15	5
Mortar	2	12	4	9	11
50mm pedestal gun	2	6	6	6	7
Antitank guns	1	2		1	
Field guns	1	5	1	6	1

THE *352.INFANTERIE-DIVISION* ARRIVES

Lower Normandy was frequently used to train and rebuild Germany infantry divisions, which were then sent back to the Russian Front. While the *716.Infanterie-Division* was defending the coast in the autumn of 1943, a new unit arrived immediately to its south in the St. Lô area. *Kampfgruppe Normandie* (Battlegroup Normandy) was first organized on 12 October 1943 from the "torso" of the shattered *321.Infanterie-Division*. The *321.Infanterie-Division* had been decimated on the Russian Front in the summer and fall of 1943 and the survivors sent back to France. The Germans called these crippled divisions "torsos" because they had lost the muscle of their combat units in fighting, but still had a relatively intact core of headquarters, supply, and artillery units. German divisions maintained two accounts of unit strength—the overall divisional strength and the "fighting" strength (*Gefechtsstärke*). A fully equipped division with about 12,000 troops would have a *Gefechtsstärke* of about 6,000 troops. This is an important factor to keep in mind when assessing combat losses. While it might seem that divisional casualties of 4,000 men represented only a third of its troops, in reality it represented two-thirds of its fighting strength.

Kampfgruppe Normandie was later joined by survivors from the *268.Infanterie-Division* and *Grenadier-Regiment.546*. On 5 November 1943, *Kampfgruppe Normandie* was redesignated as the *352.Infanterie-Division*.[8] Unlike the *716.Infanterie-Division*, the new division was organized and equipped as a regular infantry division with a full complement of troops, trucks, and horses. It also differed from the neighboring static infantry divisions

Lt. Gen. Dietrich Kraiss was commander of the *352.Infanterie-Division* on D-Day. He had commanded several infantry divisions on the Russian Front in 1941–43 before again being assigned the formation of a new division from the shattered remnants of units smashed in Russia. MHI

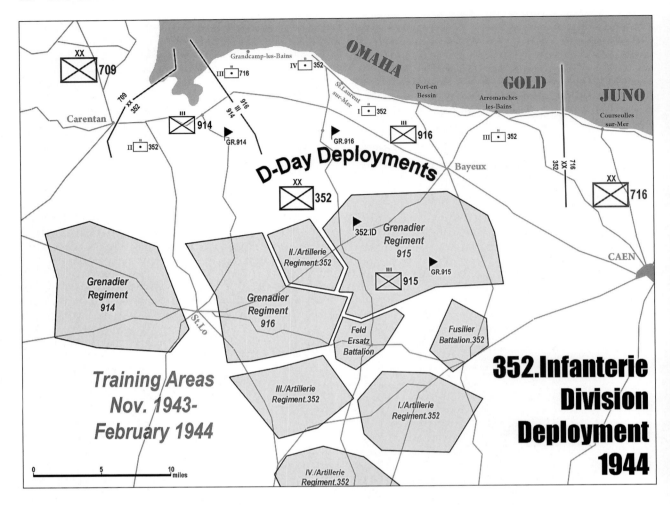

Training Areas Nov. 1943–February 1944

D-Day Deployments

352.Infanterie Division Deployment 1944

since it was manned primarily by German troops, with a smaller percentage of *Volksdeutsch* or Soviet volunteers.[*] The divisional headquarters, led by Lt. Gen. Dietrich Kraiss, expected the division to be shipped back to the Russian Front once its rebuilding and training in France were finished.[9]

The *352.Infanterie-Division* was sometimes referred to as an "attack division" in Allied intelligence briefings. This was a misunderstanding. This division was rated at Combat Value One, while the static divisions in Normandy, such as the

716.Infanterie-Division, were rated at three or four. But the division was in no sense an elite or special unit. It stood out simply because so many other units in France were of such poor quality.

Aside from receiving better-quality troops, the *352.Infanterie-Division* received a better supply of weapons, consisting mainly of standard German types, not the hodgepodge of captured weapons issued to the static divisions.[**] Its divisional artillery used the standard German 105mm LFH 18/40 field gun rather than captured types. In addi-

---

[*]As of February 1944, the division included 9,934 German troops and 515 "Hiwi" Red Army volunteers, who were used for support but not armed as were those in the *Ost-Bataillons*. Although the official records recorded the strength as primarily German, unit memoirs suggest that the division had about 20 percent *Volksdeutsch*, mainly Poles and Alsatians.

[**]For example, as of January 1944, the division had 8,220 98k rifles and 3,870 other German-manufactured small arms, but only 26 captured small arms, mainly Soviet PPSh sub-machine guns.[10]

The strongest sector of the *352.Infanterie-Division* was not Omaha Beach, but rather Strongpoint Group Vire, located between Utah Beach to the west and Omaha Beach to the east. This sector was packed with artillery, including two battalions of field artillery, most of *Grenadier-Regiment.914*, and two other infantry battalions from the *716.Infanterie-Division*. This sector was designed to shield the port of Grandcamp-les-Bains as well as the Vire River estuary. This area was overrun by the U.S. Army on 7–9 June during the effort to link up Omaha and Utah Beaches.

tion, it had armored support in the form of a company of fourteen Marder III 75mm *Panzerjäger* (tank destroyers) and fourteen StuG III assault guns; none of the static divisions had armored companies. The *352.Infanterie-Division* was the best German infantry division in Lower Normandy.

When Rommel first visited the *716.Infanterie-Division* in Normandy on 29 January 1944, he was dismayed by the overextension of the division in such a critical sector. His tour led him to believe that this portion of the coast was a plausible, if unlikely, location for an Allied landing. As mentioned earlier,

Rommel saw the physical similarity of the area to Salerno. Equally important, this portion of the coast was at the elbow where the Cotentin Peninsula juts northward toward the vital port of Cherbourg. Rommel realized that the Allies were unlikely to attack Cherbourg frontally because of its extensive defenses. A more plausible scenario would be an amphibious landing near the Vire River estuary to cut off the Cotentin Peninsula prior to storming the port from the land side. He was not worried primarily about the Plage d'Or, the future Omaha Beach, but rather the entire area from Port-en-Bessin westward toward the Vire River estuary. This sector, roughly thirty-five kilometers (twenty-two miles) wide, contained two small but useful ports at Port-en-Bessin and Grandcamp-les-Bains, and the Vire River estuary offered other smaller landing sites. In addition, Rommel recognized that the open beaches on the Plage d'Or between Port-en-Bessin and the cliffs at Pointe-et-Raz-de-la-Percée were well suited to amphibious landings.

Rommel needed to win the approval of the *Wehrmacht* high command (OKW) in Berlin to retain the *352.Infanterie-Division* in France and not send it off to the Russian Front as planned. He received this permission in early February 1944. As part of a new effort at "enhanced defense preparedness," the *7.Armee* was allotted the *352. Infanterie-Division* for its efforts in Lower Normandy so that it could be deployed for "rapid use on the coast" at the first moment after an Allied landing.[11] The division was authorized to move behind the *716.Infanterie-Division* into the sector of Bayeux-Trévières-Isigny-St. Lô. The locations of regimental command posts were approved on 15 February 1944.

Several units of *Kampfgruppe Meyer* of the *352.Infanterie-Division* were bicycle mobile on D-Day, including *Füsilier-Bataillon.352* and *I./Grenadier-Regiment.915*. These troops are from an antitank section armed with the 88mm *Panzerschreck*, the German equivalent of the U.S. Army bazooka antitank rocket launcher. MHI

A young German soldier from the *352.Infanterie-Division* captured on D-Day, seen on a U.S. ship back to a prison camp in Britain. The troops of the *352.Infanterie-Division* were recruited mainly from the 1925–26 cadre and so were mostly eighteen to nineteen years old on D-Day. NARA

By February 1944, the *352.Infanterie-Division* was not yet fully equipped and had a strength of only 9,934 troops. However, its divisional artillery, *Artillerie-Regiment.352*, was better prepared than the division's infantry regiments since it was based on the experienced troops of the old *321.Infanterie-Division*, who had survived the Russian campaign mostly intact. The *7.Armee* had already authorized a forward deployment of the artillery on 26 January 1944 as a temporary expedient to reinforce the weak *716.Infanterie-Division*, and the units began moving on 11 February 1944.[12]

Having won permission to keep the *352.Infanterie-Division* in France, Rommel continued to push the OKW in Berlin to permit its use directly on the beach and not merely as a reserve formation. This was part of his broader effort to have as much firepower immediately on the beach as possible and to not rely on counterattack forces. Rommel wanted to deploy all three of the division's infantry regiments directly on the coast, but the OKW was unwilling to permit this.[13] The OKW finally compromised in early March 1944, allowing the forward deployment of most of the division alongside the *716.Infanterie-Division*. However, Berlin con-tinued to stipulate that the division be ready to move on short notice and that a *Kampfgruppe* including at least one infantry regiment be kept behind the coast to serve as a mobile reserve for the *84.Korps* in this sector.[14]

The *352.Infanterie-Division* did not reach full strength until March 1944 with 12,734 troops. In total, about 50 percent of the officers in the division were new and inexperienced. There were few sur-vivors of the Russian cauldron in the infantry regi-ments. In contrast, the division's artillery regiment was largely intact from Russia. Even after reaching full strength, the division still had a shortage of about 30 percent of its non-commissioned officers.[15]

Starting in March 1944, two infantry regiments began taking over the western sector of the *716.Infanterie-Division* from Carentan to St. Lau-rent, while the third regiment—plus the divisional *Füsilier* (Reconnaissance) battalion—would remain in the training area near St. Lô to act as a ready reserve for the *84.Korps* or for rapid deployment to other sectors if needed. The rapid-reaction force was later called *Kampfgruppe Meyer* after the regi-mental commander of *Grenadier-Regiment.915*, Lt. Col. Karl Meyer.

THE DEFENSE OF THE OMAHA BEACH

The sector of the coast from Carentan to Ouistreham first defended by the *716.Infanterie-Division* was designated as Coastal Defense Sector H (KVA H: *Küsten Verteidigung Abschnitt H*). Rommel was especially concerned about the western portion of this defense sector around the Vire River estuary at the Cotentin Peninsula elbow. As a result, when Coastal Defense Sector H was broken in two, the *352.Infanterie-Division* was assigned to Sector H2 on the Vire estuary and the *716.Infanterie-Division* was left with Sector H1 farther east toward the Orne estuary.

The divisional Sector H2 included three Strongpoint Groups (StPG: *Stutzpunkt Gruppe*): StPG Vire, StPG St. Laurent, and StPG Bessin. The middle of these, Strongpoint Group St. Laurent, was later known as Omaha Beach. The division positioned *Grenadier-Regiment.914* on the western side of its defense zone around Strongpoint Group Vire, which covered the Vire River estuary and the port of Grandcamp-les-Bains along a ten-kilometer (six-mile) stretch of coastline.* *Grenadier-Regiment.916* covered a larger sector of the coast, from the cliffs east of Grandcamp-les-Bains near Pointe-du-Hoc, past the Plage d'Or, and over to Port-en-Bessin, encompassing Strongpoint Groups St. Laurent and Bessin in an area about twenty-five kilometers (sixteen miles) wide. The reasons for the disproportion in forces between the east and west wings of the division were the terrain and Rommel's assessment of the threat. The Vire River estuary and the port of Grandcamp-les-Bains were viewed as especially valuable to an invading force and were already heavily protected by the Strongpoint Group Vire concentration. The section farther east, which included the future Omaha Beach, was viewed as a less attractive objective for Allied landings, and significant portions of the area, including the Pointe-et-Raz-de-la-Percée to the west of Omaha Beach and the coast near Ste. Honorine, were shielded by rocky cliffs.

To minimize the disruption to the existing defense scheme, the units of the *716.Infanterie-Division* in Sector H2 were not moved, but rather absorbed by the *352.Infanterie-Division*. This force nominally consisted of the division's *Grenadier-Regiment.726*, but in reality, the regimental staff and its second battalion remained with the parent division farther to the east. As a result, three infantry battalions and one artillery battalion of the *716.Infanterie-Division* were subordinated to the *352.Infanterie-Division*.[16] The *III./Grenadier-Regiment.726* was attached to *Grenadier-Regiment.914* and deployed along the coast from the Grandcamp-les-Bains area over to the west side of Omaha Beach near Vierville. The *I./Grenadier-Regiment.726* was subordinated to *Grenadier-Regiment.916* and sandwiched between its two battalions on the Plage d'Or, the future Omaha Beach. The remaining infantry unit was *Ost-Bataillon.439*, which Rommel did not trust to guard the coast. Through the end of 1943, this Cossack battalion had been headquartered in Vierville and assigned the Vierville sector of the future Omaha Beach.[17] On D-Day, it was deployed away from the coast on the Vire River estuary near Isigny.

Although the two battalions of *Grenadier-Regiment.726* remained in nominal charge of two of the most vital defense sectors on divisional maps, the actual picture on the beach was different. Existing strongpoints along the coast remained manned by *Grenadier-Regiment.726*, and companies of *Grenadier-Regiment.914* and *Grenadier-Regiment.916* were brought forward from their training areas near St. Lô into the towns immediately behind the beaches. There were not enough accommodations for the new troops from the *352.Infanterie-Division* in the coastal strongholds, so they were garrisoned in French homes in the nearby towns and villages. Once the invasion alert message was transmitted, these units were expected to deploy forward immediately and reinforce the troops of *Grenadier-Regiment.726* in the bunkers and trenches along the coast.

---

*The town of Grandcamp-les-Bains is today known as Grandcamp-Maisy after it amalgamated with the neighboring village of Maisy in 1972.

A German rifleman in a trench during the fighting on the Cotentin Peninsula in Lower Normandy on 22 June 1944. He is armed with the standard *Gewehr* 98k and is wearing a *Zeltbahn*, a camouflaged tent shelter panel that doubled as a raincoat. MHI

THE OMAHA BEACH GARRISON

Rommel's efforts to reinforce the coast west of Bayeux substantially added to the defenses on Omaha Beach. Prior to the arrival of the *352.Infanterie-Division*, Omaha Beach was defended by three infantry companies. In addition, the battalion's heavy weapons company, *8./Grenadier-Regiment.726*, provided some of its troops to man various crew-served weapons in the defense nests along the beach.

The immediate defenses on the beach were reinforced by two companies from *Grenadier-Regiment.916*, with *5.Kompanie* stationed in St. Laurent and *8.Kompanie* stationed in Colleville. Two other companies from *II./Grenadier-Regiment.916* were three to four kilometers (two miles) behind the beach along the coastal road, with *6.Kompanie* at Formigny and *7.Kompanie* at Surrain. Other troops from *Grenadier-Regiment.916* were also on Omaha Beach: for example, *13.Kompanie* (infantry guns) and *14. Kompanie* (antitank guns) from the regimental heavy weapons companies had a portion of their troops and heavy weapons assigned to the beach. On 4 June 1944, some elements of *Grenadier-Regiment.914* were deployed in Strongpoint Vierville. Two sections from *3./Grenadier-Regiment.914* were assigned to WN72 and set up positions among the existing bunkers and defenses.[18] It is possible that the rest of the company was assigned to the other defense nests of Strongpoint Vierville, but further details are lacking.

An additional source of troops arrived in the Omaha Beach area in mid-March because of the fortification construction. *Landesbau-Pioneer-Bataillon.17*, an engineer construction unit, was transferred to the Bayeux sector to assist in the revived fortification construction on the beaches. The staff, the battalion's *2.Kompanie*, and the battalion's equipment column were garrisoned in St. Laurent-sur-Mer, while *1.Kompanie* was garrisoned in Colleville.* While these were not infantry troops, they were armed and subsequently saw combat on D-Day.

WN62 is the best-detailed defense nest on Omaha Beach since two of its troops later wrote memoirs, so it provides a good example of the interface between the units of *Grenadier-Regiment.726* and *Grenadier-Regiment.916*. Prior to the buildup effort in the spring of 1944, WN62 had a strength of twenty-one troops, all from the *716.Infanterie-Division*. On D-Day, its strength increased to thirty-nine, including twenty-seven from *3.Kompanie/Grenadier-Regiment.726*, an artillery forward observer team from *1./Artillerie-Regiment.352*, and four soldiers from *14.Kompanie/Grenadier-Regiment.916*, who manned the heavy weapons that were added to the defenses in WN62.

---

*The other two companies were deployed in Ver-sur-Mer. These companies were usually smaller than infantry companies, typically about 110 men.[19]

TABLE 5: *716.INFANTERIE-DIVISION* INFANTRY UNITS AT OMAHA BEACH		
Strongpoint	**HQ**	**Unit**
Strongpoint Vierville	Manoir de Than	11./GR.726
Strongpoint St. Laurent	WN67, near St. Laurent train station	10./GR.726
Strongpoint Colleville	WN63, Colleville	3./GR.726

German infantrymen inspect captured GI equipment, including a wool cap, during the fighting on the Cotentin Peninsula in June 1944. MHI

In total, the units subordinate to the *352.Infanterie-Division* had about 800 to 1,000 troops on Omaha Beach on D-Day—about 450 in the defense nests, with the rest in houses and trenches near the beach and in the villages a short distance behind the beach.[*] There were several hundred additional reinforcements in the area who were able to reach the beach later in the day.[**] Two other units that would be involved in counterattacks on D-Day were a company of the divisional tank destroyer battalion and the divisional engineers, located fifteen kilometers (nine miles) to the southwest of the beach.

The most significant *352.Infanterie-Division* reserve was *Kampfgruppe Meyer*, based around *Grenadier-Regiment.915* and the division's *Füsilier* battalion stationed about twenty kilometers (twelve miles) southeast of Omaha Beach near Bayeux.[***] This battle group was almost taken away from the division in the days before the invasion when the OKW planned to send it to reinforce *Festung St. Malo*, the fortified port at the junction of Normandy and Brittany. However, the order was rescinded on 2 June 1944 before the unit moved. This was of considerable significance to the Omaha Beach fighting, as one of the battle group's battalions played a key role in reinforcing the eastern wing of the German defenses and blocking the advance of the 1st Infantry Division out of the beachhead on D-Day.

The other major participant in the counterattacks after D-Day was *Schnelle-Brigade.30* (Fast Brigade 30), a bicycle infantry formation that served as a mobile reserve for the *84.Korps* near Coutances. Although a few troops arrived on D-Day, the bulk of the unit did not arrive in the Omaha area until D+1 (7 June).

The effect of Rommel's effort to reinforce the Omaha Beach sector with the *352.Infanterie-Division* was further amplified by the failure of Allied intelligence to detect the division's presence. Instead of facing only three companies of infantry, the U.S. Army unexpectedly faced a defending force about three times its size and much better armed. This intelligence failure is detailed later, in Chapter 8.

---

[*]Since there is no detailed list for dispositions on D-Day, estimates are needed. The figure of 450 troops in the resistance nests is based on a rough calculation from the example of WN62, where strength went from twenty-one on 15 June 1943 to thirty-nine on D-Day. Assuming that the other resistance nests had comparable increases, this would suggest that the 15 June figure rose to about 450 troops.

[**]In support of a 2007 BBC-Two *Timewatch* documentary "Bloody Omaha," Dr. Simon Trew of the Royal Military Academy Sandhurst prepared a memorandum entitled "How strong were the German beachfront defences at Omaha Beach?" in which he estimated 1,050 to 1,100 troops, not counting potential reinforcements nearby.

[***]The *Grenadier-Regiment.915* was headquartered in St. Paul du Vernay, southeast of Omaha Beach.

TABLE 6: *352.INFANTERIE-DIVISION* ORDER OF BATTLE, D-DAY 1944		
352.Infanterie-Division	**Molay-Littry**	**Gen. Lt. Dietrich Kraiss**
Grenadier-Regiment.914	**Neuilly-la-Foret**	**Lt. Col. Ernst Heyna**
I./GR.914	Osmanville	
II./GR.914	Catz	
Grenadier-Regiment.915	**St. Paul-du-Vernay**	**Lt. Col. Karl Meyer**
I./GR.915	Juaye	
II./GR.915	Lantheuil	
Grenadier-Regiment.916	**Trevieres**	**Lt. Col. Ernst Goth**
I./GR.916	Ryes	
II./GR.916	Formigny	
Grenadier-Regiment.726	**Sully**	**Lt. Col. Walter Korfes**
I./GR.726	Maisons	
III./GR.726	Jucoville	
Ost-Bataillon.439	Isigny	
Artillerie-Regiment.352	**Molay-Littry**	**Lt. Col. Karl Ocker**
I./AR.352	Etreham	
II./AR.352	St. Clement	
III./AR.352	La Noë	
IV./AR.352	Asnières-le-Bessin	
Füsilier-Bataillon.352	Caumont-l'Evente	
Panzerjäger-Bataillon.352	Mestry	
Pioneer-Bataillon.352	St. Martin-de-Blagny	

CHAPTER 5

Fire and Brimstone

IN MODERN INDUSTRIALIZED WARFARE, artillery has been the primary battlefield killer. The role of German artillery in the D-Day battles has generally been overlooked. Since one of the underlying themes of this book is the casualty discrepancy between Omaha Beach and the other D-Day beaches, it is important to understand the German firepower used against the invasion.

There are no authoritative sources of data on the causes of the casualties on Omaha Beach.[1] As mentioned earlier, even the overall number of casualties is still murky. Nevertheless, some idea of the likely sources can be gathered by examining the causes of wartime casualties in other World War II battles. In general, artillery and mortar fire tended to be the primary cause, with small arms a distant second. A U.S. Army Medical Department study of wound ballistics in World War II found only a single detailed statistical assessment of the cause of casualties. This study, conducted during the Italian campaign, found that 11 percent of the casualties were from small arms and 89 percent from artillery, mortars, and grenades. During the Canadian attack on the Gothic Line in Italy in August–October 1944, about 12 percent of casualties were from small arms and 59 percent from artillery.[2] During the XIX Corps penetration of the Siegfried Line in October 1944, the U.S. Army found that about 18 percent of casualties were caused by small arms and about 80 percent by artillery and mortars.[3] Another study from Korea found that small arms were responsible for 7.5 percent of casualties and artillery, mortars, and grenades for about

92 percent.* There is no particular reason to expect that the sources of casualties on Omaha Beach were markedly different from those of other battles in the same time frame. This suggests that the most lethal weapons were mortars and artillery weapons.

Artillery would include the direct-fire artillery and mortars located in the strongpoints near the beach and the field artillery located some distance from the beach.

---

*Most medical studies of casualties lump together casualties caused by artillery, mortars, grenades, and mines since it is usually impossible to distinguish the source of the blast and fragmentation injuries; gunshot wounds tend to be distinctive.[4]

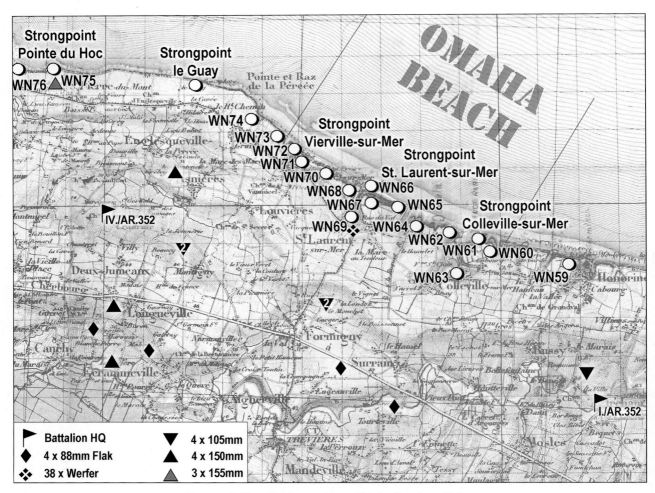

German Artillery Deployment near Omaha Beach on D-Day

OMAHA BEACH ARSENALS: THE *716.INFANTERIE-DIVISION*

Prior to the arrival of the *352.Infanterie-Division* in March 1944, the defense of Omaha Beach was in the hands of infantry companies of the *716.Infanterie-Division*. The arsenal available to this *Bodenständig* division was significantly different from standard infantry divisions such as the *352.Infanterie-Division*. Besides the normal allotment of infantry weapons covered in the standardized table-of-organization-and-equipment, the static divisions had a separate *Bodenständig* arsenal. This arsenal did not actually "belong" to the division. If the

division moved, the static weapons remained behind in the fortifications. This static arsenal was allotted to the defensive strongpoint, not the unit.

Static divisions on the Atlantic Wall were generally issued a motlier assortment of basic weapons than standard infantry divisions. In some cases, even the infantry rifles were war-booty weapons. In the specific case of the *716.Infanterie-Division*, the picture was mixed. Its basic infantry weapons, including rifles and pistols, were the standard German types, such as the Karabiner 98k rifle.* (See

---

*Details of the weapons holdings of the division are available for different dates on several *Kriegsgliederung* (military organization charts, corresponding to the U.S. Army TO&E).[5] The *Gliederung* for 1 January 1944 indicated that the division did not have any foreign infantry weapons, but those details were not listed. A later *Gliederung* from 1 March 1944 indicated that a small number of foreign weapons were in use, including eighty-six Czech, thirty-eight Polish, and thirty-five Yugoslav rifles.

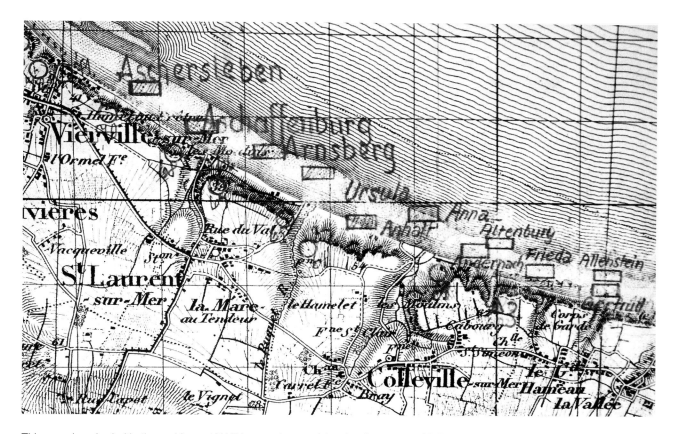

This map, long buried in the archives at NARA, reveals one of the deadly secrets of D-Day. It is a hand-drawn map by the artillery officers of *Artillerie-Regiment.352* showing the code names for the aim points (*Zielpunkt*) on Omaha Beach. In the months prior to D-Day, German artillery officers had carefully pre-registered the beach area to ensure a speedy and accurate bombardment in the event of invasion. NARA

Table 7. A detailed listing of the division's weapons is contained in Appendix 1.[6]) While the small arms were mainly standard German types, the divisional crew-served weapons were a mix, including standard German weapons such as the MG 34 light machine gun, obsolete types such as the World War I sMG 08 heavy machine gun, and various war booty weapons such as the French leMG 116(f) light machine gun.

In contrast to the divisional weapons, the division's static arsenal consisted mainly of war-booty weapons. As can be seen below, the static arsenal added substantial firepower to the division including 177 machine guns, 75 mortars, 48 antitank guns, 57 fortification guns, and 41 field guns. This more than tripled the division's heavy weapons from 92 to 398 mortars and artillery weapons.

The static arsenal fundamentally changed the firepower of the *716.Infanterie-Division*. For example, the defense nest WN62 on Omaha Beach, a platoon-size position, contained no fewer than seven machine guns, two mortars, two antitank

German artillery was especially effective on D-Day because the local units carefully registered their targets and conducted practice barrages before D-Day. The last major practice was eight days before the landing. This shows a practice artillery barrage off the coast, with a row of Cointet obstacles visible in the foreground. MHI

TABLE 7: *716.INFANTERIE-DIVISION* CREW-SERVED WEAPONS ARSENAL

Type	Divisional	Static	Total
Machine guns	376	177	553
Antitank guns	24	48	72
Mortars	72	75	147
Fortification guns		57	57
Field guns	20	41	61

guns, and two field guns—in other words, the firepower of an infantry unit much larger than a mere platoon.

Although the static arsenal substantially boosted the firepower of the division, a potential drawback was the lack of standardization. Many of these weapons used ammunition that was different from the German types, and in many cases the ammunition was no longer being manufactured under the German occupation.[7] The solution to this supply problem was to store substantially more ammunition in the strongpoints than in normal infantry divisions. In Normandy, the standard for rifles was 3 units-of-fire for the coastal defense units compared with 1.5 for normal divisions, and the standard for machine guns was 6 units-of-fire for the coastal defense units versus 2 for normal divisions.*

The ammunition situation for the *7.Armee* in Normandy on D-Day was adequate for the short term. Reports from the spring indicate there was ample ammunition for small arms, machine guns, and mortars, with enough supplies to last rifles and machine guns for 52 days, sub-machine guns and pistols for 120 days, light mortars (50mm) for 81 days, and medium mortars (81mm) for 25 days. Artillery ammunition was in much less abundant supply, with eight days' worth for light field howitzers (105mm) and seven days' worth for heavy field howitzers (150mm).[8] Ammunition supplies continued to increase in the months prior to D-Day. Holdings at the nine army ammunition depots (AML: *Armee-Munitions-Lager*) went from 16,742 tons on 1 April 1944, to 18,738 tons on 1 June 1944.[9] Divisional records for the *716.Infanterie-Division* indicate that ammunition supplies were higher than the basic requirements.

One of the developments in Normandy that may seem perplexing was a decision by Rommel's Army Group B headquarters to reduce ammunition stockpiles along the Normandy coast in late May 1944, only weeks before the invasion. During an inspection tour by Rommel in mid-May, accompanying ordnance specialists discovered that ammunition held in the *716.Infanterie-Division* coastal strongpoints was suffering from unacceptable

---

*The *Wehrmacht* used two primary methods for cataloging ammunition holdings. The German equivalent of the U.S. Army's unit-of-fire was *Ausstattung*, a standardized figure for the amount of ammunition needed for three days of fighting.[10] At the beginning of the war, the *Ausstattung* for an infantry division for some typical munitions was 3 million rounds of small-arms ammunition (95 metric tons), 22,500 mortar rounds (53 metric tons), 9,864 rounds for 105mm light field howitzers (227 metric tons), and 1,800 rounds for 150mm heavy field guns (108 metric tons). Some quartermaster records catalog ammunition holdings by "days of fighting," a somewhat different metric from the unit-of-fire.

deterioration. As a result, units were ordered to turn in some of their stockpiles to rear-area ordnance depots where the ammunition could be better maintained. The intention was to reduce the holdings by about half, but to increase them for selected weapons. The table below shows the actual holdings, as well as the intended holdings after the reduction.[11] It is by no means clear how much of this ammunition transfer actually occurred, given the late date.

TABLE 8: AVERAGE AMMUNITION HOLDINGS (IN ROUNDS) OF *716.INFANTERIE-DIVISION*, MAY 1944

	Strongpoints (StP)	Resistance Nests (WN)	Intended Holdings
Rifle	297	247	90–100
Light MG	20,700	13,800	6,000–7,500
Heavy MG	37,800	25,200	10,000–12,000
50mm mortar	624	468	540–800
81mm mortar	600	450	300–450
75mm PaK 40 AT gun	600	450	675–1,000
88mm PaK 43/41 AT gun	800	600	800–1,200

LANDING CRAFT KILLERS

The coastal defenses in Normandy were armed with a number of weapons not commonly deployed in normal infantry divisions, and it is worth describing them in a bit more detail here. The 50mm pedestal-mounted tank gun (5cm *KwK Behelfssockellafette*) was one of the most common weapons in Atlantic Wall defenses, with more than 1,800 dotting the coast. This weapon was one of a family of 50mm tank guns originally designed for the *PzKpfw III* tank, the backbone of the *panzer* force in the early years of the war. With the advent of the heavily armored Soviet T-34 and KV tanks, the gun was no longer viable as a main tank gun. In 1942, these

guns were declared surplus to tank construction and taken over by the *Wehrmacht*'s fortification office for coastal defense. Of the 1,800 guns available, about 500 went to the Norwegian coast, while the rest went to France and the Low Countries.[12]

Even though the 50mm gun was no longer state of the art for tank fighting, it was a superb weapon for coastal defense against landing craft. Like most tank guns, it had a fast-action breech and a high rate of fire, on the order of twelve to twenty rounds per minute for a well-trained crew. It was very effective against unarmored targets such as landing craft, using either high-explosive or armor-piercing

One of the most deadly but underappreciated German weapons on Omaha Beach was the 50mm pedestal gun or, by its official German title, the 5cm *KwK Behelfssockellafette*. These used surplus 50mm tank guns from the *PzKpfw III* on a special pedestal mount to create a multi-purpose coastal defense weapon. This particular example is preserved at the Utah Beach museum and is still in its original concrete *Ringstand*. AUTHOR

The 50mm pedestal gun was based on two similar guns but with different barrel lengths. This is an example with the shorter L/42 gun tube.

On Omaha Beach, the 50mm pedestal gun was mounted in open *Ringstands* and in R612 bunkers. They were particularly effective against landing craft because of their high accuracy and rapid fire. This is a survivor of the battle with the longer L/60 gun tube, preserved at the Omaha Beach museum west of Vierville. AUTHOR

The 50mm pedestal guns were frequently shielded by a camouflage umbrella prior to combat, as seen in this example in the *Festung Cherbourg* sector. This was often removed before combat, and so not evident on D-Day photos. NARA

ammunition. Even if not the most modern antitank gun in the German arsenal, it could still penetrate the armor of Sherman tanks at typical short ranges.

Most of the strongpoints on the D-Day beaches had one or two of these weapons, often along the shoreline. They were usually deployed to cover antitank traps or other major obstructions. On Omaha Beach, most of the critical exit draws had guns on either side of the draw. The most common method of deployment was in a *Ringstand*, which, as the name implies, was an open, circular concrete pit with no overhead protection. These were mounted nearly flush to the ground, providing a small target to an attacker. Some of the 50mm pedestal guns were mounted in full casemates;

there were several examples of these on Omaha Beach.

Another gun common in Normandy was the 75mm FK 235(b) field gun. This was the German designation for the Belgian *Canon de 75 mle TR "tir rapide"* (rapid-fire), the standard field gun of the Belgian Army in World War I and license-manufactured by Cockerill in Liege on the basis of the German Krupp Mod. 1905. While not an especially modern field gun, it was still a very lethal weapon against infantry. Several of these were deployed in the Omaha Beach area, but they have been widely misidentified over the years because of their similarity to other varieties of German Krupp field guns.[13]

The German Army had a substantial inventory of war-booty French antitank guns, of which the 47mm PaK 181(f) (*Canon de 47 antichar mle. 1937*) was the best. Although a bit dated as an antitank weapon, it was still highly effective against other targets such as landing craft. One of these was deployed in an earth gun pit in WN68 on D-Day. AUTHOR

Having captured a large inventory of French 75mm M1897 field guns, the German Army modernized them by transferring the gun assembly to the more modern carriage of the 50mm PaK 38. This was designated as the 75mm PaK 97/38 in German service. These were widely used in Normandy, and a single example was located at Omaha Beach in a small bunker carved into the cliff face below the WN73 defense position to the west of Vierville. AUTHOR

CONCRETE KING TIGER

The most powerful weapon on Omaha Beach was the 88mm PaK 43/41, a towed version of the weapon in the King Tiger tank. This gun had been designed as an antidote to Soviet heavy tanks such as the KV-1. When finally reaching the field in significant numbers in 1943, it did not prove especially popular and was nicknamed the *Scheuntor* (barn door) because of its massive size. Although an enormously potent gun, it was too heavy and unwieldy for battlefield use on the Russian Front. It weighed 4.4 metric tonnes, and so could not be easily man-handled by its crew when deployed. Since its prime mover was usually kept away from the

gun during combat, this made it unusually vulnerable compared to smaller antitank guns. In its place, the heavy *Panzerjäger* units began to receive a self-propelled version, the *Nashorn*, in 1943 that was mounted on a medium tank chassis. As a result, the 88mm PaK 43/41 became available for fortification use and was the most potent antitank gun deployed in the Atlantic Wall. Even though it was designed as an antitank gun, it was used as a multipurpose weapon in coastal defense and, as will be related in chapter 10, was one of the most lethal weapons used against landing craft.

The standard divisional antitank gun in 1944 was the 75mm PaK 40. This was not commonly issued to Atlantic Wall static divisions, but there were several on Omaha Beach from the *352.Infanterie-Division*. This example is preserved at the Raversijde *Atlantikwall* museum on the Belgian coast. AUTHOR

The most powerful gun located on Omaha Beach was the 88mm PaK 43/41. This massive weapon proved too heavy and unwieldy for field use, but was excellent when firing from the well-protected R677 bunkers. AUTHOR

The very substantial size of the 88mm PaK 43/41 filled up the interior of the R677 bunkers, as seen in this example located in the Varreville strongpoint of the *709.Infanterie-Division*, north of Utah Beach. NARA

OMAHA BEACH ARSENALS: THE *352.INFANTERIE-DIVISION*

The arrival of infantry companies of the *352.Infanterie-Division* in the Omaha Beach area in March 1944 increased the amount of firepower in this sector. In terms of infantry along the coast, it increased the Omaha Beach garrison from about three infantry companies to about five infantry and two engineer companies, with a commensurate increase in firepower. A German infantry company at this stage of the war had about 180 men. Besides the usual rifles, pistols, and sub-machine guns, its crew-served weapons included thirteen light machine guns—usually the MG 42 on a bipod—and two heavy machine guns, which were the same MG 42 but on a heavier tripod.

What is less clear is the amount of heavy weaponry added to the beach defenses along with the infantry companies. Each infantry battalion of *Grenadier-Regiment.916* had a heavy-weapons company with an additional three light machine guns, six heavy machine guns, six 81mm mortars, and four 120mm mortars. It can be presumed that these weapons reinforced the defenses on Omaha Beach.

German infantry regiments had an organic infantry gun company and an antitank gun company. These were often parceled out to the battalions rather than kept intact. There is evidence that the antitank company of *Grenadier-Regiment.916* dispatched at least two 75mm PaK 40 antitank guns to the Omaha Beach area, but the total may have been larger.[*]

---

[*]Memoirs from soldiers stationed in WN62 indicate that a 75mm PaK 40 and its crew from *14./Grenadier-Regiment.916* were stationed there on D-Day. A second 75mm PaK 40 is shown here in a newly discovered photograph. A third 75mm PaK 40 was scheduled for installation in the partially completed casemate in WN70, and may have been the unidentified 75mm gun in this defense nest on D-Day. Since the *716.Infanterie-Division* had so few of these new weapons, most were probably from the *352.Infanterie-Division*.

FIELD ARTILLERY FIREPOWER NEAR OMAHA BEACH

From a firepower standpoint, the most important consequence of the forward deployment of the *352.Infanterie-Division* was the addition of several of its field artillery batteries to the defense of Omaha Beach. Until this point, there were no field artillery units stationed in the immediate Omaha Beach area. The only field artillery in the sector prior to Febru-ary 1944 was a battalion from the *716.Infanterie-Division*, the *III./Artillerie-Regiment.1716*. This battalion had three batteries of 100mm Czech field guns, all deployed in the heavily fortified Maisy sector to the west of Omaha Beach. These were targeted on the beaches on the eastern side of the Vire estuary and not on Omaha Beach.

Among the hodgepodge of war-booty weapons on Omaha Beach was a single example of the 76.2mm *Infanterie Kanone-Haubitze* 290(r), the German designation for the Soviet 76mm Model 1927 regimental gun. An R612 gun bunker for this weapon was being built in WN64 on the eastern side of the E-1 St. Laurent draw; however, the bunker was not completed on D-Day, and the gun was used from an earth pit. This example is preserved at the Batterie Todt Museum on Pointe Gris Nez on the Pas-de-Calais. AUTHOR

The standard divisional gun in *Artillerie-Regiment.716* was the 100mm *leichte Feldhaubitze* 14/19(t). This Czech Skoda design was a standard divisional gun in the Austro-Hungarian army in World War I, modernized in 1919, and widely used by German static divisions in France. This particular example is from *1./Artillerie-Regiment.716*, stationed in Merville; on D-Day these were located in gun bunkers that were the targets of a British airborne attack.

When elements of the *352.Infanterie-Division* started moving forward in February–March 1944, they brought with them the divisional field artillery, and three batteries of the 1st Battalion (*I./Artillerie-Regiment.352*) were deployed immediately behind Omaha Beach to provide fire support for *Grenadier-Regiment.916*. Each of these batteries consisted of four 105mm leFH 18/40M field howitzers, the standard German divisional field gun. The ammunition supply was 2,700 rounds per battery, which was a standard unit-of-fire.* According

to the battery commander, Maj. Werner Pluskat, one of the batteries was assigned to target Port-en-Bessin and so did not fire on Omaha Beach on D-Day.

The regiment's heavy battalion, *IV./Artillerie-Regiment.352*, was moved into the sector between Grandcamp-Les-Bains and Omaha Beach. The precise deployment of this battalion remains a mystery.[14] A single 150mm heavy howitzer battery from *IV./Artillerie-Regiment.352* was subordinated to *I./Artillerie-Regiment.352*, located near Asnières-

---

*The division history indicates that *Artillerie-Regiment.352* had a single unit-of-fire (*1.Munitions Ausstattung*). The standard daily allotment for a 105mm light field howitzer was 225 rounds, and the *Ausstattung* for a battery (three days of combat) was 2,700 rounds.[15]

TABLE 9: *352.INFANTERIE-DIVISION* FIELD ARTILLERY NEAR OMAHA BEACH

Location	Unit	Forward Observer	Weapon Type
Château d'Etreham	HQ, I./AR.352	WN59	
Hill 29 and 61, Montigny*	2./AR.352	WN73	105mm LFH 18/40M
Hill 63	3./AR.352	WN59	105mm LFH 18/40M
Houtteville	1./AR.352	WN62	105mm LFH 18/40M
Crauville	HQ, IV./AR.352	WN74?	
Asnières-en-Bessin	1x./AR.352	WN73	150mm sFH 18
Ecrammeville	11./AR.352	Chateau south of Vierville	150mm sFH 18
Longueville	1x./AR.352	WN73?	150mm sFH 18

*This battery was split, with two guns near Hill 29 and the other two near Hill 69.

en-Bessin immediately to the west of Vierville.[16] This added another 1,800 rounds of artillery ammunition to the defense.* Both of the other batteries of *IV./Artillerie-Regiment.352* apparently were in range of Omaha Beach.** Presumably, the regiment's heavy battalion was deployed in this sector since it could support either the *Grenadier-Regiment.914* to its west or *Grenadier-Regiment.916* to its east, while at the same time providing coverage of the coast that formerly had been targeted by the damaged coastal battery at Pointe-du-Hoc.

Although the presence of four to six artillery batteries might not seem such a major change in firepower, these batteries had very lethal consequences for the American troops on Omaha Beach for several reasons. The batteries had adequate time to carefully plot their positions. Each battery had a forward observer, often the battery commanders themselves, in the strongpoints overlooking Omaha Beach. Key targets near the beach were pre-registered, and each of these *Zielpunkte* (aim points) was given a code name. As a result, the battery's forward observers would simply telephone or radio back to the battery with a simple codeword to fire a number of rounds towards the beach. In the weeks before the invasion, the batteries fired practice rounds to ensure that the pre-registered targets had been properly calculated.

Most importantly, the batteries were not discovered prior to D-Day. Allied intelligence was not expecting the *352.Infanterie-Division* in the area, and so did not search for their associated artillery batteries. The artillery batteries were well-camouflaged, using overhead netting. While the Allied aerial reconnaissance flights may have photographed these sites, they didn't appear markedly different from dozens of other minor military objects in the fields near the beach.

---

*The *Ausstattung* for the 150mm sFH 18 field howitzer was 150 rounds per day per gun, for a total of 1,800.

**The daily map of *AOK.7* confirms the location of *IV./Artillerie-Regiment.352* in the sector west of Vierville. In addition, the *352.Infanterie-Division* telephone log shows that the battalion was reporting on the situation in Vierville at 1721 hours, indicating it was in this sector. Many sources indicate that one battery was located in Longueville, which is about five kilometers (three miles) to the southwest of Vierville, and well within range of all of Omaha Beach. The 29th Division captured prisoners from *11./Artillerie-Regiment.352* who indicated that the battery was located in Ecrammeville, about 6.5 kilometers (four miles) to the southwest of Vierville; its forward observation post was reported to be in the area on the south side of Vierville near the chateau. It is not clear if it was deployed there on D-Day or moved into the sector on 6–7 June as part of the effort to halt the American advance out of Vierville.[17]

One of the most dangerous bunkers on Omaha Beach was this seemingly innocuous outpost on the forward crest of the hill in defense nest WN62. This was the forward observation post for Lt. Bernhard Frerking, the battery commander for *1./Artillerie-Regiment.352*. He directed fire from his 105mm howitzer battery against the E-3 Colleville draw and neighboring areas from this outpost until it was hit by destroyer fire in the early afternoon of D-Day. Other forward observer posts were located in WN59 and WN73. AUTHOR

In contrast, the field artillery batteries of the *716.Infanterie-Division* were well known. Six of the nine batteries were deployed in gun bunkers and so singled out for attention by Allied air and naval bombardment. Even when the pre-invasion bombardment failed to destroy them, it often chewed up the communication links between the batteries and forward observers, which severely degraded their accuracy. The most extreme example was the "Merville Battery" (*1./Artillerie-Regiment .1716*), which was subjected to a British airborne raid in the pre-dawn hours of D-Day.

The commander of *Artillerie-Regiment.352* also tried to strengthen the artillery in the Omaha Beach area by coordinating his land-based guns with the army's local coastal patrol units. Elements of *6.Artillerie-Trägerflottille* were stationed in the harbors of Grandcamp and Port-en-Bessin, on either side of Omaha Beach. These coastal patrol units were equipped with *Artillerie-Fährprähm* Typ C2, a converted landing barge, somewhat similar to the Allied LCG(L) used on D-Day for shore bombardment. The converted landing craft were armed with two turreted naval guns, usually 88mm or 105mm, in addition to flak guns. The attempt to link the land and naval artillery units proved futile—on D-Day the flotilla in Port-en-Bessin was trapped in the early morning hours because of the low tide, and the four artillery craft were scuttled by their crew in the harbor.

The standard divisional field gun in the German army was the 105mm IFH 18, seen here in the coastal defense role in the *AOK.15* sector south of Boulogne early in the war. This is the early configuration of the weapon, with the original square cross-section trails. NARA

Three battalions of *Artillerie-Regiment.352* were equipped with the 105mm *Leichte Feld Haubitze* 18/40, a modernized version of the basic IFH 18, which used a lighter-weight carriage based on the 75mm PaK 40 design. This can be distinguished by its circular cross-section trails. AUTHOR

The four batteries of *IV./Artillerie-Regiment.352* were equipped with the 150mm *schwere Feldhaubitze* 18, the standard German Army heavy field gun. This weapon had an effective range of 13.3 kilometers (8.3 miles) with a 43.5kg (96lb) high-explosive projectile. AUTHOR

One of the most lethal infantry weapons on Omaha Beach was the 81mm mortar, with both the standard German 81mm GW 34 and war-booty 81mm GW 278(f) French Stokes-Brandt versions in use. This example was located in an open-earth entrenchment rather than in a Tobruk. NARA

ROCKET ARTILLERY

As a means of rapidly reinforcing the firepower of the *84.Korps* in Normandy, Rommel secured a special allocation of 100,000 rounds of rocket artillery in mid-May 1944.[18] The *716.Infanterie-Division* had been supplied with twenty-one *schwere Wurfgerät* 41 28/32 multiple rocket launchers by May 1944.[19] These were nicknamed *Heulende Kühe* (Howling Cows) by the Germans and "Screaming Meemies" by the Americans. The launchers were a simple metal frame that could accommodate four large-caliber artillery rockets in their transport/launch pallet. The standard rockets for this launcher were the 280mm *Wurfkörper Spreng* with a 50kg (110lb) high-explosive warhead, and the 320mm *Wurfkörper* M FL 50, which contained a 45kg (100lb) incendiary warhead. These solid-fuel rockets had an effective range of 1.9 to 2.2 kilometers (1.2 to 1.4 miles).

Additional launchers were delivered to this sector later in the month, presumably to the *352.Infanterie-Division*. The U.S. Army found thirty-eight of these launchers in dugouts in the Le Montmain area of St. Laurent near WN69 after the fighting. There also have been reports of artillery rocket fire in the Colleville area, so it is possible that small numbers of these rocket launchers were deployed there as well.[20]

The number of launchers does not correspond to standard German organizational schemes. The heavy rocket battalions generally were deployed as three batteries each, with six launchers per battery for a total of eighteen; a regiment had three battalions,

The heaviest firepower on Omaha Beach on D-Day came from thirty-eight of these 28/32 *schweres Wurfgerat* sWG 41 rocket launchers, seen in the illustration here. Each launcher frame could accommodate four rockets, which were launched from their wooden shipping crates. The launch batteries were equipped with a mixture of 280mm high-explosive rockets (left) and 320mm incendiary rockets (right). These were ripple fired, with the salvo taking six seconds. AUTHOR

280mm   **320mm**

with fifty-four launchers. It often has been suggested that these rockets were operated by troops from *Werfer-Regiment.84*, but various accounts suggest that specialists from a *Werfer* unit trained the local infantry units how to fire these devices. The number of rockets supplied to the Omaha Beach sector is not known, but based on standard units-of-fire, there may have been as many as 1,250 rockets available.*

As can be seen from the chart below, the rocket launchers added considerable firepower to the German defenses. On the other hand, their lack of accuracy and a lack of data on the actual ammunition expenditure on D-Day make it difficult to assess their overall role in the D-Day artillery balance. The chart below is approximate, since complete details of artillery expenditure on D-Day are lacking.

*The standard *1.Munitions Ausstattung* for a *schwere Werfer Abteilung* was 450 of the 280mm rockets and 150 of the 320mm rockets. The number of launchers in the Omaha Beach area was slightly more than two *Abteilung* in strength.

TABLE 10: GERMAN FIELD ARTILLERY FIREPOWER AT OMAHA BEACH			
Artillery Batteries	**Projectiles**	**Projectile Weight (kg)**	**HE Weight (kg)**
105mm x 2 batteries	5,400	79,920	7,560
150mm x 3 batteries	5,400	234,900	27,540
28/32 rocket x 38 launchers	1,250	101,635	60,950
Total	*12,050*	*416,455 (460 tons)*	*96,050 (105 tons)*

The 28/32 sWG launchers were deployed in thirty-eight pits near St. Laurent, as seen here.

NARA

FLAK REINFORCEMENTS

Rommel also negotiated with the *Luftwaffe* to transfer its flak units closer to the beaches, both to provide air defense for the coastal units and to act as an improvised antitank barrier behind the beach defenses. The only unit readily available in the Bayeux area was *Flak-Regiment.32* of the *Luftwaffe III.Flak-Korps*. This unit deployed thirty-six 88mm guns in this sector, of which twenty-four 88mm guns were located directly behind Omaha Beach along the RN13 coastal highway three to five kilometers (two to three miles) inland. They were supplemented by thirty-two mobile 20mm anti-aircraft guns and twenty-four mobile 37mm guns. There is very little evidence that the batteries were used as improvised field artillery on D-Day, though they were used in the antitank role in the subsequent Normandy fighting.

THE FIREPOWER BALANCE

While most histories acknowledge the role played by the forward deployment of the *352.Infanterie-Division* in the subsequent debacle on Omaha Beach, the implication has generally been that this was because of the increase in infantry near the beach. As suggested in this chapter, a more plausible explanation for the high casualty count on Omaha Beach was the substantial increase in artillery firepower on Omaha Beach from both the overlooked *Bodenständig* arsenal in the strongpoints and the substantial increase in field artillery that accompanied the *352.Infanterie-Division* into the beach area. While the infantry, mines, and obstacles trapped the U.S. troops on the beach and fixed them in place, it was most probably the artillery that did the majority of the killing on D-Day.

The *716.Infanterie-Division* had three of these 150mm sFH13/1 *Geschützwagen Lorraine* in their *Bodenständig* arsenal for artillery support. According to U.S. after-action reports, one was encountered near the southern end of the E-3 Colleville draw on D-Day. MHI

The most common type of *Panzer Drehturm* on Omaha Beach used the war-booty French APX-R turret, a type used in 1940 on the Renault R-35 and Hotchkiss H-39 light tanks. They were usually mounted on a buried Tobruk, as seen here with this example at St. Merceur. NARA

One of the rare weapons seen at Omaha Beach was the VK.3001 *Panzer Drehturm*. Only four of these tank turrets were transferred to the Atlantic Wall, and two of these were at Omaha Beach. These have been misidentified over the years as PzKpfw III turrets because of the similarity of many Krupp turret designs, but this illustration shows some of the distinctive differences, such as the hatch layout on the turret roof. AUTHOR

One of the best defenses in WN68 in the D-3 Les Moulins draw was this VK.3001 *Panzer Drehturm* armed with a 75mm tank turret in WN68, shown after its capture on D-Day.

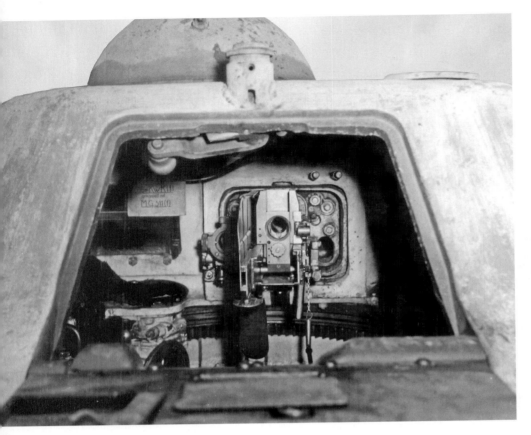

This is a view through the rear turret hatch of *Panzer Drehturm* 37mm(f) based on a war-booty French APX-R. It was armed with a short 37mm gun and a co-axial machine gun. As can be seen, the turret interior was so small it had only a one-man crew. NARA

Another common *Panzer Drehturm* seen in Normandy used the war-booty turrets from World War I French Renault FT tanks (in this case the riveted polygonal type with 37mm gun). This Tobruk was mounted in the harbor area of Grandcamp-les-Bains in the Strongpoint Group Vire in the western sector of the *352.Infanterie-Division*. NARA

To stiffen the defenses along the coast, Rommel cajoled the *Luftwaffe* into moving more heavy flak close to the beach. Two dozen 88mm flak guns of *Flak-Regiment.32* were positioned along the coastal road behind Omaha Beach. MHI

Artillerie-Regiment.352 tried to enlist the support of the *6.Artillerie-Trägerflottille* for artillery fire support on D-Day. This army coastal artillery unit was stationed in the harbors of Grandcamp-les-Bains and Port-en-Bessin on either side of Omaha Beach. Three *Artillerie-Fährprähm* Typ C3 were in Port-en-Bessin harbor on D-Day but were scuttled by their crew after they were trapped by the high tide. Each of the craft was armed with two 88mm gun turrets, plus flak guns. NARA

CHAPTER 6

The Devil's Garden

DURING THE BATTLES AROUND EL ALAMEIN in 1942, Rommel's *Afrika Korps* and Montgomery's British 8th Army made extensive use of minefields and battlefield obstacles. The German troops dubbed these danger zones the "Devil's Garden." The Devil's Garden served many tactical objectives.[1] With both sides badly overstretched across vast desert wastes, the Devil's Garden was a way to defend sectors in place of scarce manpower. Both men and tanks fell victim to buried mines. Minefields were not easily avoided and were especially costly to remove in the heat of battle when under fire. Besides increasing enemy casualties, the Devil's Gardens slowed the momentum of enemy attacks and delayed an enemy's transit through kill zones, where they could be pounded by artillery. A key role of obstacles and mines was to fix an enemy force in place in order to give the artillery the time to destroy it. There was a deadly synergy when the obstacle belts delayed an enemy force inside the kill zone while it was smashed by gunfire.

Rommel's experience with the Devil's Garden in North Africa convinced him of its enormous value on the modern battlefield. These danger zones seemed especially valuable in anti-invasion tactics. One of Rommel's prime tactical requirements to defeat an Allied landing was to delay the enemy attack as long as possible on the beaches until the *panzer* reinforcements arrived. Rommel expected that the beachhead would have to be contained for at least forty-eight hours. He immediately began pleading with Berlin to dispatch large supplies of mines to fortify the potential invasion beaches. However, mines were not sufficient for beachhead defense. To begin with, minefields could not be laid on the beaches themselves. German army mines were not waterproof, and immersion in seawater would corrode their fuzes and render them harmless. Early experiments found that even mines with waterproof fuzes were not especially useful in tidal areas since the wave action unburied them and washed them up onto the beaches. Rommel decided that another approach was necessary—the erection of vast fields of obstacles along the beaches to serve as a barrier against both landing craft and tanks.

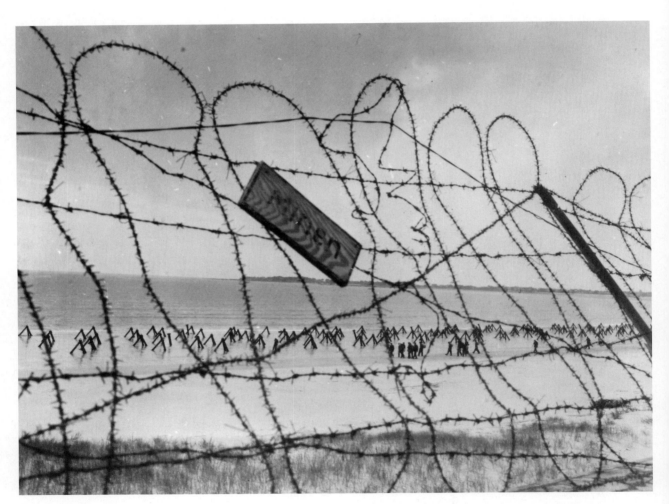

The Devil's Garden was a layered defense consisting of obstacles in the tidal zone, followed by mines, antitank traps, and other obstructions on the beaches. NARA

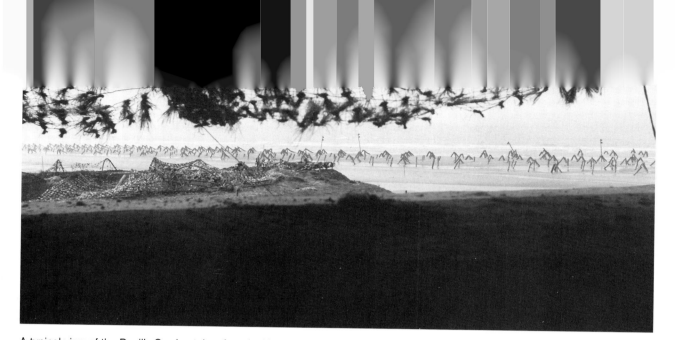

A typical view of the Devil's Garden taken from inside a bunker in the eastern sector of the *716.Infanterie-Division* near the Orne River in 1944. LIBRARY OF CONGRESS

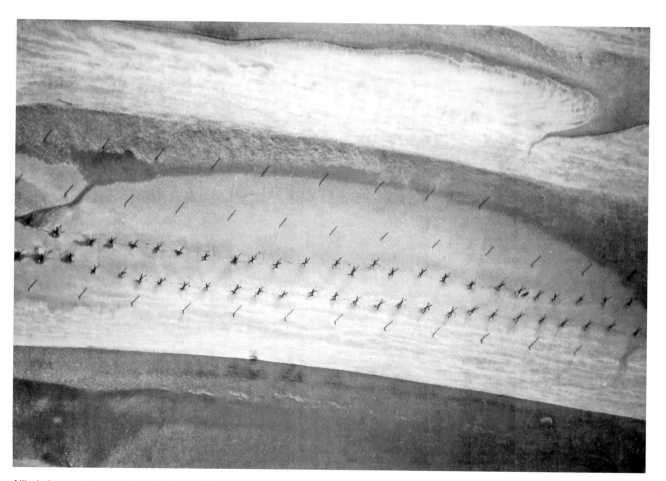

Allied planners became deeply alarmed in early 1944 when aerial reconnaissance photographs taken over the Lower Normandy landing beaches revealed spreading fields of anti-craft obstacles. NARA

THE MINE BATTLE

Rommel's plan to mine the invasion beaches fell into two main categories—anticraft mines against landing craft and landmines against troops and tanks.

Defense against amphibious attack at sea was a *Kriegsmarine* responsibility. The 1942 Dieppe raid prompted the *Kriegsmarine* to investigate controlled minefields in shallow water. This was a very traditional form of coastal defense dating back to the mid-nineteenth century, but it was a subject that had been largely neglected by the *Kriegsmarine* for many years. Controlled mines consisted of minefields that were detonated from control stations on shore rather than by contact fuzes on the mines themselves. The *Kriegsmarine* used a variety of weapons in this role, including the RMA(K) mine and improvised devices based on captured French depth charges nicknamed the Franz WB (*französisch Wasserbombe*: French naval mine). However, controlled minefields were time-consuming to deploy, and the mines were not plentiful. As a result, in Normandy these were limited to major port areas such as Cherbourg and Le Havre.

A cheaper alternative was needed for the beaches between the major ports. The *Kriegsmarine* developed an inexpensive, mass-produced, shallow-water anticraft mine called the Coastal Mine-A (KMA: *Küstenmine-A*), which consisted of a concrete base containing a 75kg explosive charge surmounted by a steel tripod frame with the triggering device. Although cheap and effective, these mines became available too late in 1943 to be laid along the entire coastline. They were first laid along the high-priority sectors of the Channel coast from Boulogne southwestward towards Le Havre, and this project was completed in early June 1944, around the time of the D-Day landings. The next area scheduled to be mined was the Seine estuary around Le Havre, which was to begin on 10 June, but this project was cancelled because of the invasion.

The most lethal anticraft mine in the *Kriegsmarine* arsenal was the new KMA mine. This was a simple and inexpensive design consisting of a concrete base with an explosive charge inside and a simple metal frame holding the impact fuze on top. Although a great worry to Allied planners, manufacture began too late and few, if any, of these were deployed off the Lower Normandy coast by D-Day. This rare surviving example is preserved at the Overloon, Netherlands, museum. AUTHOR

The shortage of the new KMA mines led to local improvisations such as the *Nussknacker* (Nutcracker) mines. These used war-booty French artillery projectiles mounted on a concrete base. The vertical metal post triggered the detonation when struck by a landing craft. These particular examples were found on the beach at Dunkirk in the summer of 1944. NATIONAL ARCHIVES CANADA P-174349

Rommel was unhappy about the slow pace of navy mine operations and badgered his staff to come up with expedients that could be manufactured using locally available materials. In March 1944, Naval Group West developed and tested the *Nussknackermine* (Nutcracker mine), an improvised copy of the KMA using a concrete base containing an explosive device, such as a French high-explosive artillery projectile, with a pivoting steel rod that pressed against the projectile fuze when a landing craft came in contact with it. Other improvised coastal mines were based on the same concept, though their technical details differed. Deployment of the Nutcrackers began in April 1944, but once again priority went to locations away from Normandy, such as the Channel coast and Brest. The improvised mines proved to be a mixed blessing. The munitions used in the mines were not designed for immersion in water, and leakage resulted in erratic performance. Nutcrackers often were damaged or moved by tidal currents, and the triggering beam often was ren-

dered harmless by prolonged exposure to seawater and tides.

With the *Kriegsmarine* unable to shield the extended shorelines between the main ports, Rommel pressed the army into the anticraft business. As detailed below, the army was already erecting obstacles along the coast, and it was possible to enhance these with mines. One of the most common approaches was the *Minenpfahl* (mine pole), which consisted of a vertical stake created from logs or telephone poles, with a Teller antitank mine mounted on top. A more elaborate device was the *schwimmende Balkenmine* (floating wooden mine), which was made by fastening several Teller mines on a wooden raft. These floating mines were fixed in place with a concrete anchor. The *Armsperre* was a similar idea, except it was fitted with only a single mine. In practice, the various army mine schemes suffered from the vulnerability of landmines in a nautical environment. Seawater seeped into the casings, disabling the contact fuzes, and tidal action knocked down the stakes or disrupted the sea anchors.

The shortage of anticraft mines led to improvisations in Normandy such as the Balkan mine, which consisted of a simple wooden raft with several Teller mines attached. This was anchored to the seabed using a cheap concrete anchor. MHI

The use of Teller mines on stakes was one of the most common forms of anti–landing craft defenses on the D-Day beaches. MHI

LANDMINES

Rommel's grim memories of British minefields in North Africa made him a fervent proponent of mine warfare. Through the end of 1943, the *Wehrmacht* had already laid about 1.8 million mines in belts along the coast from the Netherlands through southern France. This didn't satisfy Rommel, who felt that these minefields were simply not dense enough to deter an Allied landing. Rommel wanted to expand the coastal minefields to 50 to 100 million mines. Regardless of Rommel's intentions, the supply of mines from Germany was simply not enough. Toward the end of 1943, OB-West was receiving fewer than 100,000 mines per month. Rommel's frequent requests to Berlin increased the supply. Indeed, the memoirs by Hitler's naval aide, Vice Admiral Friedrich Ruge, are filled with accounts of Rommel's obsessive demands for more and more mines along the coast. By March 1944, the *7.Armee* had laid about 800,000 mines, while the *15.Armee* on the Pas-de-Calais had laid over 1.4 million.[2] (See Table 11.) As was the case with so much of the fortification work, the Pas-de-Calais area was favored with mine supplies. This area reached a density of 2,000 mines per kilometer by mid-March 1944,

compared to only 510 mines per kilometer in Lower Normandy. The *716.Infanterie-Division*, assigned to the Overlord beaches, laid 62,000 mines up to February 1944, and increased this to 100,000 by March 1944. Because of Rommel's insistent prodding, the minefields on the Pas-de-Calais and Normandy coast expanded almost four-fold since late 1943.

The predominant mine deployment pattern on the Atlantic Wall was to create flanking minefields to shield the strongpoints. They were not widely deployed on the beaches because of the technical issues of water-seepage and erosion. The maps in Chapter 7 show the deployment pattern for mines on Omaha Beach based on surviving German maps.[3] It should be noted that these maps are undated and are probably from late 1943. There were probably additional minefields planted on Omaha Beach, and there was also some use of hasty minefields created using small antipersonnel mines that were simply laid on the surface. The minefields were usually marked with warning signs, and it was not uncommon for the *Wehrmacht* to use false minefield signs in areas that had not been planted with mines as a cheap expedient to discourage passage of enemy troops.

	WBN	AOK.15	AOK.7	AOK.1	AOK.19	
Field Army						Total
Sector	Netherlands	Channel Coast	Normandy	Atlantic Coast	Mediterranean	
10 Oct 43	172,622	582,049	567,759	286,695	171,945	1,781,070
12 Nov 43	196,362	615,130	602,246	205,303	217,041	1,836,082
31 Dec 43	233,431	656,394	639,721	325,767	258,834	2,114,147
10 Jan 44	235,029	672,778	645,677	327,112	273,265	2,153,861
11 Feb 44	252,661	833,629	693,046	364,746	311,511	2,455,593
11 Mar 44	354,759	1,258,694	818,971	387,480	392,130	3,212,034
10 Apr 44	527,238	1,866,476	1,202,803	581,823	710,863	4,889,203
10 May 44	586,205	1,924,518	1,492,454	737,935	1,138,411	5,879,523
10 Jun 44	691,911	2,107,946	1,744,457	862,451	1,365,899	6,772,664

TABLE 11: LANDMINE DEPLOYMENT IN OB-WEST, 1943–44

The shortage of conventional landmines prompted another of Rommel's improvisations—mines converted from surplus artillery projectiles. There were hundreds of thousands of rounds of French naval gun ammunition in the arsenals. These were converted into mines by fitting contact fuzes and were planted in the ground like conventional landmines. There was also a far less conventional use of artillery mines. The French coast has many cliffs, and these were booby-trapped with special types of improvised mines made from old French artillery projectiles. The *Minengranaten* (projectile mines) were simply artillery rounds strung on the cliff with impact fuzes that would fall off and explode if disturbed. The *Rollminen* (rolling mines) were similar hanging artillery projectiles, lashed to the cliff by ropes that could be cut by local troops to drop the devices to the beach below, detonating the explosives. These types of improvised mines were encountered by U.S. troops on the western side of Omaha Beach on D-Day.

One of the improvised "roller mines" used on the cliffs on either side of Omaha Beach consisted of war-booty French artillery shells that were suspended on the cliffs by cable and detonated on impact when released to fall on the beaches below. NARA

ROMMEL'S ASPARAGUS

Since it proved impractical to lay minefields on the tidal flats and beaches, Rommel sought other methods to interrupt the flow of landing craft to the beaches. He decided to erect dense fields of obstacles—soon dubbed "Rommel's Asparagus" (*Rommelspargel*) by the local German troops—along the coast. Rommel argued that the obstacle belt would prevent the landing craft from reaching the shelter of the shoreline. In combination with enhanced fortifications and firepower, this would create an extended killing zone along the beach. Instead of landing near the protective seawalls so common on the Channel coast, the infantry would have to disembark hundreds of yards from shore and be exposed to prolonged fire as they attempted to reach the sanctuary of the shoreline. In contrast

to his arguments about defensive tactics, Rommel's program for improved coastal defense was welcomed by Rundstedt and the other senior *Wehrmacht* commanders, who felt that the army had been too long neglected in the Atlantic Wall construction compared to the *Kriegsmarine*.

Rommel began by requesting that the engineer command in Berlin deliver as many surplus obstacles as could be gathered from derelict German fortification lines such as the *Westwall*, as well as obstacles from French, Belgian, and Czech fortification lines. Beyond this, he assigned his own engineer units to create obstacles using local resources. Since there were not enough engineer troops to undertake such a massive effort, he ordered local divisional commanders to assign their infantry

This view of the beach off Grandcamp-les-Bains gives some sense of the density of the anticraft stakes found on the Normandy coast. This small port was located immediately to the west of Omaha Beach and was the focal point of the Strongpoint Group Vire defenses of the *352.Infanterie-Division*. A careful look at one of the stakes toward the center of the photo shows a high vertical post attached. These were mortar-marking stakes, used by nearby mortar Tobruks for precision targeting. NARA

troops to the mission, even if it meant cutbacks in tactical training.

One of the most common obstacles were *Hochpfählen* (high stakes), created from lumber or telephone poles. While a simple and effective barrier, they proved to be unusually difficult to erect. When troops tried to dig pits to plant the stakes, the waterlogged soil simply collapsed before the pit was deep enough. Engineer troops finally suggested the use of pile drivers, but this took forty-five minutes per stake, and there were not enough pile drivers available. During a visit to Hardelot-Plage on 3 February 1944, Rommel was shown a technique developed locally by troops who used a high-pressure water hose instead of a pile driver to emplace wooden stakes. This took only three minutes per stake, and fire hoses were widely available. Rom-

mel immediately saw the merits of this technique, and orders were dispatched along the Normandy coast. In some sectors, such as Sword Beach, the rocky conditions did not permit the use of fire hoses, and the slower pile drivers had to be used. The new technique was so successful that troops quickly ran out of available supplies of telephone poles and so were dispatched to neighboring woods and forests to chop down trees.

The stake obstacles were a source of lingering annoyance to local German army units. Although the water hose method proved very effective to help plant the stakes, local tidal conditions soon undermined the sand at the bases. Early spring storms knocked down whole fields of stakes. Some local commanders were also dubious of their value. In mid-February 1944, the *7.Armee* in Lower Nor-

One of the innovations that made the Devil's Garden possible was the use of fire hoses as a means to quickly plant high stakes. This trick was displayed to Rommel during his visit to Hardelot-Plage on 3 February 1944, and he quickly disseminated the technique throughout the Army Group B command. MHI

To increase the lethality of the ramps, mines were mounted on top. The sawtooth device to cut up the bottom of landing craft was an innovation suggested by Rommel's naval aide, Vice Admiral Friedrich Ruge. MHI

Experiments by *7.Armee* found that the vertical stake obstacles could be easily brushed aside by an onrushing landing craft. As a result, a more substantial tripod configuration called a *Hemmbalk* was developed. A typical example of this type of timber ramp with a Teller mine in place was photographed here at Barneville-sur-Mer. MHI

One of the most typical obstacles at Omaha Beach was the Cointet device, also known as the Belgian Gate or C-Element. This particular example is still preserved at the Omaha Beach Museum. AUTHOR

The Belgian Gates were extremely difficult targets for the Gap Assault Teams because of their size and durability. The prescribed method for demolishing them was to place plastic explosive at several points, as shown on this training dummy erected at one of the assault training camps in Britain in 1943–44. Such an elaborate and time-consuming process proved nearly impossible when the engineers were under fire on D-Day. NARA

mandy tested some of the obstacles using a British landing craft that had been captured at Dieppe in 1942. The landing craft plowed through most of the obstacles, especially the stakes. As a result, more substantial *Hemmbalken* (beam obstructions) were designed, based on a tripod design instead of a single stake. The vertical stakes remained in use but were often reinforced by the addition of mines, as mentioned above. Ruge, Rommel's naval aide, suggested the addition of *Stahlmesser* (steel sawteeth) to cut into the lower hulls of the landing craft that passed over submerged obstacles. The motto at Rommel's headquarters was "better to do something imperfect than nothing at all."

The limited value of the stakes encouraged Rommel to use more substantial obstacles. The best of these were called "C-Elements" by the U.S. Army. These were a large steel obstruction designed by Col. Leon De Cointet in 1933 for the Maginot Line. The French army rejected their manufacture for France, but the idea caught on in Belgium. The Belgian army wanted to erect barriers along the frontier to obstruct roads in times of crisis, but could not use traditional antivehicle obstructions such as concrete barriers in peacetime. The Cointet obstacle was designed to be moved and fixed into place by lashing it to a small concrete post that could be anchored off the road. The Cointet obstacles, also known as "Belgian Gates," were quite large and heavy, weighing 1.4 metric tons, and were difficult to move without specialized equipment. About 75,000 were manufactured for Belgium and used with some success in the 1940 campaign. Rommel managed to secure the large inventory of these obstacles for his anti-invasion plan. They began showing up on the Normandy coast in February–March 1944.

One of the more common types of antitank obstructions in Normandy was the Czech hedgehog, based on a Czechoslovakian army design used in the Czech fortified zone along the German frontier in the late 1930s. Rommel's program led to many of these devices being moved to the Atlantic Wall. The Czech hedgehogs usually were embedded in a concrete block. AUTHOR

Another common steel obstruction was the *Tschechenigel* (Czech hedgehog), steel antitank obstacles that came from prewar Czech fortified areas. They were fixed in shallow water by embedding their steel arms in concrete anchors. Besides these captured obstacles, tetrahedron obstacles were mass-produced in Germany or locally assembled by engineer troops in Normandy from steel girders or cast from concrete.

Another type of antitank obstacle was the steel tetrahedron. To be effective, these had to be planted in concrete. This particular barrier was erected on the eastern side of the Orne River near Merville in early 1944. LIBRARY OF CONGRESS

Since steel was in short supply, many of the tetrahedrons used at Omaha Beach were locally manufactured types using concrete instead of steel. These examples can still be found near the Vierville draw. AUTHOR

Barbed wire has been an essential ingredient in field fortifications for a half-century and was used extensively in Normandy in 1944, as in this example on the beach of Strongpoint Franceville on the eastern side of the Orne River. LIBRARY OF CONGRESS

In addition to the obstacles in the tidal zone, a variety of antitank obstacles were erected on the beaches. These included *Betonigel* (concrete caltrops/tetrahedrons) and steel antitank obstructions such as the *eiserne Hemmkurven*, a prefabricated, curved antitank ramp. The most effective antitank obstacles were concrete-reinforced antitank ditches and special antitank walls. On Omaha Beach, several large antitank ditches were completed prior to D-Day, but they mostly used log reinforcement since concrete was in limited supply.

Rommel was also concerned about the risk of paratroopers and gliders landing behind the beach defenses, as had been done at Sicily in July 1943. As a result, there was an active antiglider program. This consisted of erecting stakes in open fields behind the beaches. Another technique was damming small rivers to create flooded areas. In the case of Omaha Beach, an elaborate flooding program was undertaken in the farm fields on the bluffs. However, natural drainage completely undermined this effort, and the flooding program proved to be a flop.

One of the most effective antitank defenses on the Normandy beaches was the deep antitank ditch, especially those lined in concrete, such as this one in Strongpoint Riva-Bella (Sword Beach). These would trap any tank foolish enough to try to cross it, but were mainly intended to create a barrier at key beach exits. Usually these antitank ditches were protected by fortified antitank guns to prevent breaching by engineers. LIBRARY OF CONGRESS

Most of the antitank ditches on Omaha Beach were of the earthen variety, often with log retaining walls. They were used as emergency casualty evacuation stations by U.S. medics on D-Day, as seen here. MHI

This was part of the antitank ditch near the E-1 St. Laurent draw. It was only partially complete, and not yet reinforced. NARA

Another type of antitank obstacle that was adapted to the Devil's Garden was the curved ramp. These were heavy steel devices intended to stop tanks and landing craft. These are seen in early 1944 off the shores of Pornichet in the St. Nazaire area.
LIBRARY OF CONGRESS

Rommel ordered large areas behind potential invasion beaches to be flooded to discourage paratroop and glider landings, as well as to frustrate exit from the beaches. This is the village of Baupte near Carentan on the western side of the *352.Infanterie-Division* sector that was flooded in February 1944. LIBRARY OF CONGRESS

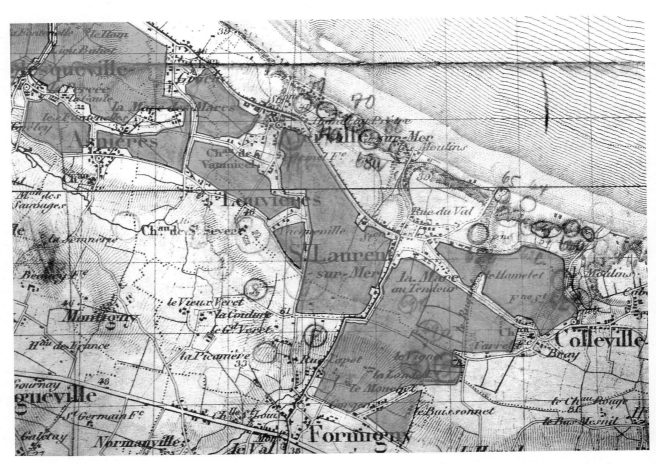

This is a map found by the 1st Infantry Division after D-Day showing the scheme to inundate the area behind Omaha Beach. According to German accounts, this effort failed because of water shortages and drainage issues. NARA

Rommel placed high value on mines as a means to entrap and delay enemy landing forces. However, mines could not be placed directly on the beaches because of the problems of water immersion and erosion. Instead, minefields were placed beyond the tidal areas, as seen here on a beach in the *15.Armee* sector. MHI

Here, an engineer from the 5th Engineer Special Brigade uses a minesweeper during mine-clearing operations shortly after D-Day. The rectangular devices in the foreground are war-booty French antitank mines that were widely used by the Germans on Omaha Beach. NARA

Mines proved to be a persistent problem on Omaha Beach even after D-Day. This U.S. Army engineer team is seen sweeping for mines along the road in the D-1 Vierville draw on 7 July 1944, a month after the landings. NARA

SECRET WEAPONS

There were two secret programs to reinforce the defenses, neither of which succeeded. The German engineers had developed a static flamethrower, which could be emplaced near key positions and then remotely activated. These were designated as *Abwehrflammenwerfer 42* and had an effective range of about fifty meters (fifty-five yards) and a duration of five to ten seconds. Several dozen of these were planted in the Omaha Beach defenses, mostly on the eastern side near Colleville. So far as can be determined, none were successfully used on D-Day.

The other device planned for the defenses was the Goliath remote-control demolition vehicle. This resembled a miniature tank, but was packed with a 60kg (130lb) high-explosive demolition charge. The Goliath was remotely operated via a trailing wire linked to the control box. The wire reel was 650 meters long (710 yards). The plan was to create a concrete hanger for each Goliath near the beach and then launch them against landing craft or tanks. The garrison at Omaha Beach received their first shipment of Goliaths in the days before the invasion, so they were not deployed in time. They arrived somewhat sooner at neighboring Utah Beach but saw little combat use.

One of the less successful devices planted on the Normandy beaches was the *Abwehrflammenwerfer 42* fortification flamethrower. It could fire a burst of flaming fuel about fifty meters (fifty-five yards) for five to ten seconds. A few dozen of these were mounted in the defenses around Colleville on Omaha Beach, but there are no known instances of their use. This particular example was uncovered near Fort de Foucarville later that summer. NARA

The Goliath remote-control demolition vehicles were supposed to be used to attack landing craft and other high-value targets on the landing beaches. The allotment to Omaha Beach arrived too late for them to be properly deployed. These examples were captured near Utah Beach. MHI

The Goliaths were supposed to be operated from special concrete bunkers carved into the shoreline, like the one seen here. MHI

Although no Goliaths were known to have been used on D-Day, at least a few were employed in the subsequent fighting. This one was captured by a Ranger patrol behind the beachhead after D-Day. The soldier to the right is holding the control cable. NARA

ENGINEERING THE DEVIL'S GARDEN

The unit responsible for erecting "Rommel's Asparagus" in Lower Normandy was Fortification Engineer Staff-11 (*Festung Pioneer Stab.11*), the fortification engineer staff of *84.Korps*. This unit had little manpower of its own, but was used to direct the infantry garrisons stationed along the coast. It was organized into three groups, two of which managed the obstacle construction program and the third of which was responsible for mine-fields. The *84.Korps* covered about 320 kilometers (200 miles) of coastline, and about 205 kilometers (127 miles) were planted with Rommel's Asparagus by the time of the D-Day landings. Most beach areas suitable for amphibious landings had these obstacle fields. The areas not covered by obstacles were mostly the beaches that were edged with high cliffs. These cliffs, known in French as *Falaises*, were the French cousins of the better-known White Cliffs of Dover on the English side of the Channel.

In the case of Omaha Beach, the eastern shoulder of the landing zone was a stretch of cliff known as the Pointe-et-Raz-de-la-Percée, while the western shoulder abutted the Plateau du Calvados, a line of cliffs that stretched from Colleville westward to Port-en-Bessin. The Normandy coast received a lower density of obstacles than nearly any other Atlantic Wall sector (see Table 12).

Omaha Beach was shielded by about 3,700 obstacles, including 450 ramps, 2,000 stakes, 1,050 Czech hedgehogs, and 200 Belgian Gates. These followed a standard pattern. The Belgian Gates formed the first line of obstacles about 800 meters (875 yards) from the high-water mark. These were followed by a line of wooden or metal ramps. The final line closest to shore was made up of the smaller steel hedgehogs or concrete tetrahedrons. Stakes were scattered among the other lines of obstacles for reinforcement and to seal gaps.

TABLE 12: ATLANTIC WALL BEACH OBSTACLES, 1 JUNE 1944

Army	15	15	15	7	7	7	1	1
Corps	67	47	81	84	74	24	80	86
Sector	Calais	Dieppe	Le Havre	Normandy	North Brittany	South Brittany	Atlantic Coast	Bayonne
Coast length (km)	329.5	125.5	253.5	300.0	450.0	816.0	596.0	221.9
Coast with obstacles (km)	142.7	119.2	174.7	205.0	136.0	220.0	520.8	117.9
Concrete stakes	2,171	9,600	?	4,634	4,092	1,137	—	—
Wooden stakes	48,191	60,631	75,020	10,939	29,334	23,483	35,545	38,047
Steel stakes	10,584	21,465	9,416	?	?	1,316	—	—
Concrete tetrahedrons	1,849	5,167	4,163	4,912	1,721	25,239	15,832	3,214
Nutcrackers	4,797	1,964	2,433	?	445	146	—	—
Other types	22,898	9,747	7,513	4,722	11,683	6,990	1,113	—
Belgian Gates	644	6,631	4,256	2,375	3,202	3,674	933	400
Czech hedgehogs	9,461	7,849	16,269	15,932	4,420	1,703	1,426	10
Curved antitank ramps	2	—	4,836	2,252	476	1,248	—	—
Mines (in tidal area)	14,779	15,757	20,123	6,589	10,195	6,335	2,541	—
Obstacle density (per km)	705	1,032	709	223	407	295	105	353

Deadly Geography

ANYONE WALKING ALONG THE D-DAY BEACHES today will notice the striking differences between Omaha Beach and the other four beaches. The topography of Omaha Beach played a contributory role in the higher casualties suffered there on D-Day, as German fortification engineers were able to exploit the geographical features of Omaha Beach to make it a deadly killing ground.

The British and Canadian beaches to the east of Omaha Beach were located near small coastal towns. The topography is mostly flat, although there is a hill on the western side of Gold Beach. In some cases, these beaches consisted of alternating villages interspersed with fields. Juno Beach, the Canadian objective, consisted of no fewer than four separate seaside villages. Sword Beach, on the other hand, consisted of three intermingled villages in one long, built-up strip. Gold Beach consisted of two major towns on either extreme, with a flooded area of coastal marsh in between.

The other distinctive feature of these beaches was the presence of seawalls near the towns. To protect the towns against the harsh tidal effects of the sea, most of these towns were edged by substantial protective walls. The seawalls had two mutually opposing effects on the Allied invasion plans. On first glance, they presented an immediate and imposing barrier against quick exit off the beach, since the walls were in many cases too high for troops to easily climb. They were also far too substantial for tanks to surmount without specialized equipment. On the other hand, the seawalls had one obvious advantage for the attackers since British infantry could shelter under the seawalls after racing across the beach. The Germans attempted to circumvent

The British and Canadian beaches were dominated by seaside towns and villages, often with protective seawalls. This is Beach Nan-Red in St. Aubin-sur-Mer, part of Juno Beach, where the Canadian North Shore Regiment landed on D-Day. The village defenses were designated as WN27 by the *9./Grenadier-Regiment.736* of the *716.Infanterie-Division*, which held this stretch of beach. On the beach is a crashed P-47 Thunderbolt. NARA

This is a panoramic view of Omaha Beach (with draws numbered) taken shortly after the war from over Colleville-sur-Mer, looking westward toward the Pointe-et-Raz-de-la-Percée promontory in the upper right of the image. It also provides a view of the extensive *bocage* (hedgerows) that would cause the U.S. Army so many problems in the subsequent Normandy fighting. MHI

this problem by creating gun positions that could fire along the seawall with enfilade. Nevertheless, these defensive works were very limited in number, and once eliminated by tank fire or infantry action, the seawalls provided useful protection to infantry soon after landing.

The seawalls were not an impenetrable barrier for tanks, and British planners were well aware of their presence. Tank landing zones took advantage of natural exits past the walls. Since many of the villages relied on fishing, there were often small harbors carved into the seafront that could be exploited by attacking forces for beach exit. Where the walls could not be avoided, specialized engineer tanks (the "Funnies") could overcome obstacles with bridging and fascine tanks.

Likewise, the towns presented a mixed picture for attackers and defenders. On the one hand, the sturdy construction of the shoreside buildings gave the Germans many natural defensive points for their own infantry. On the other hand, once British and Canadian infantry surmounted the seawalls and advanced into the town, the buildings offered a measure of shelter against German small-arms fire and artillery. An American assessment of the German coastal defenses in the towns concluded that they "required more men to man than could possibly be made available . . . [and] concentrated too much of the available strength in towns where only troops familiar with the maze of passageways, mine fields, etc. could man defenses efficiently. Reserves unfamiliar with the layout could not fight to best advantage."[1]

Utah Beach, on the far western side of the Allied landing zone, was topographically more similar to the British/Canadian beaches than to Omaha Beach, though fundamentally different in its lack of towns and buildings near the beach. The beach was extremely flat aside from the natural irregularities of the dunes. In contrast to the British/Canadian beaches, it was very sparsely inhabited and lacked any extensive housing or seawalls near the shore. From the German perspective, Utah Beach was one of the more difficult beaches to defend because of the lack of troops and fortifications. Infantry fortifications had to be located up against the shore edge in order to have clear lines of fire against troops moving across the beaches. Positioning fortifications immediately on the shore edge made them vulnerable to both the Allied naval gunfire and coastal erosion. From the attackers' perspective, once the thin crust of defensive positions near the beach was overcome, the terrain did not favor any defense in-depth. Utah Beach was one of the few beaches to be successfully defended by an extensive inundation program behind the beach. This limited access off the beach to a handful of causeways. In theory, these should have been easily defended, but on D-Day the threadbare defenses in this sector rapidly collapsed.

OMAHA BEACH TERRAIN

This sketch was done after D-Day for the U.S. Army engineers' after-action report and shows the five prominent draws that dominated the tactics on D-Day. MHI

In contrast to the flat terrain at the other D-Day beaches, Omaha Beach was dominated by high bluffs. The beach was nestled between two stretches of cliffs—the Plateau du Calvados on the eastern side and the Pointe-et-Raz-de-la-Percée on the western side. These soft sandstone cliffs gradually transitioned to a line of bluffs about forty-five to sixty meters (150 to 200 feet) above sea level. These bluffs were steep enough that they could not be traversed by vehicles or tanks. The only access off the beach for vehicular traffic was down a series of ravines, called "draws" or "exits" in Allied planning documents. There were five of these, numbered D-1, D-3, E-1, E-3, and F-1. The letters were associated with the beach code names—D-1 was located in the "Dog Beach" section, E-1 in the "Easy Beach" section, and F-1 in the "Fox Beach" section.

Of the five draws, not all were equally valuable. The F-1 Cabourg draw on the far eastern side of the beach, known locally as *La Révolution*, was a shallow basin that petered out before reaching the village of Le Grand Hameau. The E-1 St. Laurent draw, known locally as *Le Ruquet*, was somewhat deeper than F-1 but lacked a good connection to a major road.

The three remaining draws offered the best access off the beach. The D-1 Vierville draw contained the only paved road that connected to the coastal road that paralleled the beach.[*] The D-3 *Les Moulins* ("Windmills") draw led to the town of St. Laurent-sur-Mer. The E-3 Colleville draw was the most substantial of the three and was a shallow valley locally known as *Vallée du Ruisseau des Moulins* ("Valley of the Windmill Stream"), leading from the beach to the town of Colleville-sur-Mer.

Not surprisingly, the three main draws became the centerpiece for German defense of Omaha Beach. Each draw was the center of a strongpoint (StP: *Stützpunkt*) large enough for an infantry company, consisting of a cluster of defense nests (WN: *Widerstandnest*) for platoons or squads. The tactical intention of this layout was to cork the ravines with fortified positions to prevent invading troops from exiting from the beach.

---

*The coastal road was called Route National 814 at the time; today it is called D514.

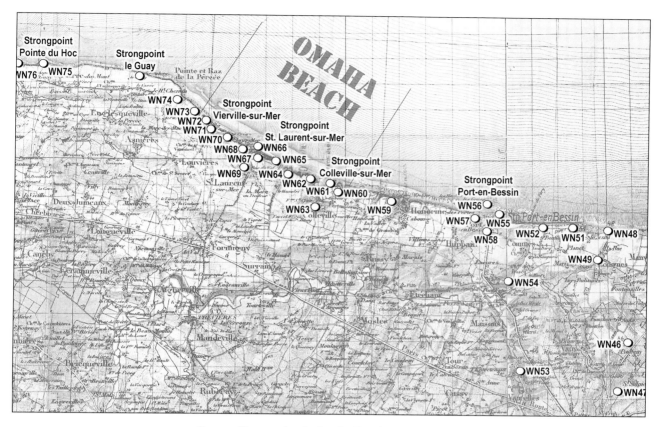

German Strongpoints in Omaha Beach Area on D-Day

There were far fewer buildings along Omaha Beach than on the British/Canadian beaches. The most substantial accumulation of buildings was the small hamlet of Hamel-au-Pretré on the western side of the beach. There was also a cluster of buildings in the Vierville draw, including a casino and hotel. In the spring of 1944, the German army began a systematic campaign to level most of the coastal buildings to provide better fields of fire. Some of the sturdier stone buildings were left on the beach to serve as reinforced infantry positions.

The strongpoints on Omaha Beach were modest tactical fortifications and in no way comparable to the massive coastal batteries that so dominate the iconography of D-Day.* One of the reasons that Allied planners selected the Colleville-Vierville beach for the D-Day landings was the almost complete lack of fortified positions in the summer of 1943 when the decision was made. Although there were some entrenchments and a few reinforced gun positions, there were no significant bunkers in mid-1943. German officers, when first posted to Omaha Beach, were surprised at the paucity of large bunkers. Lt. Hans Heinze, with the headquarters of the newly arrived *II./Grenadier-Regiment.916*, took a walk along the beach with a fellow officer in February or March 1944 and later recalled: "At the end of the tour, we were so astonished that we could not believe it was true. I think we expected the same sort of effort as the *Westwall* or something similar. There was nothing significant on the whole beach."[2]

---

*The two classic films about Omaha Beach, *The Longest Day* and *Saving Private Ryan*, both used images of the impressive Longues-sur-Mer battery in their depictions of the beach defenses.

TABLE 13: TROOPS AND WEAPONS IN STRONGPOINTS AT OMAHA BEACH, 15 JUNE 1943[3]

WN	60	61	62	63	64	65	66	67	68	69	70	71	72	73	74	Total
Officer										1						**1**
NCO	1	2	3	4	1	3	1	2	1	7	1	1	2	1	3	**33**
Troops	10	16	18	24	9	18	10	12	11	21	9	14	13	12	12	**209**
Rifles	9	16	16	9	6	17	8	15	8	51	8	14	12	8	15	**212**
SMG	1	3	3	4	1	3	1	1	1	7	1	1	2	1	1	**31**
Pistols	2	2	3	12	3	1	1	3	2	10	1	0	2	4	1	**47**
LMG	1	2	2	1	2	1	3	1			3	1	2	2	1	**22**
HMG		1	1		2	2	1	1			3	1		2		**14**
Mortars	2	1	2		2	1					2	2				**12**
37/47mm						1			1							**2**
50mm		2				1	1	1					1			**6**
Field guns	2		2												1	**5**
Flame-throwers	12	12	12			6	1		1			1		8		**53**

The *Wehrmacht*'s winter 1943 *Bauprogramm* (construction program) planned to add a handful of gun bunkers to this stretch of beach. Rommel's invigoration of the anti-invasion effort led to a much more extensive construction effort in the spring of 1944. Dozens of small Tobruks were added by the spring construction program, and the number of gun bunkers was substantially increased. Much of this construction did not start until February and March 1944. Most of the better gun bunkers on Omaha Beach were not completed until April and May 1944. One reason that the U.S. Army was so unprepared for the scale of defenses on Omaha Beach was their relatively late appearance. The big 88mm bunker in WN61 in the Colleville draw was not finished until late April 1944, and its companion bunker in the Vierville draw was still under construction in early May 1944 and not finished until later in the month.[4] The defenses in the center of Omaha Beach were among the last to be started in the spring of 1944, and so many were uncompleted on D-Day.

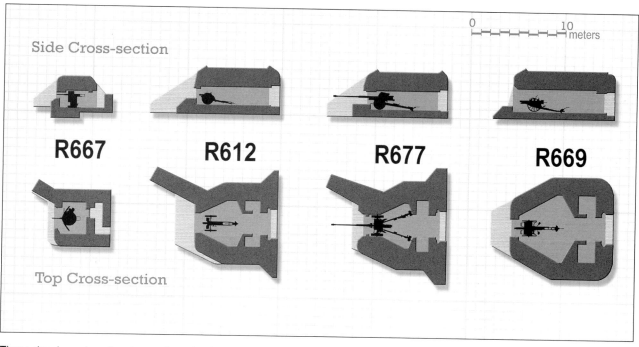

These drawings show four types of gun bunkers found on Omaha Beach. The R667 was typically armed with the 50mm pedestal gun, such as the example in WN65 in the St. Laurent draw. Several R612 were under construction on D-Day, including one in WN64 in the St. Laurent draw for one of the small war-booty Soviet 76mm regimental guns. The R677 was typically used for the big 88mm PaK 43/41, such as in WN61 and WN72; the wall shielding the embrasure would always face toward the sea. The R669 was a general-purpose bunker for field artillery and was used in WN62 to house the Belgian 75mm field guns; those were a modified version of the type shown here and had embrasure shield walls. The small closets seen behind the main fighting room are ammunition storage rooms. AUTHOR

TOBRUK DEFENSES

Gun bunkers were not especially common on Omaha Beach, and the most common type of concrete defense works were the so-called *Verstark-feldmässig* (reinforced field positions). These were not considered bombproof since they had open roofs and were built to the lower B1 construction standard with thinner concrete walls and less resistance to naval gun fire. They were supposed to be fully buried to make up for their less robust construction, leaving only the weapon opening exposed. The Tobruk was the most common concrete defensive position in the Atlantic Wall. The name stems from their origins during the fighting around Tobruk in North Africa in 1942, where Italian construction engineers found that a simple way to create a concrete-reinforced foxhole was to simply take a length of concrete sewer pie and bury it vertically in the ground.

The German Tobruks eventually evolved into a whole family of small defensive works.[5] They were used principally to protect crew-served weapons such as machine guns and mortars. They were officially classified as *Ringstand*s, since their most apparent feature was the circular opening for the weapon's mount. They were typically a small rectangular design with a small shelter for ammunition supply and crew protection during artillery bombardments. Some designs became much more elaborate and included more substantial shelters. Some Tobruks were incorporated into larger structures as a supplementary means of defense for major bunkers.

Tobruks were constructed for specific uses. The common machine-gun Tobruks usually had an open *Ringstand* but no other major structural detail. The Tobruks built as mortar pits often had a concrete table built into the center of the *Ringstand* for mounting the weapon, especially when the intended armament was one of the smaller 50mm mortars.

Tobruks were also widely used as the basis for a *Panzer Drehturm* (tank turret mount). There were large numbers of surplus tank turrets available in France, especially those from French tanks captured in 1940. On Omaha Beach, the most common type was the APX-R turret, a French turret mounted on the Renault R-35 infantry tank and on the Hotchkiss 35H and 38H cavalry tanks. This turret was armed with a short 37mm gun and a coaxial machine gun. Another common type was the turret of the World War I Renault FT light tanks. These *Panzer Drehturm* were one of the better defensive positions on Omaha Beach since the tank turret was impervious to most infantry weapons and the Tobruk was a very small target for naval bombardment.

Another common form of *Ringstand* found on the D-Day beaches was a type of open gun pit for 50mm pedestal guns. This bore little similarity to the Tobruk other than the circular gun opening on top. Unlike the Tobruk, the basic version did not include a shelter for the crew.

STRONGPOINT VIERVILLE-SUR-MER

Strongpoint Group Vierville, on the western side of the beach, was defended primarily by troops of the *11.Kompanie, Grenadier-Regiment.726*. It consisted of four defense nests: WN74, WN73, WN72, and WN71. WN74 was located above the cliffs, where the Pointe-et-Raz-de-la-Percée promontory poked out into the sea. It actually had very limited lines of fire against Omaha Beach and principally served as a western shoulder for this defense sector, linking it to defensive works farther west on the cliffs, such as the Strongpoint Le Guay radar station. It had at least three field guns along the cliff edge that were within range of Omaha Beach.

WN73 was located in the high ground on the western side of the D-1 Vierville draw and saw a considerable amount of combat on D-Day, mostly in the fighting with the 2nd Rangers. It consisted mainly of trench lines and earth gun pits for an infantry defense of the bluff. There were several stone buildings in the defense nest that were used as defense points on D-Day.

WN72 was the smallest, but most important, of the defense nests in this strongpoint. It was designed to physically block the entrance to the Vierville draw, thereby cutting off access to the main paved road off the beach. The centerpiece of

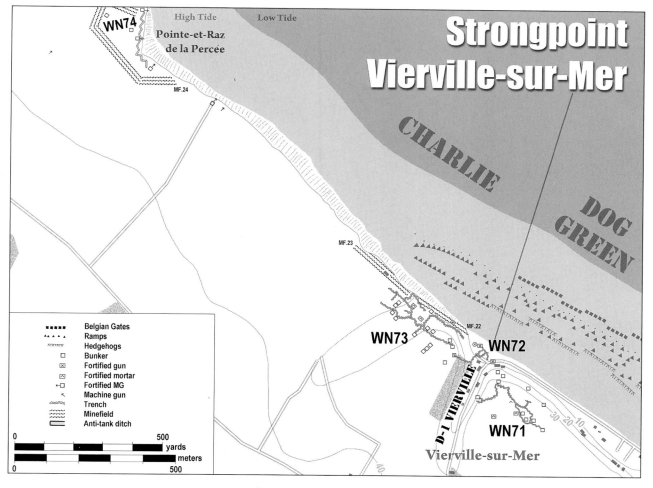

Strongpoint Vierville-sur-Mer

This is a view from the bluffs under the WN71 defense nest looking eastward toward the seaside resort of Hamel-au-Prêtre, with the WN70 defense nest on the bluff above. General Cota's group from the 116th Infantry made their way over the bluff in this sector. MHI

This non-standard machine-gun nest was built into the crest of the hill in the WN71 defense nest, overlooking the D-1 Vierville draw. AUTHOR

This is a contemporary view of Strongpoint Vierville taken from the coast road near Hamel-au-Prêtre looking westward toward the D-1 Vierville draw and the cliffs of Pointe-et-Raz-de-la-Percée to the far right. On D-Day, the 116th Infantry used this section of the beach as a rallying point before moving up the bluffs on the left. AUTHOR

Strongpoint Le Guay between Omaha Beach and Pointe-du-Hoc was a combined *Luftwaffe/Kriegsmarine* radar station. This shows the damaged FuMO 2 Calais radar, part of the *Kriegsmarine Imme* station of *2.Funkmessabteilung* (radar regiment) in WN75. NARA

This is a low-altitude aerial reconnaissance photo showing Strongpoint Le Guay on the cliffs east of Pointe-du-Hoc. The circular antenna of the FuSE 65 *Wurzberg-Riese* air search radar of the *Luftwaffe "Igel"* station of *9./ Luftnachrichtenregiment.53* (air surveillance regiment) is about all that is visible of the site from this angle. NARA

This is a contemporary view of the far western end of Omaha Beach. The WN73 defense nest was located on the top of the bluff to the left, and the rectangular opening for the 75mm PaK 97/38 gun can be seen midway up the hill. Capt. Ralph Goranson's Company C, 2nd Rangers, climbed the cliffs seen in the center of the photo to attack WN73 above. To the right is the Pointe-et-Raz-de-la-Percée; WN74 was located on the top of that bluff. AUTHOR

This non-standard gun bunker was built into the steep hill at the base of the WN73 defense nest and contained a 75mm PaK 97/38 gun that faced toward the D-1 Vierville draw. AUTHOR

This is a contemporary view of Omaha Beach from the WN73 defense nest looking eastward toward the D-1 Vierville draw. Goranson's Company C, 2nd Rangers, first reached the bluff from the cliffs below and to the left in the small gully immediately in front of this photo. AUTHOR

WN72 was a "Concrete King Tiger"—an R677 bunker with an 88mm gun sitting in the middle of the exit and blocking access to the ravine. This bunker and antitank wall were not completed until later May 1944, which is one reason that the U.S. Army was unprepared to deal with this formidable fortification. This casemate was typical of the better German gun bunkers. To limit its vulnerability to naval gunfire, its embrasure was located on the eastern side of the structure, with the gun firing in enfilade up along the beach. There was a wall shielding the embrasure from the sea, another typical feature of these coastal bunkers. Its construction standard was Category B, meaning side walls of two-meter-thick (6.5 feet) steel-reinforced concrete.

This level of thickness could withstand naval gunfire up to 8-inch (203mm) guns and so was essentially impervious to artillery fire except through its embrasure. These casemates were quite time-consuming and expensive to build, requiring seventeen metric tons of rebar steel, four tons of other steel for armor doors and other structures, and 380 cubic meters of concrete weighing some 915 metric tons. They were actually far better protected than the King Tiger tank but had an Achilles heel in the form of their open embrasure. There were two of these 88mm bunkers on either end of Omaha Beach, providing a deadly crossfire across the entire landing area. The other one was in WN61.[6]

Calm and peaceful today, this was one of the deadliest stretches of Omaha Beach on D-Day. The WN71 defense nest was located on the hill in the center of the photo, while the big 88mm bunker in WN72 can be seen at the far right. The terrain has changed considerably since the war, with the stone seawall having been added to limit erosion. The 88mm bunker has been rebuilt with the National Guard memorial on top. AUTHOR

This photo was taken in the months after D-Day from inside the 88mm bunker in WN72 in the D-1 Vierville draw. WN71 was located on top of the hill seen here. NARA

To further cork up the exit, a massive concrete wall about thirty-eight meters (125 feet) in length was built on the eastern shoulder of the bunker, projecting into the neighboring hill. The wall was staggered near the bunker to permit foot traffic, but the access was too small for vehicles. This wall essentially sealed off the Vierville draw from traffic and became the primary obstruction when U.S. troops tried to exit from the western end of Omaha Beach on D-Day.

To cover the western side of the Vierville draw, in March–April 1944, a heavily reinforced bunker was built for a 50mm pedestal gun with twin firing ports facing east and west. This type of *Doppelschartenstand* was not a standard design approved in Berlin, but was found at a number of Normandy sites as a way to offer better coverage than casemates with a single embrasure. To top it off, the bunker had a World War I Renault FT tank turret mounted on the upper corner to provide close defense.

The eastern side of the Vierville draw was protected by WN71, which was located on the top of the bluff overlooking WN72. (German defenses on

The H677 bunker was the cork in the opening of the Vierville draw. The bunker itself was a formidable obstacle, but the German engineers also had constructed a substantial tank wall on the south side of the bunker, preventing access to the Vierville. The antitank wall can be seen to the left on this architectural model of the bunker. AUTHOR

Omaha Beach took maximum advantage of the defensive potential of the bluffs.) By Omaha Beach standards, it was not especially well fortified and consisted mainly of earth field fortifications. It was considered easy to defend since the nearby hill was so steep. Its only main armament was a single 75mm gun in an open field position. An R612 anti-tank gun bunker was being constructed for this gun, but it had not been finished by the time of D-Day. There were a number of *SK* (special construction) machine-gun bunkers overlooking the beach. These were not standard designs, but local improvisations to blend in better with the local terrain.

This illustration shows the layout of the *Bauwork* Nr. 968 *Doppelschartenstand* built by the Scheidt construction firm in WN72 in the spring of 1944. It was armed with a 50mm pedestal gun that could fire either east or west along the beach through the two embrasures. There was a war-booty Renault FT tank turret on the upper rear corner for site defense.

This is a contemporary view of the double-embrasure 50mm gun bunker located in WN72 in the D-1 Vierville draw. The Pointe-et-Raz-de-la-Percée can be seen to the far left. As can be seen by comparing this photo to the illustration here, the bunker has been substantially modified since the war, losing its protective walls and becoming enveloped in the expanded coastal road. AUTHOR

This is a postwar panoramic view of Strongpoint Vierville taken from the west over the Pointe-et-Raz-de-la-Percée and looking eastward toward the D-1 Vierville draw. MHI

STRONGPOINT ST. LAURENT-SUR-MER

Strongpoint St. Laurent-sur-Mer was the central defense work on Omaha Beach, covering the D-3 Les Moulins draw, and was defended primarily by troops of the *10.Kompanie, Grenadier-Regiment .726*. It also included a smaller defense nest, WN70, in the seaside village of Hamel au Prêtre. The WN70 defensive works consisted mainly of trench lines and a few small Tobruks in the hill overlooking the beach houses.

The main defenses of Strongpoint St. Laurent were three defense nests clumped together around the access roads of the D-3 Les Moulins draw. The central element of this defense work was an enor-mous antitank trench more than 600 meters (2,000 feet) long that blocked all vehicular access to the D-3 draw. The shoulder of the antitank trench was covered by another large antitank wall. The WN66 defense nest was a series of defensive positions along the beach, including several Tobruks. The main weapon in this defense nest was a 50mm pedestal gun mounted in a *Ringstand*.

There were two defense nests on the hills on either side of the draw—WN68 on the western side and WN67 on the eastern side. Strongpoint St. Laurent was the last of the three strongpoints on Omaha Beach to be heavily reinforced with

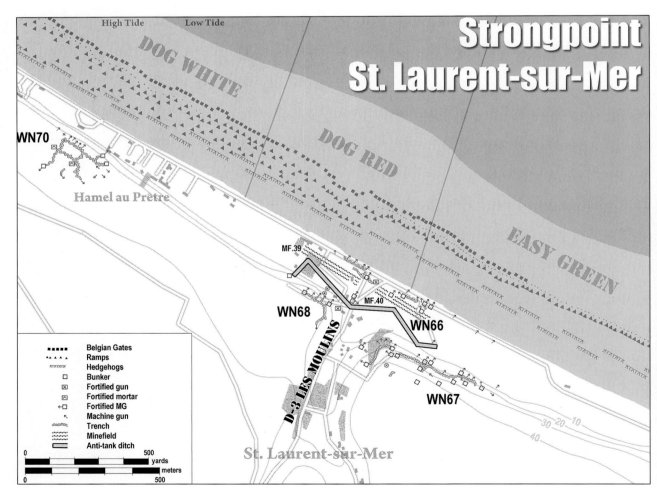

Strongpoint St. Laurent-sur-Mer

This is an overhead reconnaissance photo taken over Strongpoint St. Laurent on D-Day showing the massive antitank ditch that blocked access to the D-3 Les Moulins draw.

WN66

WN68

WN67

Although the Germans demolished most structures along the beach to provide better fields of fire, some of the sturdier buildings were left for infantry positions. This house, *Les Sables d'Or* (Sands of Gold), in WN66 on the beach at the mouth of D-3 Les Moulins draw was used as a rallying point for Maj. Sidney Bingham during his attempts to storm Strongpoint St. Laurent. NARA

Either side of the D-3 Les Moulins draw was covered by camouflaged machine-gun bunkers nestled into the tops of the crests of the hills on the side of the draw. These were not a standard design, but were custom-built to fit the terrain. AUTHOR

bunkers, and the defense nests at this location (including several gun bunkers) were still under construction on D-Day. The most unusual bunker in WN68 was a *Panzer Drehturm* fitted with the turret from the VK.3001 heavy tank with a 75mm gun. This tank was a predecessor for the later and more famous Tiger I heavy tank, but never reached production. A handful of VK.3001 tanks were built, and two turrets from these were sent to Omaha Beach. One was fitted to a bunker on the western side of the WN68 defense nest. Plans were underway to mount the second on the eastern side in WN67, but on 5 June 1944, the truck carrying the turret became stuck in the mud. After it was pulled out, the site was strafed by Allied

fighters, putting an end to the day's work. As a result, the second turret was found abandoned at the site on D-Day by advancing U.S. troops.

Besides the main defenses near the beach, Strongpoint St. Laurent also included its most critical command post. WN69 was a battalion headquarters located in a bunker between the beach defenses and the town of St. Laurent. This site also held the main communication hub on Omaha Beach, which contained the main exchange for the field telephone network from the seacoast defense nests, and connected the Omaha Beach defenses to other German strongpoints along the Lower Normandy coast.

This is a view from the eastern edge of Easy Green Beach looking westward toward the D-3 Les Moulins draw. The draw is in the depression between the WN67 and WN68 defense nests. MHI

This is a view looking directly into the E-1 St. Laurent draw, taken shortly after the war, after U.S. Army engineers had cleaned up most of the German obstructions. The two main defense nests, WN67 and WN68, were located on the hills on either side of the draw. MHI

Besides the many concrete fortifications, the Omaha Beach defenses consisted of extensive field entrenchments like these in WN67 on the east shoulder of the D-3 Les Moulins draw. NARA

STRONGPOINT COLLEVILLE-SUR-MER

Strongpoint Colleville-sur-Mer was one of the most heavily defended sites on Omaha Beach and was manned primarily by troops of the *3.Kompanie, Grenadier-Regiment.726*. When the beach defenses were first organized in 1942, the command network was divided between the two strongpoints on the western side, which reported through the St. Laurent command center, and Strongpoint Colleville, which reported through the command post farther east behind Port-en-Bessin. This situation remained in place on D-Day, with the Vierville and St. Laurent strongpoints under the command of the *II./Grenadier-Regiment.916*, while Colleville was under the *I./Grenadier-Regiment.726*.

The central defensive cluster for Strongpoint Colleville consisted of WN61 and WN62, which sat on either side of a 500 meter (1,640 feet) wide antitank ditch, completely blocking access into the valley beyond. WN62 dominated the site and was located on the bluff on the western side of the E-3 Colleville draw. The most prominent features at the site were a pair of R669 bunkers on the crest of the hill, each armed with a 75mm FK 235(b). This was the German designation for the *Belgian Canon de 75 mle TR*, the standard field gun of the Belgian army in World War I, based on the *Krupp Mod. 1905*. While not an especially modern field gun, it was still a very lethal weapon against exposed

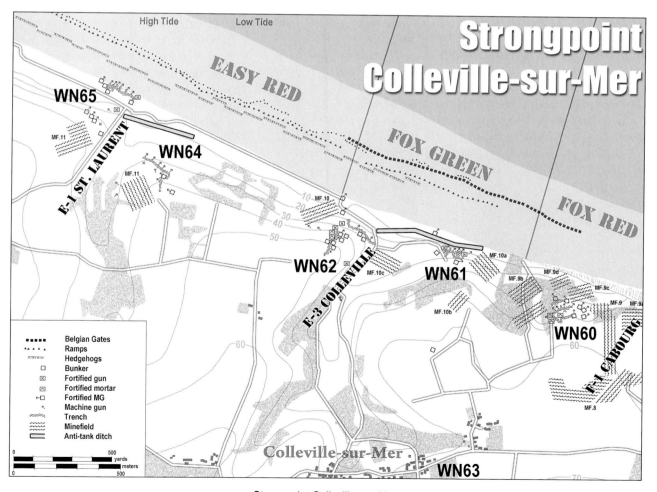

Strongpoint Colleville-sur-Mer

The geography of Omaha Beach lent itself to the defense. This is a view out the embrasure of one of the 75mm gun bunkers in WN62, looking westward toward the Pointe-et-Raz-de-la-Percée. As can be seen, even the defenses on the eastern side of the beach had clear firing lines across most of the beach. AUTHOR

This is a view of the E-3 Colleville draw looking down the shallow valley locally known as the *Vallée du Ruisseau des Moulins* ("Valley of the Windmill Stream"). As can be seen, WN62 was perched on a substantial hill, while WN61 was near shore level. This photo was taken shortly after the war, by which time the big antitank ditch across the mouth of the valley had been plowed under by U.S. Army engineers. MHI

troops on the beaches below. The two gun casemates faced westward toward Easy Red Beach and had excellent coverage over a large portion of Omaha Beach. Farther down the hill was a small cluster of defensive works. There was a single 50mm pedestal gun in an open pit, serving to shield the antitank ditch farther below, and there was a second 50mm pedestal gun around the side of the defense nest, intended to cover the valley below. There were also numerous machine-gun and mortar entrenchments, several in their own Tobruks.

The WN62 defense nest is the best-known and best-documented site on Omaha Beach. Several German soldiers from the site survived the war, two of whom wrote memoirs. In addition, the site is located near the U.S. cemetery, so it is widely visited by tourists. One of the gun casemates is topped by a memorial to the 5th Engineer Special Brigade, and so the site is sometimes called "Engineer Hill."

WN61 was one of the smaller, but more powerful, sites on the beach and was a counterpart of WN72 on the other side of the beach. It was located on the low ground on the eastern side of the Colleville tank trap. It contained another of the "Concrete King Tigers," an R677 bunker with 88mm PaK 43/41 gun facing westward. This casemate was protected by an APX-R *Panzer Drehturm* behind it. In addition, there was another 50mm pedestal gun mounted in a *Ringstand* to cover the tank trap.

This is an Allied reconnaissance photo taken in May 1944 showing the massive antitank ditch blocking the E-3 Colleville draw, with the WN61 defense nest to the right.

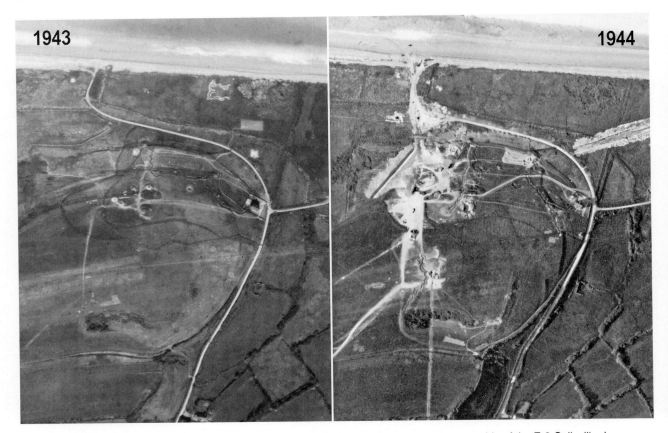

This is a pair of overhead Allied reconnaissance photos of the WN62 defense nest on the west side of the E-3 Colleville draw. These photos show the extensive fortification work that was undertaken between April 1943, when the photo on the left was taken, and May 1944, when the reconnaissance photo on the right was taken.

A contemporary view from the WN62 defense nest looking eastward toward the Plateau du Calvados, with the E-3 Colleville draw immediately below. AUTHOR

A contemporary view of the lower of the two R612 bunkers with 75mm FK 235(b) field guns in the WN62 defense nest on the hill on the west side of the E-3 Colleville draw. It was commanded by Cpl. Heinrich Brinkmeier of *3./Grenadier-Regiment.726* and was knocked out by tank fire from the 741st Tank Battalion on D-Day, with most of the four-man crew wounded. AUTHOR

This is a contemporary view of the same R612 bunker in WN62 but from the rear, showing the back entrance and rear protective wall. This bunker was set up to provide crossfire along the beach, and the embrasure pointed westward. This is a useful view to show the proximity of the site to the beach at high tide—about 130 meters (142 yards) to the sand below. AUTHOR

A view from the west side of WN62 looking eastward and showing both of the R612 bunkers in the defense nest. The upper bunker has been used as the base for the memorial to the 5th Engineer Special Brigade. AUTHOR

While WN61 and WN62 covered the main Colleville exit, there were two smaller clusters of defense works covering two other smaller beach exits on either side. WN64 and WN65 were located on either side of the E-1 St. Laurent draw. The Le Ruquet ravine was not one of the better exits off the beach and so was not especially well protected. The best defensive work in the site was a 50mm pedestal gun mounted in a H667 casemate in WN65 on the western side of the draw. This particular bunker is very well known because it was later used by U.S. troops as a command post and widely photographed. It is still very well preserved today and contains the only original 50mm pedestal gun still on Omaha Beach. A second R667 gun case-

mate was being built in WN64 on the hill opposite to help seal off the ravine, but it was not complete on D-Day.

The easternmost defense work on Omaha Beach was the WN60 defense nest on the cliffs overlooking the F-1 Cabourg draw. This position had a large number of Tobruks and entrenchments, as well as two open gun pits for Belgian *Canon de 75 mle TR*, like those used in WN62. The field gun on the western side of the hill had a particularly good vantage over the beach, especially toward the Colleville draw. However, the F-1 ravine was a poor beach exit for vehicles. The cliffs below the defense works provided a natural shelter for any force landing there, as would become evident on D-Day.

This is one of the best-known bunkers on Omaha Beach, an R667 containing a 50mm pedestal gun, located in WN65 on the western side of the E-1 St. Laurent draw. It was heavily photographed on D-Day and the days after, as it was used as an American command post after its capture. The nearby scenery has changed since the war because of local efforts to prevent beach erosion, and there are now more substantial dunes to the right by the shoreline. The memorial to the left is dedicated to the 2nd Infantry Division, which came ashore here after D-Day. AUTHOR

This panoramic view taken after D-Day shows Omaha Beach from the vantage point of the WN60 resistance nest. This provides a clear idea of why the topography of the beach favored the defenders, since so many sites on bluffs provided clear fields of fire for German weapons. NARA

The WN60 defense nest on the extreme eastern side of Omaha Beach was located on top of the cliffs of the Plateau du Calvados. During the D-Day landings, the 3/16th Infantry landed too far east and took shelter under the cliffs here before moving up the F-1 Cabourg draw in the center of this contemporary photo. AUTHOR

The *2./HKAR.1260* in WN76 at Pointe-du-Hoc deployed six 155mm *Kanone* 418(f). These were war-booty French 155mm GPF guns from World War I. They were originally deployed in open concrete "kettle" gun pits as seen here. Later in 1943, the battery troops erected standard camouflage umbrellas over the guns for concealment. ALAIN CHAZETTE

Construction of six R679 gun bunkers for the guns at Pointe-du-Hoc was undertaken by the Scheidt construction firm in 1944, but they were only partly complete on D-Day because of the Allied spring bombing campaign and so were never occupied. AUTHOR

TABLE 14: GERMAN BEACH STRONGPOINTS, OMAHA BEACH

	Gun Bunkers	Tank Turrets	AT Guns	Field Guns	Tobruks, Ringstands	Mortars
StP Colleville						
WN60		1		2x 75mm FK235(b)	3	4
WN61	1	1	88mm, 50mm		4	
WN62	2		2 x 50mm PaK	2x 75mm FK235(b)	3	2
WN64	1			76mm iKH290(r)	1	2
WN65	1		37mm, 2x 50mm, 75mm PaK 40		3	2
StP St. Laurent						
WN66	2	1	2x 50mm		2	2
WN68		2	47mm, 50mm		1	
WN70	1				4	2
StP Vierville						
WN71			75mm PaK 40		3	2
WN72	2	1	50mm, 88mm		3	
WN73	1		75mm 97/38 PaK 231(f)		3	3
WN74				76mm Skoda, 3x 75mm FK235(b)		
Total	*11*	*6*	*16*	*9*	*30*	*19*

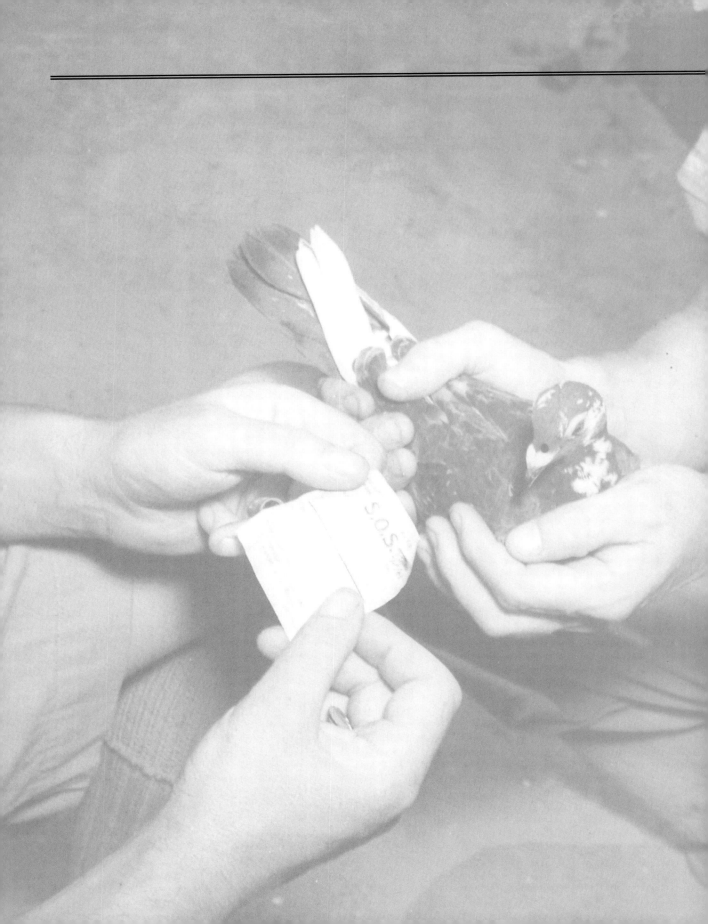

CHAPTER 8

The Pigeon Patrol

ON SATURDAY MORNING, 3 JUNE 1944, Sgt. Günter Witte was on guard duty at Les Pieux, a small coastal village on the Cotentin coast, west of the fortified port city of Cherbourg. Witte served with the *HKAA.1262*, an army coastal artillery regiment. Curiously enough, his weapon was not the usual *Wehrmacht Gewehr* 98k rifle, but instead a civilian shotgun. Peering into the haze, he spotted his target—a pigeon. With a few shots, he brought down the bird and raced over to retrieve it. On its leg was a small metal capsule and, within it, a small coded message. With pride, he showed it to his commander, who ordered him to take it to the regimental headquarters by bicycle. After his arrival at headquarters, the tiny message was sent up the chain of command to the counterintelligence section of the *84.Korps* headquarters, responsible for army units in lower Normandy.[1] This espionage message was not the first intercepted, and the German commanders were content that their antipigeon patrols were helping to frustrate Allied intelligence gathering in Normandy. The carrier pigeon was one of the main means used by the French Resistance to communicate with British intelligence, and this incident was a small part of a much larger intelligence struggle that would have a profound impact a few days later at Omaha Beach.

In an age of spy satellites and robotic drones, it is easy to forget that intelligence gathering in World War II was less a high-tech science and more the traditional art of spycraft. Over recent decades, the role of intelligence in the Allied victories in Europe has received an increasing amount of attention as a "war-winning" innovation. In particular, the "Ultra secret"—the success of Allied signals intelligence in breaking the German Enigma codes—has revolutionized our understanding of the value of intelligence in Allied decision-making. But Ultra was not all-knowing, and there were many gaps in Allied understanding of German defenses in Normandy. Furthermore, Ultra was not the primary means for Allied intelligence gathering in Normandy. Other methods were used, and to understand the successes and failures of Allied intelligence in the months leading to D-Day, it is essential to understand how they worked.

"Ultra" is the name widely used to identify a highly sophisticated Allied program to intercept and decipher coded German military radio traffic. This type of intelligence is now called SIGINT (signals intelligence). The Germans used the Enigma coding machine, as well as several other systems, to code their messages before sending them by radio. Radio signals could be picked up hundreds of miles away by friend and foe, so enciphering the messages was a vital means to protect their secrets from the ears of Allied signals intelligence units. Although the Ultra decryption efforts contributed to the Allied assessment of German defenses in Normandy, they were by no means adequate to create a detailed picture.

To begin with, Ultra depended on the interception of radio messages. However, the *Wehrmacht* tried to avoid the use of radio when possible because of the recognition that it could be intercepted, even if in code. Communication security was a vital concern to the *Wehrmacht*, based on lessons from World War I. Prior to D-Day, the *Wehrmacht*'s primary method of communication between Berlin and its far-flung subordinate commands was by means of traditional landlines, including couriers, telephones, and teletypes. Allied intelligence could not intercept any of these messages and was largely in the dark regarding German military communications within France. Ultra was more valuable when dealing with units that were obliged to use radio, including U-boats at sea and *Luftwaffe* units in the air. Army units did not need to use radio for important messages until the start of battle since they were located at fixed bases with telephone lines. When battle began and units started to move, radio communication suddenly picked up in volume and became more essential. But the *7.Armee* in Normandy was stationary until D-Day and so made very limited use of radio for important messages.

Because of these shortcomings in SIGINT, the Allies' principal means of collecting intelligence prior to D-Day were human intelligence (HUMINT) and photographic intelligence by aircraft.

Pigeons have been used by armies for centuries as a means of communication, though their role in World War II has been overshadowed by newer technologies such as radio. This carrier pigeon was being used by the U.S. Army Air Force in China in November 1944. NARA

SPY NETWORKS IN FRANCE

One of Germany's main intelligence weaknesses in France was its vulnerability to espionage from the local French population. This is a traditional problem for occupation forces, and Germany had an extensive array of counterintelligence agencies, including both the military intelligence (*Abwehr*) and the secret state police (*Gestapo: Geheime Staatspolizei*). The counterintelligence struggle in the occupied countries was complicated by the rivalry between the military police and the various state police organizations, including both the *Gestapo* and *Sipo*.[2]

The area along the French coast was a prohibited zone for most of the war to prevent espionage against German military installations such as the Atlantic Wall. Essential French civilians were allowed to remain in the zone, but the occupants were issued special passes and travel was greatly restricted.

The day-to-day business of monitoring this security zone was handled by the army itself. German Army headquarters in Normandy contained their own counterintelligence detachments.[*] Actual police functions were carried out by the Secret Field Police (GFP: *Geheime Feldpolizei*), the military counterpart of the better-known *Gestapo*.[3]

The German counterintelligence effort was made simpler by the physical barrier between France and Britain, namely the English Channel. Unlike other situations in which intelligence agents might sneak across a long border, the North Sea presented an immediate challenge for timely communication between French Resistance groups and British intelligence. Agents could be smuggled out of France over the Pyrenees Mountains in southwestern France into neutral Spain, but it was a slow and uncertain process. To speed up vital intelligence communication, the British Special Operations Executive (SOE) used three major means to communicate with the French resistance: radio, pigeons, and aircraft.

The SOE developed specialized compact radio transmitters that could be smuggled into France for use in communicating with resistance espionage rings.[4] Britain was close enough to France that special light aircraft such as the Lysander could be flown at night from southern England into Normandy. These flights were dangerous for both the aircrews and the Resistance members, since the *Wehrmacht* was obviously on the alert for any such missions. Another method of aerial delivery—the principal means to deliver radio transmitters to the French Resistance—was by parachute. The radios required highly trained operators, often French volunteers trained in Britain and parachuted back into France.

The resistance radios had their drawbacks. Although they provided a quick means to communicate with London, the radio signals also could be intercepted by German counterintelligence. The *Abwehr* set up a special program in France codenamed Operation Donar (after the mythical God of Thunder in Valhalla). This effort revolved around specialized direction-finding teams, dubbed Short Wave Monitoring Units (KWU: *Kurzwellenüberwachung*). A central control station monitored the radio bands, and when a new signal emerged, it would be tracked down by KWU teams in specially equipped, unmarked Mercedes panel trucks. The KWU units worked in teams since a radio signal intercepted by two separate direction-finding stations could be used to triangulate the location of the radio transmitter. The French radio teams knew they had to move their radios to avoid the German teams. They also were careful to limit the broadcast time since it took the German teams a few minutes to identify the radio signal and to initiate the triangulation process. This led to a cat-and-mouse game, pitting the German teams against the French radio teams—a chase that often ended with tragic consequences for the French radio operators. Of the approximately one hundred radio teams operating in France, at least ten were arrested by the Germans.[5]

---

*The Germany Army's equivalent of the U.S. Army G-2 was abbreviated Ic (*Feindnachrichten*: enemy intelligence). The subsection devoted to counterintelligence was designated as the Ic/AO (*Abwehroffizier*: intelligence officer).

Since the radios were limited in number and required experienced operators, the Resistance also used an older and more traditional communication method—the homing pigeon.[6] Hannibal had used pigeons for military communications during his traverse of the Alps in 218 B.C. In more recent times, homing pigeons became famous for their use during the siege of Paris in the 1870 Franco-Prussian War. Pigeons had been widely used by many armies over the years and extensively by the British Navy in World War I from small coastal vessels. The spread of radio communication in the 1920s and 1930s reduced the role of pigeons for military communication but did not entirely eliminate it. All the major armed forces used pigeons during World War II.

During World War II, the British armed forces had a well-organized program, though largely unknown, run by the National Pigeon Service. Young homing pigeons were raised and donated by British racing pigeon breeders, with some 200,000 pigeons donated during World War II. The homing pigeons were legendary for their ability to find their way back to their roosts. The record-holder among the WWII pigeons was a bird that traveled 1,090 miles from Gibraltar in twenty-eight days.

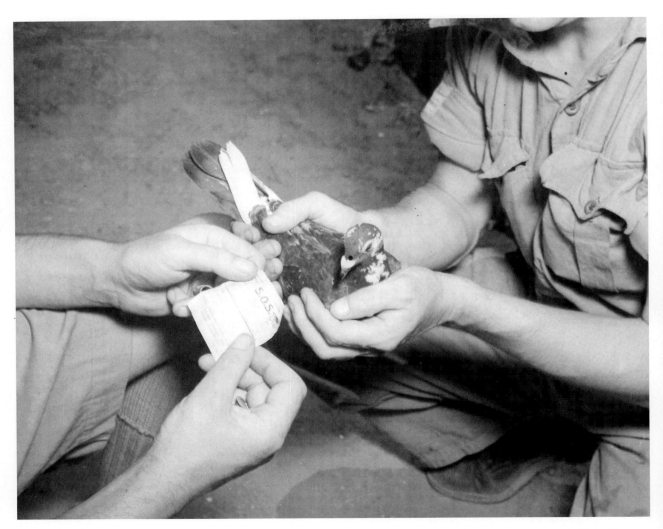

One of the more common military uses for carrier pigeons in World War II was as a means of emergency communication with downed air crews or small warships. This pigeon was used by the U.S. 9th Air Force in Libya for the rescue of bomber crews downed in the remote desert. NARA

Such long-distance missions were not common. More typical missions from France involved travel of 80 miles in two hours or 125 miles in as little as three hours.

The homing pigeons were used by a variety of military units. One of their roles was to serve as a means of emergency communication for British bombers returning from missions over Germany. In the event the bomber was shot down and the radio no longer of use, the crew could release a pigeon that would return to its roost with a message about the location of the downed crew. The story of a red checkered cock named George (numbered MEPS.43.1263) is a typical example. George had been raised by the Middle East Pigeon Service in Cairo and was carried aboard a British Baltimore medium bomber that ditched in the Mediterranean on 22 June 1943, about a hundred miles from base. The crew was unable to get the emergency radio to work properly and released George, who flew back to his roost in Berka. The crew of four men was saved by air-sea rescue based on the pigeon-borne message.

British motor torpedo boats and air-sea rescue boats in the Channel made regular use of pigeons for emergency communications. On D-Day, hundreds of pigeons were provided to British and American paratrooper units as a means to communicate back to the United Kingdom when radios were not available.

The use of homing pigeons in occupied France involved two separate programs. Operation Columba was a secret program started in 1942 to drop homing pigeon containers by parachute over occupied Europe with a small questionnaire included in the bird's carrying container. British intelligence asked people in the occupied countries to answer some questions involving nearby German occupation troops. These pigeon missions were discovered almost as soon as they started, and on 19 February 1942, orders were issued that the pigeons should be captured and turned in to centralized collection points run by the *Abwehr* intelligence service. The questionnaires were filled out by German intelligence officers with bogus information and the pigeons released back to Britain. The pigeons were called "the flying postmen" by the *Wehrmacht*. Over three-and-a-half years, some 16,554 pigeons were dropped into occupied Europe, and 1,842 pigeons returned to Britain. It remains a mystery as to how many returned with useful information and how many returned with "double-cross" messages from the *Abwehr*.

Homing pigeons were also provided to the French Resistance as an alternative to the radio transmitter. These were often delivered in groups by special aircraft drops and then distributed amongst the Resistance cells. They were especially useful in the more remote and rural areas, such as Normandy, where there were few Resistance members skilled in radio operation or Morse code.

A typical example of the resistance pigeons was captured by the *352.Infanterie-Division* in May 1944. The pigeon had been dispatched by a Frenchman living in Criqueville (west of Omaha Beach), who provided details of the dispositions of the *2./Artillerie-Regiment.1716* and the newly deployed *Flak-Sturm Regiment.1* and of obstacle construction around the small port of Grandcamples-Bains. From 20 March 1944 to 20 May 1944, the pigeon patrols in the *352.Infanterie-Division* near Omaha Beach downed no fewer than twenty-seven courier pigeons.[7] Some pigeons returned to England but failed to reach their roost; one was even found in 2012 in an English house chimney with its message still intact.[8]

THE RESISTANCE IN LOWER NORMANDY

The story of the French Resistance in Normandy is far too complicated to describe in any detail here, but a brief sketch of its activities will help explain U.S. Army intelligence problems at Omaha Beach. Popular accounts might suggest that the French Resistance was a highly organized movement operating with military precision. The opposite was the case. The Resistance was a voluntary amalgam of scattered little cells, some based around former army veterans and others based around political parties, civic groups, and religious groups. Some groups specialized in espionage, others in political agitation, and some in "direct action" military raiding.[9]

One of the earliest espionage successes involving the future Omaha Beach area was conducted by the Resistance group *Centurie*, based in Caen. This group succeeded in smuggling an agent into the headquarters of the *Organisation Todt* construction agency in Caen in May 1942, under the pretext of painting the offices.[10] The agent managed to find the plans for future fortification along the Normandy coast. The plans were smuggled to Britain and were the first information about the defenses along the future D-Day beaches. In 1943, the French Resistance group *Confrérie Notre-Dame* sent a detailed map to London that had been stolen from German offices in Caen and described the planned construction of Atlantic Wall fortifications in the Lower Normandy area.

One of the most active groups in the Lower Normandy area was the *Alliance* resistance network formed by Commander Georges Loustaunau-Lacau.[11] The group's Ferme sector in Normandy was led by Jean Roger (also known as Jean San-

The German army sealed off the Atlantic Wall coast as a restricted zone, with local French inhabitants obliged to use special passes to get to their homes. This was intended to limit access to German defense works by the French Resistance. This particular checkpoint was located at Franceville on the eastern side of the D-Day beaches and photographed in February 1944. LIBRARY OF CONGRESS

teny), code name Dragon. He owned a villa in Vierville and so had connections in the area. The future Omaha Beach was in the group's Bessin sector, headed by Marcel Couliboeuf—a teacher in Formigny, code name *Bison noir* (Black Bison)—and this sector had a radio transmitter. The Bessin sector had three cells in the area: in Bayeux, in Port-en-Bessin to the east of Omaha Beach, and in the Omaha Beach area around Vierville. The Vierville group was headed by Desiré Lemière, code name *Chordeille*, and included three other members, most of whom were postmen in the town. The *Alliance* network was not the only Resistance group in the area, and they cooperated with other groups such as the *Organisation civile et militaire* (OCM) intelligence cell of Guillaume Mercader, who was the source of pigeons for communication. Mercader was a professional cyclist and veteran of the Foreign Legion who grew up in the Bessin region. In total, there were 135 to 180

individuals involved in Resistance activity during the war in this area, of whom about fifteen to twenty belonged to the *Alliance* network.

Lemière's group was responsible for scouting the German beach defense construction in the area, a task made somewhat easier by their occupation as postmen. Much of the construction of the Atlantic Wall was by French architectural firms.[12] Many of the construction workers in the area were young Moroccans, recruited by the Germans in southern France and used as workers in Normandy because of their lack of local connections. However, they spoke French and had contact with the postmen because of their mail back home to French North Africa. Lemière's cell scouted out most of the major sites in this area, including the artillery batteries at Maisy, Pointe-du-Hoc, and Longues-sur-Mer, and the shore defenses on Omaha Beach. The group was well aware of the movement of the *352.Infanterie-Division* to the Omaha Beach sector,

A German patrol guards the entrance through an antitank wall in the *15.Armee* sector of the Atlantic Wall in 1944. The soldier to the right is from a *Luftwaffe* field division. MHI

Some of the members of the French Resistance in the Omaha Beach area (from left to right) were the head of the *Alliance* Ferme sector in Normandy, Jean Roger; head of the Vierville cell, Desiré Lemière; head of the Trévières cell, Robert Boulard; and the famous cyclist from the OCM group, Guillaume Mercader.

In spite of German efforts to isolate the Atlantic Wall from French spying, the use of French labor at the construction sites made them vulnerable to espionage. Here two French workers are completing the construction of an H677 gun bunker armed with an 88mm PaK 43/41 in StP 18 on the coast of Hermanville-Le Brèche (Sword Beach) in February 1944. This strongpoint was manned by *10./Grenadier-Regiment.736* of the *716.Infanterie-Division* on D-Day. LIBRARY OF CONGRESS

and they also identified many other important secrets, such as the removal of the guns at Pointe-du-Hoc in April 1944 to new locations away from the strongpoint. They had discovered the movement of the Pointe-du-Hoc gun battery by staying in contact with a restaurant owner in Grandcamp, where German soldiers from the battery attended the weekly Sunday dances. The group attempted to warn the Allies of these developments by sending messages via pigeons. According to German accounts, these two critical bits of intelligence were intercepted by the antipigeon patrols along the Normandy coast. As will be related in detail elsewhere, the loss of these little bits of information would prove very costly to the U.S. Army on D-Day.

On 14 March 1944, a liaison officer of the *Alliance* network was arrested in Paris. The German counterintelligence service quickly began to round up the group. Suspects were tortured, and as more names were revealed, the operatives in Normandy were arrested. On 5 May 1944, Lemière's group was arrested and sent to the prison in Caen for interrogation and torture. The fate of these *Alliance* members is not known in detail. In the wake of the D-Day invasion, many of the prisoners in the Caen prison were shot; others were sent to concentration camps—none survived.

Although German counterintelligence prevented some information from reaching Britain, a consid-erable amount of material leaked through. The *Abwehr* officer in charge of northern France and the Low Countries, Col. H. J. Giskes, wrote in a report: "The wealth of minute detail in the many docu-ments we seized showed how effective our adver-saries' activities were. . . . [They] had won the secret war."[13]

Casemate for 50mm Anti-Tank Gun -Reported Type 680

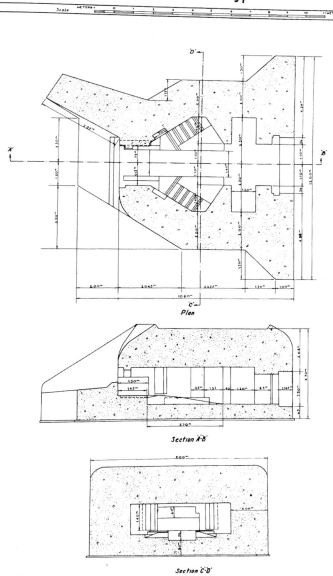

The French Resistance evidently managed to provide Allied intelligence with copies of some German bunker architectural drawings. This is a retracing of an original German plan for an R680 gun bunker, which appeared in the 10 May 1944 Martian Report. Although the drawing is extremely detailed and accurate, it is misidentified as a 50mm gun bunker when in fact it was intended for the larger 75mm PaK 40. NARA

MARTIAN REPORTS

The flow of intelligence data from France led to the creation of a special organization in London to keep track of German coastal defenses along the Channel coast. Headed by an Oxford don, John Austin, a special intelligence cell of the Combined Intelligence Section was established at Clive Steps near Whitehall in London to collate and analyze the growing information. They began issuing top-secret summaries to Allied invasion planners starting in 1942, which were code-named the "Martian Reports."[14]

The French Resistance information was only part of a much larger effort to collect intelligence on German defenses in Normandy. As mentioned earlier, signals intelligence from Normandy was a lim-

ited source because of the German Army's use of landlines. As a result, the other major source of intelligence was aerial photography. The Royal Air Force began reconnaissance flights over France in 1940, and they increased in intensity through D-Day, later supplemented by the U.S. Army Air Force.

One dilemma in conducting these missions was the need to avoid alerting the Germans to Allied interest in the Normandy coast. Since Allied planners wanted to deceive Berlin that the invasion would take place on the Pas-de-Calais, the rule of thumb was to conduct at least two photo reconnaissance flights over those sectors for every flight over Normandy. Coverage of Omaha Beach was thor-

COPY No. 170

SUPREME HEADQUARTERS
ALLIED EXPEDITIONARY FORCE

G-2 (INTELLIGENCE) DIVISION.

MARTIAN REPORT

95

THIS REPORT CONTAINS COMPROMISING INFORMATION. IT IS TO BE SHEWN ONLY TO THOSE OFFICERS WHOSE WORK MAKES IT NECESSARY FOR THEM TO SEE IT. IT IS NOT TO BE TAKEN OUT OF THE UNITED KINGDOM WITHOUT PERMISSION OF T.I.S. NO ITEM MAY BE REPRODUCED WITHOUT REFERENCE TO T.I.S.

T. I. S.
c/o No. I, A.P.D.C.,

Allied intelligence-gathering about the German defenses in Normandy culminated in the Martian Reports, which were issued to a tight circle of senior Allied commanders and planners.

ough, starting with four quarterly sorties in 1943. The pace of coverage intensified in 1944 with fifteen flights from January to May 1944, nearly half of which took place in May 1944 to keep an eye on the changing German defenses. Besides the high-altitude overhead flights, some low-level sorties were conducted. For example, a flight on 9 April 1944 was sent to obtain low-angle oblique photos from Pointe-et-Raz-de-la-Percée to Port-en-Bessin, the future Omaha Beach sector; this sortie was low enough to capture the beach obstructions in detail. As a result, the 30 April 1944 Martian Report included maps showing the locations of individual obstacles.

The reconnaissance photos were extremely useful in creating detailed maps of the D-Day beaches, showing each individual bunker, antitank ditch,

trench line, and beach obstacle. The overhead photos were far less useful in determining the details of the German coastal bunkers. The Atlantic Wall bunkers were all of a new design that had never before been encountered in battle. Overhead photos could not reveal the thickness of the bunkers, nor the contents. Allied planners had to guess the relative strength of the bunkers and the type of guns they contained. The French Resistance did manage to obtain some detailed architectural plans of certain bunker types, and these provided a much more detailed insight into the strength of the bunkers. Nevertheless, there were some serious limitations to aerial photography. The best example is provided by the coastal artillery batteries on either side of Omaha Beach—those at Point-du-Hoc to the west and Longues-sur-Mer to the east.

This is a typical example of the type of aerial reconnaissance photos included in the Martian Reports, taken on 27 April 1944 over the D-3 Les Moulins draw. NARA

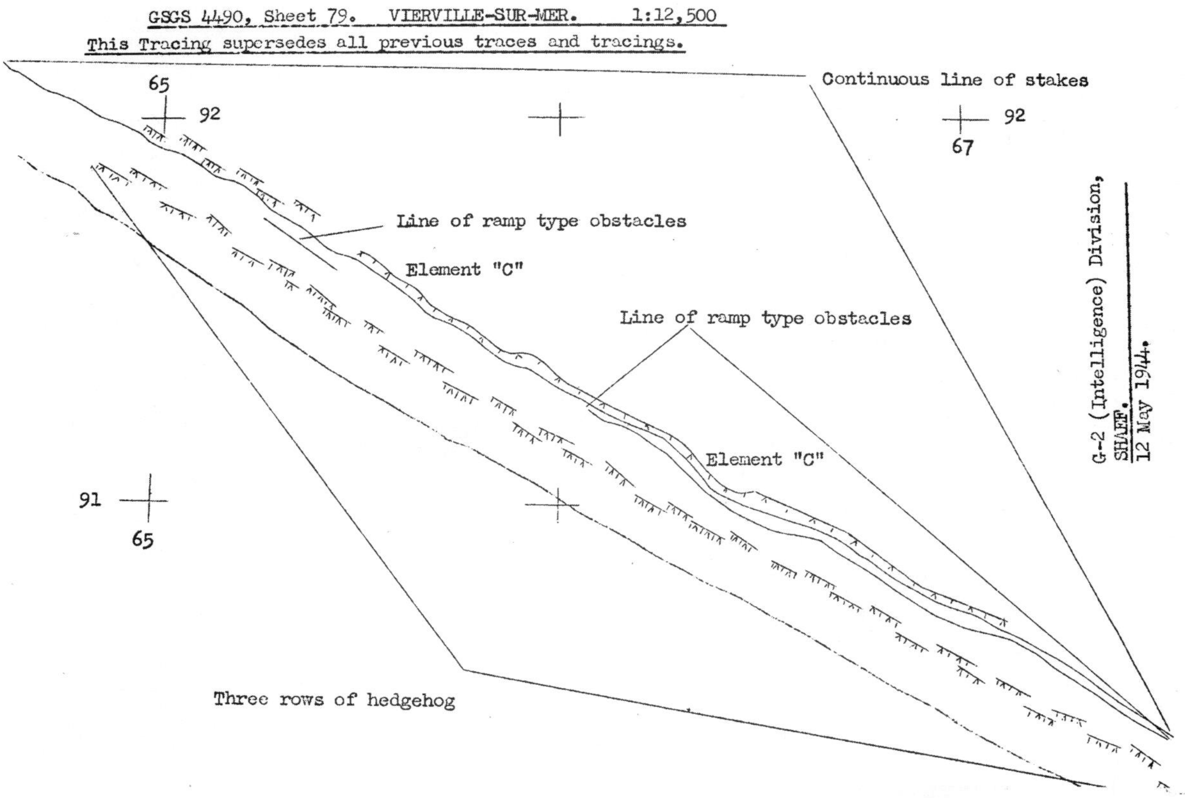

GSGS 4490, Sheet 79. VIERVILLE-SUR-MER. 1:12,500
This Tracing supersedes all previous traces and tracings.
Continuous line of stakes
65
92
92
67
Line of ramp type obstacles
Element "C"
Line of ramp type obstacles
Element "C"
91
65
Three rows of hedgehog
G-2 (Intelligence) Division,
SHAEF.
12 May 1944.

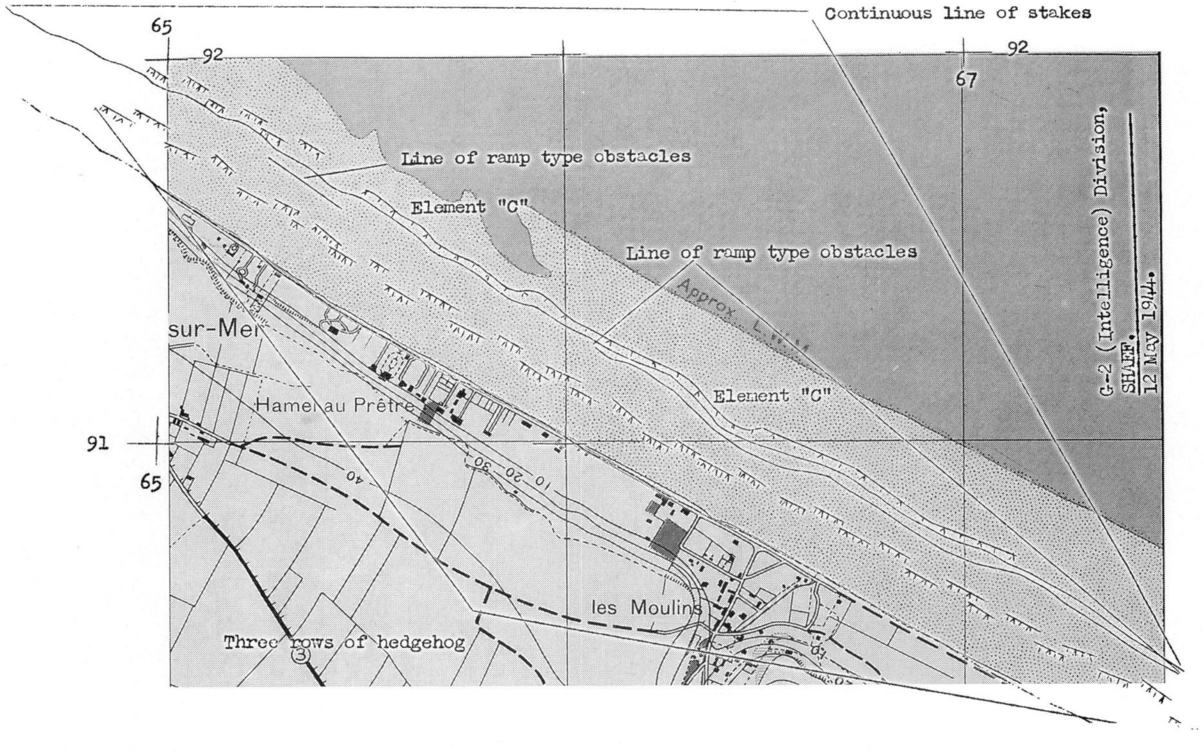

Continuous line of stakes
65
92
92
67
Line of ramp type obstacles
Element "C"
Line of ramp type obstacles
Approx. L.W.M.
sur-Mer
Hamel au Prêtre
Element "C"
91
65
les Moulins
Three rows of hedgehog
G-2 (Intelligence) Division,
SHAEF.
12 May 1944.

This shows a typical example of how the Martian Reports were used. The upper half of this image shows the mimeographed page from the 12 May 1944 Martian Report, which included the latest update on German obstacles on the western section of Omaha Beach. The obstacle sketch included Lambert map grid references so the page could be superimposed on the appropriate GSCS map (below) to better appreciate the location of the obstacle belts.

Coast Battery at LONGUES Ref. Map: GSGS-4347, Sheet 37/18 SW, 797871.

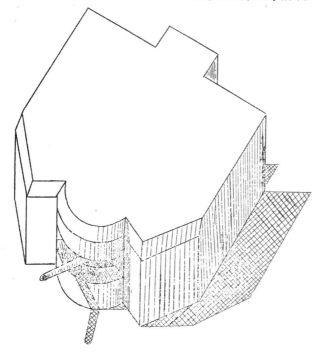

This sketch of the gun bunker at Longues-sur-Mer, based on recent overhead aerial photography, is a typical example of the type of content found in the Martian Reports. This was included in the 21 May 1944 report, shortly after the naval gun battery there had been completed. NARA

G-2 (Intelligence) Division
SHAEF.
21 May 1944

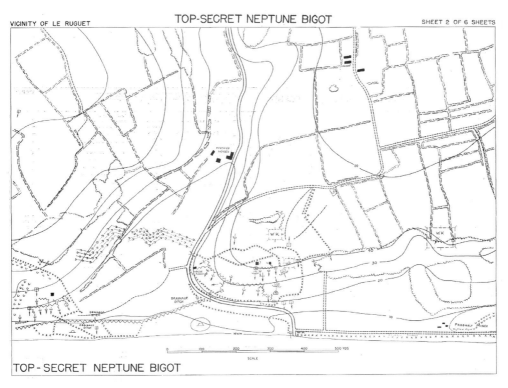

The final products of all the Allied intelligence effort were the special maps issued for the Neptune landings. This is one of the 1st Division Assault maps, in this case showing Strongpoint Colleville with WN62 in the lower center and WN61 in the lower left. MHI

AN INTELLIGENCE SHORTFALL: COASTAL GUN BATTERIES

Allied intelligence was aware of the Pointe-du-Hoc battery even before its construction was completed, based on the plans smuggled out of France by the Resistance in 1942–43. As a result, reconnaissance over-flights of Pointe-du-Hoc were frequent to keep track of the progress on the battery's construction. In May 1942, the *2./HKAA.832* (*Heeres-Küsten-Artillerie-Abteiling*: Army Costal Artillery Battalion) was deployed to Point-du-Hoc prior to the completion of its fortified positions. Allied intelligence quickly identified this battery's weapons as French 155mm GPF guns. This artillery piece was very familiar to the U.S. Army since it had been manufactured under license in the U.S. after World War I and was still a standard weapon of U.S. coastal artillery batteries in World War II. The presence of this powerful battery within range of Omaha Beach led to special plans to deal with the threat. After studying various schemes, including paratroop attack, the Operation Neptune plans for D-Day assigned a Ranger group a daring mission to scale the cliffs of Pointe-du-Hoc to knock out the gun battery prior to the landings.

In the meantime, the Allied air forces had included Pointe-du-Hoc on their list of critical targets. The Pointe-du-Hoc battery was bombed for the first time in the early evening of 25 April 1944. Two waves of USAAF A-20 Havoc medium bombers dropped about forty tons of bombs (see Table 15), destroying two of the six concrete gun emplacements and one of the six guns, and damaging two other guns. The battery moved its three surviving guns and the two damaged guns off the peninsula and back inland, where they were less

The battery of six war-booty French 155mm GPF guns located on the promontory of Pointe-du-Hoc was one of the main concerns of Allied planners. This was the first coastal battery installed near Omaha Beach and so was well known to Allied intelligence. This shows one of the guns in its original concrete "kettle" gun pit. ALAIN CHAZETTE

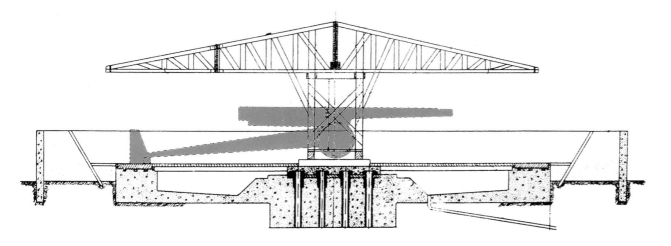

The Pointe-du-Hoc battery eventually installed camouflage umbrellas over the guns, as shown in this later illustration from the Martian Reports.

The camouflage umbrellas over the Pointe-du-Hoc gun pits frustrated Allied intelligence since they prevented the Allies from discovering the extent of damage suffered by the battery after spring 1944 bombing raids. In fact, the Germans had removed the guns to a safer location about two kilometers (one mile) behind the site and replaced the guns with telephone poles. This shows one of the gun pits after their capture by the Rangers on D-Day, with the camouflage umbrella collapsed by the early morning bomber attack and naval gunfire. NARA

TABLE 15: BOMBER ATTACKS AGAINST POINTE-DU-HOC

Date	Unit	Aircraft	Bomb Tonnage
Apr 25	416 Bomb Group	35 (2)* A-20	33.75
Apr 25	409 Bomb Group	16 (4) A-20	16
May 13	322 Bomb Group	33 (2) B-26	69
May 22	323 Bomb Group	29 (3) B-26	56
Jun 4	416 Bomb Group	43 A-20	50.5
Jun 4	409 Bomb Group	42 A-20	51
Jun 5	379 Bomb Group	35 B-17	104.25
Jun 6	8 Group (RAF)	9 (2) Mosquito	2.5 (illumination)
Jun 6	5 Group (RAF)	108 (7) Lancaster	634.8
Jun 6	391 Bomb Group	9 (8) B-26	16

*Data in parentheses indicate aircraft that sortied but aborted.

This overhead view of Pointe-du-Hoc from the after-action report shows the extent of the bomb damage to the site. MHI

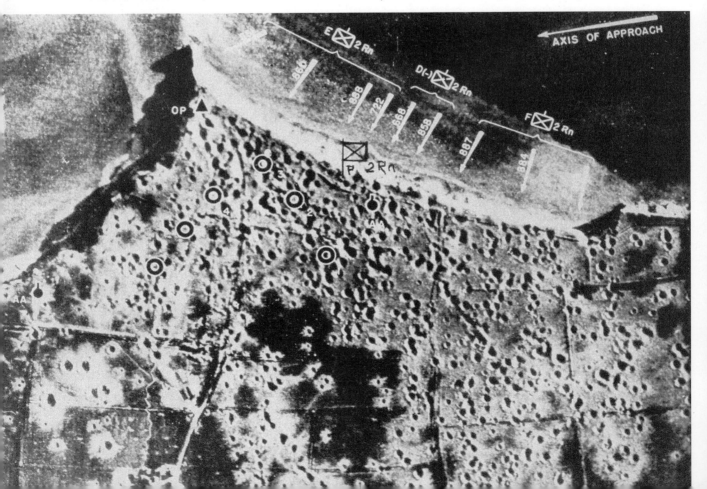

This overhead view of the western side of Pointe-du-Hoc shows the extent of the damage from the heavy bomber attack. The battery site was farther to the right and not in view on this aerial photo. The site identified as "1" in the photo is one of the flak bunkers used as Colonel Rudder's command post on D-Day. The site identified as "2" was the actual location of the three surviving guns and two of the damaged guns on D-Day. NARA

In an attempt to redeem the site, a set of six R679 bunkers (*Bau Werk* No 465–468) were being built at Pointe-du-Hoc by the Scheidt construction firm in May 1944. They were not completed by D-Day and the guns remained offsite. This photo was taken in 1954 by a U.S. Army survey team after the site had become overgrown. NARA

vulnerable to future attacks. This single air raid had put half the battery's guns out of action and greatly reduced the battery's combat capabilities by forcing its displacement back to a site away from the coast. Construction of more elaborate concrete gun bunkers continued in the hopes of eventually moving the battery back to its position overlooking the sea.

The German troops cleaned up the damage to the older open kettle emplacements, replaced damaged camouflage umbrellas over the gun pits, and substituted telephone poles for the actual guns. This proved very effective in deceiving Allied intelligence. Allied overhead photography of the site after the raids indicated damage to two gun pits, but concluded that "no definite statement can be made with regard to hits on the gun positions."[15] Later Allied raids continued to inflict damage to the site, halting the construction of the new concrete gun casemates, but German deception efforts continued to confuse Allied intelligence as to whether or not the gun battery was still in place.[16]

In the meantime, André Farina, a member of the local French *Centurie* Resistance cell, saw the repositioned guns, which were well outside the battery's restricted perimeter. He passed this information to the head of his cell, Jean Marion, who attempted to inform London by the standard means of a homing pigeon. However, this particular pigeon was one of those shot down. Under other circumstances, the Allies might have learned of the movement of the battery, bombed the exposed guns, and cancelled the hazardous Ranger mission.

The Ranger raid on Pointe-du-Hoc has become one of the central legends of D-Day. Indeed, when President Ronald Reagan visited Normandy in June 1984 on the fortieth anniversary, he chose Pointe-du-Hoc to give his commemoration speech. While no one can doubt the spirit and heroism of the

This R636a observation bunker had been completed at Pointe-du-Hoc in 1943 at the tip of the promontory and contained the battery fire-direction center on D-Day. However, it was out of contact with the guns on D-Day because of the disruption caused by the bombardment. NARA

Rangers on such a dangerous mission, it is extremely doubtful whether the raid was worth the risk. Although the three guns still posed some threat to Omaha Beach, their firepower was considerably smaller than the several batteries of 105mm and 150mm field guns of *Artillerie-Regiment.352* active in the area on D-Day. Furthermore, the bombing and naval gunfire on D-Day disrupted the communication link between the surviving guns and the fire direction center still at Pointe-du-Hoc, essentially leaving the guns blind. While they could fire on pre-registered targets, it is by no means clear that Omaha Beach was the battery's main mission.

The exaggeration of the threat posed by the Pointe-du-Hoc battery also diverted considerable resources to repeated strikes against the battery. There was a massive heavy bomber strike against Pointe-du-Hoc in the pre-dawn hours of D-Day. The USS *Texas*, one of only two battleships assigned to naval fire support at Omaha Beach, was assigned primarily to bombard Pointe-du-Hoc. At the same time, Allied planning had given far less attention to a more dangerous threat—the neighboring battery at Longues-sur-Mer.

Pointe-du-Hoc was a German army battery, while Longues-sur-Mer was a *Kriegsmarine* battery. These rival services had very different approaches to coastal artillery guns. The army batteries had very little capability to engage moving ships offshore since they lacked the suitable fire-control equipment in their command bunkers. This had already become painfully evident to the Pointe-du-Hoc battery. On 22 October 1943, three British warships appeared off Colleville at the eastern extreme of the battery's effective range. They were not engaged by the battery. When the battalion commander angrily called the Pointe-du-Hoc battery commander and asked why he hadn't attacked,

This is a view of one of the three functional 155mm GPF guns of the Pointe-du-Hoc battery, discovered and disabled by the Rangers on D-Day. COL. R. McCORMICK RESEARCH CENTER, 1ST DIVISION MUSEUM AT CANTIGNY

Bradley's U.S. First Army headquarters was established a short distance from the Pointe-du-Hoc guns. Here most of the senior U.S. D-Day commanders are given a tour of the gun site on 14 June 1944. In the front row are Gen. Omar Bradley, Air Force Gen. Henry "Hap" Arnold, Gen. Dwight Eisenhower, and Army Chief of Staff Gen. George C. Marshall. NARA

The German naval battery of Longues-sur-Mer to the east of Omaha Beach was a much more sophisticated gun battery than Pointe-du-Hoc. However, its late completion left it out of Allied special operations planning. NARA

At the last moment, there were some plans to attack Longues-sur-Mer with Rangers or paratroopers, but this was rejected by Allied planners because of the late date. Instead, the site was heavily bombed and shelled, which greatly reduced the battery's effectiveness on D-Day. The two circled items are two of the gun bunkers, while the large fire-control bunker is evident near the cliff edge in the lower left of the photo. NARA

he nonchalantly replied: "I can't hit sparrows with these guns." The battery lacked forward observers in the Omaha Beach area. The battery commander was unceremoniously sent to an artillery unit in Russia and a new commander assigned.

In contrast, the *Kriegsmarine*'s "battleships of the dunes" were designed like landlocked, concrete warships. They used the same type of fire controls used on destroyers to enable the battery to track and engage moving enemy warships. The gun positions were built around naval destroyer guns under steel-reinforced concrete casemates. They were connected to the fire-control posts by electrical cable, which automatically transmitted detailed aiming instructions to their crew. This permitted precision engagement of enemy targets, including difficult targets such as moving warships. Longues-

sur-Mer was the most sophisticated coastal gun battery near the D-Day beaches, so why wasn't Longues-sur-Mer the target of the Ranger attack instead of Pointe-du-Hoc?[17]

Part of the reason was the inertia of the planning process. Pointe-du-Hoc had been identified as a major threat from the first moment that Allied planners began to consider attacking Omaha Beach in early 1943. A special forces attack on Pointe-du-Hoc was included in all of the plans until D-Day itself. In contrast, construction of the Longues-sur-Mer battery began much later and was not completed until May 1944, a few weeks before D-Day. Allied planners might have shifted their resources from Pointe-du-Hoc to Longues-sur-Mer if they had realized how much damage had been inflicted on the Pointe-du-Hoc battery by the April–May

This shows the damage to one of the Longues-sur-Mer gun bunkers by naval gunfire on D-Day, which led to an internal ammunition explosion. NARA

1944 air raids. They also might have shifted priorities if they understood the difference between German army and navy batteries in terms of fire-control accuracy. However, they had never captured a German naval coastal battery and so had no idea of its capabilities. Allied aerial reconnaissance had spotted Longues-sur-Mer during its construction and had included it in the Martian Reports. Lacking a firm appreciation of its capabilities and unwilling to shift priorities at so late a date, they left Longues-sur-Mer to D-Day bombing attacks and naval gunfire.

In the event, the D-Day bomber attacks crippled Longues-sur-Mer. Only one of the concrete casemates was knocked out because of their solid construction, but the heavy bombardment tore up the vital communication cables between the batteries and the fire-control bunker. Unlike Pointe-du-Hoc, which failed to fire a single shot on D-Day, Longues-sur-Mer continued to fire on Allied shipping on D-Day. However, its accuracy had been significantly degraded by the air attacks, and the batteries were smothered by Allied naval gunfire. The battery never hit an Allied ship on D-Day. Fur-thermore, as a naval battery, they did not engage land targets on Omaha Beach, even though they were within range of the eastern landing beaches around Colleville.

The consequences of the intelligence shortcomings over the coastal gun batteries were not as great as other failures. Longues-sur-Mer was crippled by air attack even if it was not subjected to a Ranger attack. Recognition that Pointe-du-Hoc had been disabled might have prompted Allied planners to shift the Rangers to a more valuable mission, such as reinforcing the main attack at Omaha Beach. Indeed, a portion of the Ranger force scheduled to land at Pointe-du-Hoc was diverted to land at Vierville, and they played a vital role in adding momentum to the 116th Infantry attack on the western side of Omaha Beach. Other assets, such as bomber missions or naval gunfire, might not have been wasted on Pointe-du-Hoc. The intelligence shortcomings about German coastal artillery batteries were not profoundly consequential to the outcome of the D-Day fighting at Omaha Beach, but they are illustrative of the challenges facing Allied intelligence in planning the invasion.

THE GREATEST INTELLIGENCE FAILURE

While the intelligence issues with the German coastal gun batteries were not especially serious, another intelligence mistake had far more lethal ramifications. Allied intelligence failed to identify the transfer of the *352.Infanterie-Division* from the St. Lô area to the Normandy coast in March 1944. Allied intelligence thought the division was still located in its original garrisons around St. Lô, a day's march to Omaha Beach. The presence of this unit in the Omaha Beach area added a substantial amount of additional manpower and firepower to the German garrison, as detailed in previous chapters. This was probably the single greatest reason for the heavy American casualties on Omaha Beach. Why didn't Allied intelligence recognize this transfer?

As mentioned before, German divisions in France were not dependent on the use of radio communication for day-to-day operations prior to D-Day. For security reasons, teletypes, telephones, and other methods were used. Although the Germans were convinced that their Enigma code system was unbreakable, they tried to decrease the risk of intelligence discoveries by minimizing radio use. Even when armies use unbreakable codes, enemy radio traffic is still monitored, since it is a useful tool for identifying the location and activity levels of opposing forces. The Germans were well aware of the need for radio security and kept radio traffic to a minimum. German memoirs from officers of the *352.Infanterie-Division* reveal not only that they did not use radio, but also that in most cases they did not have telephones or telegraph available in the forward units near Omaha Beach. Instead, they relied on couriers on bicycles prior to the invasion.[18] Because of these factors, the relocation of the *352.Infanterie-Division* was not identified by the Ultra signals intelligence network.

Aerial photo intelligence was also of limited use in identifying the transfer of the division. Since the *352.Infanterie-Division* was moving into areas already occupied by the *716.Infanterie-Division*, their presence was not especially noteworthy in aerial photographs. The troops were billeted in existing French homes, so there was no evidence of

Identification of the field artillery of *Artillerie-Regiment.352* was complicated by its deployment in camouflaged gun pits, which were difficult to identify from aerial photos, especially when the presence of the parent division was not expected. This is a typical 105mm lFH 18/40 gun emplacement taken later in the campaign. NARA

tent cities or other military encampments. The few features of the additional units were invariably camouflaged. For example, the division placed its artillery battalions in field positions along the Normandy coast. Each of the gun batteries was placed under trees for camouflage or, if no trees were available, covered with camouflage nets. While the Allied aerial photos might reveal a few dozen additional camouflage nets, this was not enough evidence of the division's transfer.

Local French civilians were well aware of the division's transfer. Even though it was against the rules, many of the division's soldiers had French girlfriends. When the division began moving in February 1944 and March 1944, these friendships were broken. Likewise, French civilians close to the coast noticed the arrival of new German units since the forward infantry battalions frequently purchased eggs, milk, and alcohol from the local farmers. As a result, the French Resistance cells in the Lower Normandy region learned of the division's transfer.

The inability of the French Resistance to inform London of this vital information was because of a variety of factors. As mentioned earlier, the Resistance cells in the Omaha Beach sector began to be broken up by arrests in March–May 1944, effectively silencing one of the best sources of information. Other cells in the area attempted to contact London via homing pigeons, but German accounts suggest that these messages were intercepted by the pigeon patrols.

As a result of these problems, Allied commanders were not aware that the Omaha Beach defenses had been substantially reinforced prior to D-Day.[19] The intelligence assessments issued to senior commands prior to D-Day indicated that Omaha Beach was held only by a second-rate battalion of the *716.Infanterie-Division* and that the *352.Infanterie-Division* was in St. Lô, a day's march away. Allied plans assumed the *352.Infanterie-Division* would not appear on the battlefield until the morning of D+1 (7 June).[20] There was considerable shock on D-Day when prisoner-of-war interrogations revealed that the division's *Grenadier-Regiment.916* was present on the beach.[21]

There is some reason to suspect that at least one of the French pigeons may have gotten through to Britain. A former British intelligence officer has noted that Brig. E. T. Williams, the senior intelligence officer of Montgomery's 21st Army Group, gave a warning about a possible move forward of the *352.Infanterie-Division* to thicken up the defense between the *709.Infanterie-Division* and the *716. Infanterie-Division*. This was printed in the 3 June 1944 issue of the *21 Army Group Weekly Neptune Intelligence Review*.[22] The report noted: "It should not be surprising if we discovered that [the *716th Infantry Division*] had two regiments in the line and one in reserve while on its left, *352nd Division* had one regiment up and two to play." However, these mimeographed reports had very restricted circulation. The release of this information at such a late date went unnoticed by the senior Allied leadership, and the assessment was far from definitive. From the phrasing of the report, it seems likely that Allied intelligence was uncertain of the validity of the information. Even if senior commanders such as Eisenhower were briefed on this discovery, there was little they could have done at so late a date.

Another mystery surrounding this controversy was the subsequent myth that the presence of the *352.Infanterie-Division* on Omaha Beach was simply bad luck. The postwar V Corps G-2 Intelligence after-action report from 1945 indicated that the reason for the late recognition of the presence of the *352.Infanterie-Division* near Omaha Beach was that the division was there "for tactical exercises." The myth that the *352.Infanterie-Division* was present on Omaha Beach because of the unlucky timing of a training exercise has been widely repeated in many histories of D-Day.[23] It remains unclear whether it was based on mistaken assumptions or was a deliberate attempt to whitewash the failure. One of the first messages sent by G-2 officers on Omaha Beach on the morning of D-Day to the V Corps G-2 headquarters indicated that the *352.Infanterie-Division* had been in the Omaha Beach sector "about a month." As detailed earlier in this book, elements of the division began moving toward the beach in mid-February 1944 and the division as a whole in mid-March 1944. There were a sufficient number of prisoner-of-war interrogations in the days after 6 June to make this issue quite clear.

RAMIFICATIONS OF THE INTELLIGENCE FAILURE

The failure to detect the presence of the *352.Infanterie-Division* near Omaha Beach had several consequences for Allied planning on D-Day. To begin with, the assumption that Omaha Beach was weakly defended by a battalion of *Grenadier-Regiment.726* simply reinforced Allied preconceptions about German tactical intentions. The Allies had assessed the nature of standard German anti-invasion doctrine from their experiences at Sicily, Salerno, and Anzio. They expected to find the beach weakly defended, and they anticipated that after a modest struggle on the beachhead they would establish defense lines behind the beach and await the inevitable German counterattack. What the U.S. Army did not understand was that Rommel's new tactics were a repudiation of the traditional German tactics and that these changes were most dramatic on Omaha Beach. This is very evident in the details of the Omaha Beach landings.

The most immediate consequence of the underestimation of the German garrison on Omaha Beach was the plan to land the first waves immediately in front of the draws. Although Allied intelligence was well aware that German defenses were concentrated around the draws, the plans expected that they would be weakly defended. These plans inadvertently placed the first waves in the most dangerous German kill zones. Had the German defenses been more clearly appreciated, the landings could have been conducted in the sectors between the draws, which were much more weakly defended. Furthermore, U.S. commanders expected that the exits would be secured within about an hour of landing, permitting the arrival of the larger LCI landing craft, which could accommodate larger numbers of troops than the small LCA, LCVP, and LCM craft. The use of the larger LCI landing craft prior to the capture of the German strongpoints gave the Germans larger targets and larger numbers of vulnerable disembarking troops in the kill zones in the first hours of D-Day.

The U.S. troops in the first waves on D-Day were grossly overburdened with extra supplies and equipment on the assumption that the main fight would come a day or more after landing, not in the first moments on the beach. Usual U.S. Army practice was for infantrymen to minimize their equipment prior to a skirmish by dropping their musette bags and heavy gear before entering combat. On D-Day, they had not only their usual tactical equipment, but also additional supplies. These burdens had lethal consequences when troops had to advance across the beach under intense fire. It also increased the risk of drowning when troops were dropped off in deep water by landing craft crew wary of approaching too closely to the beach because of the intense fire.

The details of the Gap Assault Teams also displayed the U.S. Army's expectation for a very modest fight on the beachhead. The engineers were expected to employ high-explosive charges to remove the Belgian Gates and other obstructions, which required elaborate and time-consuming preparation work. This might have been possible under relatively benign circumstances, but such plans were lethal in view of the German firepower on Omaha Beach.

Allied intelligence never understood the amount of firepower added to the German static divisions.[24] The presumption was that these divisions were simply second-class units assigned to beach defense like the Italian coastal divisions on Sicily. They expected them to be armed like a normal German infantry division, except deployed in fortified positions. There was no real appreciation for the number of additional weapons reinforcing these divisions. To make matters worse, the addition of the *352.Infanterie-Division* in the Omaha Beach sector further reinforced German firepower.

Not expecting the *352.Infanterie-Division* on Omaha Beach, the Allied intelligence officers did not conduct a detailed or very deliberate search for the German division's artillery, *Artillerie-Regiment .352*. Allied intelligence had a very good appreciation of the location of the artillery batteries of the *716.Infanterie-Division* and had plans to deal with them through either preliminary air and naval bombardment or, in more extreme cases such as the

Allied planners tended to underestimate the threat posed by the Atlantic Wall defenses because of past experiences with Axis coastal defenses in the 1943 amphibious landings. There was extensive Italian fortification of the Sicilian beaches, such as these bunkers near Gela where the 1st Infantry Division landed in July 1943. However, they provided little serious resistance to the Allied landings. NARA

Merville battery, through airborne assault. While there was a great deal of concern over the threat posed by the six 155mm guns on Pointe-du-Hoc, there was no concern at all for the twelve 150mm howitzers of *IV./Artillerie-Regiment.352* or the dozen or more 105mm howitzers of the other artillery batteries. They were assumed to be in garrison near St. Lô and not likely to be present until D+1. None of the *Artillerie-Regiment.352* artillery batteries were on the naval bombardment list, nor were the rocket launchers in the St. Laurent draw. The *I./Artillerie-Regiment.352* battalion commander, Werner Pluskat, later stated that none of his guns was knocked out on D-Day, even in the presence of Allied spotter aircraft working in conjunction with the warships.

If Allied intelligence had discovered the location of the *352.Infanterie-Division* by May 1944,

they might have taken steps to diminish its effects on the Omaha Beach landings. The clearest case of Allied flexibility in response to intelligence developments was the discovery of the deployment of the *91.Luftlande-Division* behind Utah Beach in mid-May 1944. This made the planned landing of the 82nd Airborne Division around St. Saveur-le-Vicomte too risky. At the last moment, its drop zone was shifted to the Merderet River area and the 101st Airborne drop zone was shifted slightly south so that both divisions would control an easily defensible area between the beaches and the Douvre and Merderet Rivers. Had Allied intelligence discovered the *352.Infanterie-Division* in the Omaha Beach sector, a number of steps could have been taken, including the reinforcement of naval bombardment and more realistic plans for the first waves of the landing.

Had the U.S. Army appreciated the scale of defenses on Omaha Beach, other tactical approaches would have been possible. There were three hundred amtrac amphibious tractors in the United Kingdom, a technical innovation that had proven very successful in the Pacific Theater for assaulting heavily defended beaches. This is an ordnance yard in the United Kingdom in March 1944 with LVT-1 and LVT-2 amtracs. NARA

The U.S. Army Chief of Staff, Gen. George C. Marshall, had deliberately transferred two corps commanders from the Pacific theater, Maj. Gen. J. Lawton Collins and Maj. Gen. Charles Corlett, to serve in the Normandy campaign. This was done with the expectation that they could help brief the European staff on lessons from recent amphibious warfare in the Pacific. Corlett had been involved in the most recent army landing in the Pacific at Kwajalein in February 1944 and was well aware of the different tactics needed in the Pacific to deal with contested landings against strong Japanese beach defenses. Corlett was adamant that the Omaha Beach landings needed to be reconsidered in terms of naval firepower and landing tactics. He was well aware of the risks of landing on a fortified beach and of the imperative to smash the enemy beach defenses prior to the landing and to move the infantry through the enemy kill zone

on the beach as quickly as possible. In the Pacific, the Japanese beach fortifications were subjected to a much more prolonged naval bombardment than was planned for Normandy.[25] In addition, new tactics had been tested since the Tarawa landing in November 1943 using amphibious tractors (amtracs) in the first waves to get the vital first wave ashore as quickly as possible to reduce their vulnerability in the beach kill zone. There were 300 amtracs available in Britain on D-Day, but they played no significant role in the Normandy operation. Corlett was extremely bitter about the dismissive attitude of the Normandy planners toward his concerns.[26] Yet the core problem was not the parochialism of the European planners to the Pacific veterans, but rather a fundamental misunderstanding of German tactical intentions after Rommel took command of the anti-invasion effort and changed anti-invasion tactics.

CHAPTER 9

Day of Reckoning

THE *WEHRMACHT* HAD MANY INDICATIONS that an Allied invasion of Fortress Europe was imminent, but they did not know where or when. Units along the Normandy coast had been on heightened alert for several days before D-Day and were weary of the frequent alarms and subsequent stand-down orders. The garrison on Omaha Beach had been alerted repeatedly in early June with instructions that an Allied landing would soon take place. On 3 June, the *84.Korps* informed units that an invasion was imminent. On 4 June, they first reported it would occur in twenty-four hours, then cancelled the warning with news it had been postponed. On 5 June, the *84.Korps* reported that it might occur in the next twenty-four hours. The continual alerts led to skepticism about future warnings—a skepticism that was further reinforced by the stormy weather on 4–5 June 1944.

Around 0100 hours on 6 June, the staff of the *352.Infanterie-Division* was alerted by *84.Korps* headquarters that Allied paratroops had begun to land around Caen. D-Day had begun. It was still not clear whether the landings were simply a diversion or a raid, so Alarm Level II was sent down the chain of command to the division's subordinate units. This meant that the units of the *352.Infanterie-Division* located in the villages behind Omaha Beach were put on full alert and sent forward to the beach defenses. The first reports of enemy activity from the *352.Infanterie-Division* took place around 0200 hours when elements of *Grenadier-Regiment.914* on the Vire River near Carentan began encountering American paratroopers. The first reports of Allied ships off Port-en-Bessin took place around 0300 hours.

At 0300 hours, the *84.Korps* activated the divisional reserve, *Kampfgruppe Meyer*. This consisted of Meyer's *Grenadier-Regiment.915* and *Füsilier-Bataillon.352*. The *I./Grenadier-Regiment.915* and *füsiliers* were mounted on bicycles, while *II./Grenadier-Regiment.915* was transported on requisitioned French civilian trucks. The battle group was stationed immediately to the south of Omaha Beach and was ordered to move westward through the Cerisy woods to St. Jean-de-Daye in anticipation of action against the American paratroop operation in the Carentan sector. The unit began moving westward around 0400 hours. The premature commitment of this battle group was one of the few lucky breaks for the U.S. Army in the Omaha Beach sector that morning. *Kampfgruppe Meyer* spent most of D-Day on a wild goose chase, delayed at first by uncooperative French truck drivers and repeatedly strafed after daylight by roving Allied fighter-bombers. The premature activation of this unit temporarily removed the main German reserve near Omaha Beach.

Although the landings by the 82nd and 101st Airborne Divisions were supposed to occur in the area behind Utah Beach to the west of Omaha Beach, navigation errors resulted in the landings of paratroopers behind Omaha Beach. As a result, there was sporadic contact between the German Omaha Beach garrison and scattered American units. There were a number of reports from defense nests in the St. Laurent area about Allied ships off the coast, but the pre-dawn weather was overcast and foggy, and many of these reports were dismissed at divisional headquarters.

In the pre-dawn hours, the Allied heavy bombers struck a number of high-priority targets including Pointe-du-Hoc and the neighboring *Luftwaffe* radar station at Strongpoint Le Guay. The *IV./Artillerie-Regiment.352* reported being struck by bombs in the early morning hours, probably an overshoot from the attacks on the coastal radar station.

THE GERMAN VIEW OF THE LANDINGS

One of the best vantage points overlooking the Omaha Beach area was the observation bunker in WN59 to the east, used as a command post by Maj. Werner Pluskat, who commanded the *I./Artillerie-Regiment.352*. Pluskat had arrived at the bunker around 0200 hours, but the scene was calm with little evidence of any enemy action. Pluskat thought it might be another false alarm. Around 0500 hours, as the sun began to rise and the fog started to lift, Pluskat scanned the horizon with his binoculars. He began to see traces of a vast armada. He turned to his aide, Lieutenant Theen, and exclaimed: "Take a look . . . My God, it is the invasion!" He immediately telephoned the divisional intelligence officer, Maj. Paul Block, back at the divisional command post near Littry: "There must be 10,000 ships out here. It's unbelievable. It's fantastic. It must be the invasion!" Block was skeptical: "Now look Pluskat, are you really sure it's that many ships? The Americans and British combined don't have that many ships." Angry and excited, Pluskat replied: "For Christ's sake, come and look for yourself!"*

---

*WN59 was not actually on Omaha Beach—it was farther to the east on the Plateau du Calvados. This incident was immortalized in the movie *The Longest Day*, with Pluskat's role played by the German actor Hans Christian Blech. The scene was based on Cornelius Ryan's interview with Pluskat, which can be found in the Ryan collection at the Ohio University archive. Pluskat's recollections are somewhat controversial among some veterans of the *352.Infanterie-Division*. Hein Severloh, who served in Pluskat's unit as the orderly for Lieutenant Frerking at the battery observation post at WN62, stated that Pluskat was not on duty on D-Day morning at WN59 as he claimed, but back at his apartment to the rear. After the publication of Severloh's memoirs, Pluskat threatened to sue him for libel. Regardless of the authenticity of Pluskat's recollections to Ryan, there can be little doubt that the same scene played out at several of the observation bunkers overlooking Omaha Beach. As a minor detail, it's worth noting that the scenes in *The Longest Day* were filmed in the massive fire-control bunker at Longues-sur-Mer. Pluskat's actual bunker was far more modest and only recently has been rediscovered by Dutch bunker buffs.[1]

Lt. Hans Heinze, with the headquarters of *II./Grenadier-Regiment.916*, was perched in a tree overlooking the beach with binoculars:

Until dawn, the beach was quiet. Around dawn, the fog thickened. I took another glance a half-hour later and I could distinguish something coming out of the fog. I took my binoculars, cleaned the lens and gave them to my messenger to take a look. He could not distinguish anything. Then a strong wind blew and the scene opened before us. The landing craft approaching the beach deployed, but most of the large ships remained behind. . . . Everything was quiet. Before us, the immense panorama of an invasion fleet. At the fore, the small landing craft, larger craft, followed by destroyers, and then the huge ships. Everything was quiet, completely quiet.[2]

The scene was repeated all along the beach. Ships appeared out of the mist, only to disappear again as the Allied task force activated its smoke-screens. A young soldier in WN62 recalled: "The sight was eerie, and it was now clear that things were about to get ugly. I knelt in my foxhole and prayed."[3] Another soldier nearby recalled: "Heavy warships were lined up as if on Sunday parade. The whole spectacle was quite a sight to see until the bombardment began."[4]

BLASTING THE BATTERIES

The first attacks near Omaha Beach took place to the east and west against the coastal gun batteries. At 0446 hours, Mosquito bombers of the RAF's 8 Group swooped over the gun emplacements at Pointe-du-Hoc and dropped illumination flares to strip away the pre-dawn darkness. They were followed at 0450 hours by wave after wave of 108 Lancaster heavy bombers of the RAF 5 Group, which dropped nearly 635 tons of bombs on the peninsula, pulverizing what was left of the gun casemates. The naval gun battery at Longues-sur-Mer east of Omaha Beach had been bombed repeatedly on 29 April, 21 May, 27 May, and 2 June. The final two attacks had left the battery area cratered and two of the casemates severely damaged. The most important consequence of the pre-invasion bombing was the destruction of the elaborate communications network and telephone cabling, which made it impossible to use fire directions from the forward bunker.[5]

Even though both batteries were only marginally operative on D-Day, the Allies were intent on silencing any remaining activity. Pointe-du-Hoc was listed as Target No. 1 for the U.S. Navy's Bombardment Force C. At 0550 hours, the battleship USS *Texas*, flagship of Rear Adm. C. F. Bryant, began pounding the strongpoint with its 14-inch guns, firing some 250 rounds. One of the spotter planes from the *Texas* orbited over Pointe-du-Hoc to call in artillery corrections. The destroyer USS *Satterlee* attacked known pillboxes on the western side of Pointe-du-Hoc. Before the dust had even settled, another nine B-26 bombers of the 391st BG arrived overhead around 0630 hours and dropped sixteen tons of bombs on the strongpoint. The Longues-sur-Mer battery also received the attention of naval gunfire, starting with the cruiser HMS *Ajax* at 0530 hours. One of the guns at Longues managed to fire a few rounds in response, but the Pointe-du-Hoc battery remained inactive in its improvised site away from the cliffs.

The preliminary bombardment did not touch any of the field guns of *Artillerie-Regiment.352* in the Omaha Beach sector. The *IV./Artillerie-Regiment .352* to the west and southwest of Omaha Beach had more than double the firepower of Pointe-du-Hoc, but its presence there was completely unknown to Allied planners.*

---

*On 31 May–1 June 1944, the Allied air forces had compiled a list of artillery targets that had been attacked over the previous few weeks, with notes to provide guidance about which batteries needed further attention. None of the artillery batteries near Omaha Beach had been spotted.[6]

THE NAVAL BOMBARDMENT

Fire Support Group O began to approach Omaha Beach shortly after dawn. The warships were assigned specific targets with specific ammunition allotments. At 0545 hours, the battleships and destroyers began the preliminary naval bombardment, which lasted only forty minutes until 0625 hours. While there were two older battleships in the group, the USS *Texas* was not assigned targets on Omaha Beach, but instead sent to bombard Pointe-du-Hoc. For the German garrison at Omaha Beach, the naval gunfire proved to be frightening but largely ineffective.

The initial naval bombardment was scheduled to be followed by a heavy bomber attack conducted by the U.S. Army Air Force's 2nd Bomb Division with 446 B-24 Liberator heavy bombers and 1,285 tons of bombs. The attack plan, Field Order 328, was extremely cautious to prevent bomb drops into the approaching flotilla of landing craft, which were expected to be 400 yards to a mile from shore when the air attack began. An added problem was that the USAAF had decided to bomb perpendicularly to the beach rather than parallel in order to avoid flak. This meant the Pathfinders leading the bombers had only a few seconds to accurately time the drop, since the bomber stream would be flying over Omaha Beach at more than 100 yards per second. The Pathfinders were relying on H2X radar to identify the water's edge, but the field-order instructions insisted on a visual identification of the beach before the release signal was issued. In the event, as the bombers approached Omaha Beach, cloud cover was too thick for visual identification of the beach, and the Pathfinders followed instructions and delayed the release so that the mean point of impact would be no fewer than 1,000 yards away from the forward wave of landing craft. This meant the 329 bombers dropped their 13,000 bombs well behind the German defenses, causing little or no damage.

The final phase of the naval bombardment began at 0610 hours when five small LCG(L) closed on the beach and added their gunfire. These gun craft were landing craft, tanks (LCTs), that had been converted into bombardment monitors by the addition of a pair of 4.7-inch naval guns in their hold. The five craft were assigned to attack individual houses and bunkers. Three of the monitors were assigned to bombard the buildings and bunkers in WN71 at the access to the Vierville draw with 120 rounds each. One monitor was assigned to the bunkers of WN61 in the Colleville draw and the last to the bunkers along the water's edge in WN65. From accounts by nearby landing craft, the LCG(L) monitors repeatedly battered away at bunkers, but there is very little evidence that any of these bombardments had much effect. The German bunkers' thick concrete was proof against far heavier weapons than the 4.7-inch guns of the monitors.

The final wave of the naval bombardment involved the LCT(R) rocket ships. Each of these nine craft was armed with 792 to 1,066 RP-3 5-inch rockets. These rockets contained a 60lb high-explosive warhead, so each craft was capable of firing some twenty-three to thirty tons of high explosive, with the intention of pulverizing an area about 160 by 760 yards. The plans called for the craft to approach to within 4,500 yards of the coast, fire thirty-six incendiary rockets in twelve salvoes of three each for ranging purposes, then proceed toward the beach at six knots, firing more ranging salvoes every thirty seconds until a "dry burst" on the land was achieved. At this point, they were to salvo their high-explosive rocket load. These salvoes were intended to provide drenching fire on the most important targets on the beach, including the Vierville, St. Laurent, and Colleville draws. Unfortunately, the rockets proved to be wildly inaccurate and most appear to have missed their targets.[*]

---

[*]There is a discrepancy between the description of the rocket targets in Operations Order No. 3-44. The description of many of these targets indicates specific bunkers and other targets in the strongpoints, but their geographic coordinates suggest that many of the targets in the Colleville and St. Laurent area were the beach obstacles.

TABLE 16: WEIGHT (IN TONS) OF NAVAL FIRE ON GERMAN STRONGPOINTS AT OMAHA BEACH[10]			
	Gunfire	Rockets	Total
StP Colleville	12	112	*124*
StP St. Laurent	171	84	*255*
StP Vierville	24	56	*80*
Pointe-du-Hoc	203	—	*203*
Other	27	—	*27*
Total	**437**	**252**	**689**

A German soldier in WN62 recalled: "All the rockets landed in front of us. Some hit the beach but most landed harmlessly in the water. Still, a soldier next to me was injured by a bit of shrapnel. Metal splinters fell around us, followed by dirt. The noise died down followed by a strange silence. The landing craft came closer. . . ."[7]

Most accounts of the naval bombardment have been laudatory, and the official U.S. Navy evaluation concluded that "the naval gunfire plans were sound, realistic, and effectively carried out . . . the effect of naval gunfire on coast and beach defenses was a major factor in enabling the troops to land and start their advance inland."[8]

From the German standpoint, this assessment is mistaken. No doubt the bombardment was terrifying to the German troops. But there is no evidence to suggest that any of the significant defensive works on Omaha Beach were knocked out by the bombardment. In the case of the only defensive work where detailed coverage is available, WN62, the casualties among the troops amounted to only a single soldier lightly wounded.* The German bunkers on Omaha Beach, with the exception of the Tobruks, were built to B Standard and were largely resistant to naval gunfire from destroyers' guns, which numerically constituted the bulk of the gunfire. In the event, the naval bombardment was of too short a duration to have any substantial effect on the German defenses.[9]

The sector which received the most naval gunfire, Strongpoint St. Laurent, is not well covered in surviving German records, but neither is there much indication from later inspections of the bunkers that much damage had been inflicted. A disproportionate share of the coverage of the beaches was diverted to Pointe-du-Hoc, which merely served to "bounce the rubble." This battery site had been smashed already in pre–D-Day bombardments totaling 380 tons of bombs, followed by another 650 tons on D-Day morning. The two most vital Omaha Beach targets—the Colleville and Vierville draws—received very modest gunfire bombardment, and the final rocket attack was entirely ineffectual.

---

*It's worth noting that the two survivors from WN62 who wrote memoirs, Franz Gockel and Hein Severloh, were both in open field entrenchments through the bombardment and not in bunkers. Both survived.

THE ASSAULT BEGINS

The amphibious assault began to arrive off Omaha Beach around 0530 hours. It consisted of the LCTs of Assault Group O-1 carrying the 741st Tank Battalion on the eastern side, heading for Easy Red and Fox Green Beaches near Colleville; and Assault Group O-2 carrying the 743rd Tank Battalion, heading for Dog Green and Dog White Beaches near Vierville.

Despite heavy seas, the two companies of DD amphibious tanks of the 741st Tank Battalion began to leave the LCTs of Assault Group O-1 around 0535—about an hour before H-Hour—at a distance some 5,000 yards from shore. All sixteen tanks of Company C sank after launch off Fox Green Beach. Company B fared little better, losing all of its tanks except for two that swam ashore and three that were delivered directly to the beach on LCT-600 on the far western side of Easy Red Beach. During the last fifty yards to the beach, the LCT-600 was straddled by three artillery hits ten to thirty yards from the craft. This fire was coming from *1./Artillerie-Regiment.352*, directed by Lieutenant Frerking in an observation bunker in WN62. Company A with M4 tanks fitted with deep-wading trunks were landed directly ashore on modified LCT(A), which had modest armored protection. The three LCT(A) that landed west of Strongpoint Colleville suffered little damage. The three that landed near WN61 and WN62 came under heavy fire. LCT(A)-2043 landed near WN61 and deposited two tanks before coming under artillery, mortar, and machine gun fire. The craft received ten mortar hits, and the remaining M4 tank with dozer blade was hit by the 50mm pedestal gun in WN61 and rendered inoperable. The gunfire from WN61 holed the craft below the waterline, causing a list; the craft managed to withdraw without sinking despite the damage. The other two LCT in this sector also were hit and damaged, but managed to withdraw. In total, Assault Group O-1 managed to deliver sixteen out of its original fifty-six Sherman tanks.[*] Many of the tanks survived for only a few minutes before being disabled by gunfire from WN61 and WN62.

Assault Group O-2 on the west side of Omaha Beach had better success landing their tanks, but suffered heavier casualties in the landing craft. Instead of launching the DD amphibious tanks in the heavy sea, all twelve LCTs headed directly to shore. As a result, Assault Group O-2 delivered forty-two of its original fifty-six Sherman tanks.[**] The elements of the flotilla on the western side closest to Strongpoint Vierville suffered the most damage. LCT-590, on the western extreme of the flotilla, took a direct gun hit and suffered five casualties to its crew. LCT(A)-2124, landing on Dog White Beach, took about ten 50mm hits. The German gunners in WN72 appear to have focused on the disembarking tanks. The DD tanks of Company B, 743rd Tank Battalion, landed closest to WN72 and suffered the worst casualties. LCT-591 unloaded its tanks near the damaged LCT-590, and its first departing DD tank off was slammed in the side by an antitank round no more than five yards from the bow ramp. Within the first hour of fighting, Company B lost seven of its sixteen tanks. The preliminary naval bombardment had started a grass fire on the slopes east of the Vierville draw, and the pall of smoke provided a limited amount of cover for the tanks landing farther east. Nevertheless, the smoke did not shield the LCT(A)-2307, which landed almost directly in front of WN70. It was hammered by intense fire from the German defense nest. A single wading tank exited, but the two remaining tank commanders refused to drive off, blaming the depth of water. After several additional attempts to land in areas under less intense fire, the young ensign gave up and returned to sea, where his craft sank from the damage sustained, the tanks still aboard.

---

[*]This included five M4A1 DD tanks from Company B, plus six M4 wading tanks and five M4 dozer tanks from Company A.
[**]This included thirty-two M4A1 DD tanks, seven wading tanks, and three dozer tanks.

As the tanks finished disembarking, the first waves of infantry approached in their smaller LCA and LCVP landing craft. This first wave landed at low tide on the outer edge of the obstacle belt and were about 500 yards from the high-water mark. In the case of units landing in front of seafront defense nests such as WN65, they were well within range of machine guns and began taking heavy fire as soon as the craft dropped their ramps. In the case of beaches where the defense nests were farther back from the shore, such as WN62, the machine-gun crews were instructed to hold their fire until the American troops entered the kill zone closer to the high-tide mark. In contrast to the machine-gun crews, the German mortar and gun crews began engaging the landing craft even before they reached the shore. A later U.S. Army report summarized the initial combat:

> As the ramps were lowered, the infantry rushed for the partial shelter of the obstacles in an attempt to gain cover, but the protection was slight and the casualties high. Men who escaped the machine gun bullets and shell bursts made their way toward the shore in short rushes, lying in the runnels and crawling through the slight defilades in the sand. They dug in behind the comparative safety of the shingle pile and the sea wall and slowly began to build up a fire line. In this they were handicapped, however, by the fact that the men had unserviceable weapons. In some instances rifles were soaked when landing craft unloaded troops in water over their heads, and other weapons were clogged with beach sand.[11]

The scale of infantry casualties depended on where the units landed. Landing craft which disembarked their boat teams immediately in front of the draws suffered the worst casualties because of the concentration of German defense nests protecting the draws. The riflemen were overburdened with gear and had to run 300 to 500 yards across open beach to reach the high tide area, only to find that there was little protection except for a swath of shingle near the high-tide mark. The shingle was a layer of pebbles and small rocks near the crest of the beach. Beyond it was the first layer of the beach defenses, consisting of lines of barbed wire and minefields. Most surviving infantry units tried to catch their breath after reaching the shingle while under mortar and artillery fire.

The heaviest casualties were suffered on the extreme western flank of the attack on Dog Green Beach in the face of the D-1 Vierville draw. These landing craft, delivering companies of the 116th Infantry, were clearly visible to the German defense nests WN71 and WN73 on the hills on either side of the Vierville draw, as well as the bunkers in WN72 immediately on the beach. The approaching landing craft were hit with 50mm gunfire and mortar fire before they even reached the beach, and once the craft reached the obstacle belt, they were within machine-gun range. One LCA was hit four times in rapid succession by mortar or gunfire and disintegrated. Company A, 116th Infantry, had 100 of its 155 men killed. It was this sector depicted in the harrowing opening scenes of the movie *Saving Private Ryan*. At the other end of the beach, two companies from the 2nd Battalion, 16th Infantry, landed in front of Strongpoint Colleville with disastrous consequences. Within moments of landing, its Company F lost six officers and half its troops. Grenadier Heinz Bongard, a machine gunner in WN60 overlooking the slaughter, recalled that "the first wave of Americans didn't engage in combat, they were already wiped out."[12]

Some units had the good fortune to land away from their intended destinations in front of the draws because of the strong tidal currents. Two companies from the 3rd Battalion, 16th Infantry, landed at the foot of the cliffs in front of WN60 near the F-1 Cabourg draw. In spite of their proximity to the WN60 defense nest, the cliffs in this sector offered protection from German small-arms and heavy-weapons fire.

The most severe casualties were suffered by the army and navy engineers assigned to the Gap Assault Teams that were supposed to demolish the German beach obstructions. These teams were delivered in the larger LCM landing craft. Many of the LCM were able to discharge part of their teams shortly after landing; however, it took time for the

WN60 was the easternmost defense post on Omaha Beach. This is the gun pit for a 75mm FK 235(b) field gun, the German name for the war-booty Belgian *Canon de 75 mle TR*. There were two of these field guns in WN60, and they were knocked out early in the morning by tank and destroyer fire. COL. R. McCORMICK RESEARCH CENTER, 1ST DIVISION MUSEUM AT CANTIGNY

The WN60 site was protected by a pair of *Panzer Drehturm* Tobruks fitted with war-booty French APX-R tank turrets.

teams to unload the large quantity of high explosives carried in the LCM for the demolition work. These were often carried on a rubber raft that had to be dragged out of the craft. In the critical few minutes of unloading, the engineer LCM became lucrative targets for the German gun crews. A gunner on the 88mm antitank gun in the bunker in WN61, Cpl. Hermann Götsch, recalled firing at one of these and was surprised when it erupted in a massive explosion, throwing the troops and their equipment in all directions.[13] The two Belgian 75mm guns in the WN62 bunkers were oriented to fire westward toward Easy Red Beach. One of the assistant gunners, Cpl. Hans Selbach, later recalled: "We took the landing craft under direct fire with our gun and we could see very precisely when it hit; it was terrible. . . ."

Of the seven LCM of the 299th Engineer Combat Battalion landing on either side of the Colleville draw, four of their craft were hit by 50mm gun fire or mortars, causing massive casualties among the Gap Assault Teams. The first to land, Team 14, on the hill below WN62, managed to get most of the army squad off the craft before a mortar or gun hit the craft, detonating the explosives and wiping out the navy team before they disembarked. One team that managed to place demolition charges on some of the obstacles was decimated when a mortar round set off the Primacord before the team had withdrawn. The Team F support LCM was hit by artillery fire and wiped out on the approach to the beach. Not surprisingly, no gaps were created in the obstacle belt immediately in front of the E-3 Colleville draw; a few partial gaps were created in the more sheltered area between the Colleville and St. Laurent draws. No Gap Assault Team survived in the area in front of the Vierville draw, and the tide pushed many of the teams off course so that they landed in the relative shelter of the area in front of Hamel-au-Prêtre. By 0700 hours, only five narrow gaps and three partial gaps had been blown through the obstacle belts, but the army and navy teams had suffered 41 percent casualties in less than half an hour. Four adjacent gaps had been cre-

ated between the E-1 St. Laurent and E-3 Colleville draws—these would prove crucial later in the morning since they were the only gaps wide enough to accommodate a large number of landing craft.

The German perspective of the initial fighting was recalled by Franz Gockel, manning a water-cooled machine gun in a trench in WN62:

> The ramp went down on the first boats and soldiers jumped into the water. Other boats followed. Men were in the water up to their knees or chest. They didn't shoot at us because they were running through the water. They all headed for the sea wall, and once they reached it they began to shoot at us. They could not see us very well and most of their shots were high and wide. None of them came up the hill and we continued to fire at them. Then they spotted us and we received heavy fire. They concentrated on our trench because of the heavy machine gun. Luckily, it was hard to hit because we were well protected. The rifle fire intensified and then the craft began firing at us with bullets striking all around. I fired two more bursts and ducked down. I was out of ammunition and had to wait for the ammo bearer to bring more ammunition. I was preparing to reload when it blew up in my face. To this day I don't know what hit it, or how I survived.[*]

Gockel's machine-gun nest was one of a number of German positions hit in the early morning of D-Day as the U.S. forces began to fight back. Before it was knocked out, Gockel estimated he had fired 10,000 rounds of ammunition.

WN61 was the most vulnerable defense in Strongpoint Colleville because of its location on the flat terrain on the east side of the E-3 Colleville draw. It was a small site with only about fifteen troops, consisting mainly of the 50mm pedestal-gun pit, the H677 88mm bunker, and an APX-R *Panzer-Drehturm* protecting the big gun bunker.

---

*Gockel was armed with a sMG 30(p) heavy machine gun, the German name for a war-booty Polish CKM wz. 30, a license-built version of the Browning 30 caliber water-cooled machine gun also used by the U.S. Army at this time.[14]

The 88mm gun bunker was well shielded from the sea by a protective wall, but around 0710 hours, an M4A1 DD tank commanded by Sergeant Geddes fired several rounds through the embrasure of the bunker, knocking out the gun. The 50mm pedestal gun had been very destructive in the first half-hour of fighting and succeeded in knocking out three M4 tanks in quick succession on the western side of the E-3 Colleville draw. This infuriated S/Sgt. Frank Strojny from Company F, 16th Infantry, who located a bazooka and began making his way toward the gun pit. He hit the gun pit with a couple of bazooka rockets without much effect, went back to the beach for more ammunition, and returned to fire six more rounds into the gun pit, finally killing the crew and setting off an ammunition fire. The 50mm gun pit was not well protected because of the shortage of infantry and was very vulnerable to a determined infantry attack.

This is a 50mm pedestal gun in a *Ringstand* in WN61 on the eastern side of the E-3 Colleville draw, covering the antitank ditch that can be seen running in front of it. What is remarkable about this photo is the amount of expended ammunition around the site, suggesting the gun played a major role in fighting the landing craft on Easy Red Beach. This gun was knocked out by bazooka fire from Sergeant Strojny of the 16th Infantry. COL. R. McCORMICK RESEARCH CENTER, 1ST DIVISION MUSEUM AT CANTIGNY

This is a view of a mortar Tobruk in WN61, which was positioned to cover the antitank ditch across the E-3 Colleville draw. The mount is for a *Fest.Gr.W.210* (f), a type of war-booty French 50mm fortification mortar, but the actual weapon has been removed before this photo was taken. What is especially interesting about this photo is the extensive data painted on the rim of the Tobruk, providing the crew with targeting data for specific locations along the coastline in front of the strongpoint. COL. R. McCORMICK RESEARCH CENTER, 1ST DIVISION MUSEUM AT CANTIGNY

The most powerful bunker on the eastern side of Omaha Beach was this 88mm H677 casemate in WN61. It was knocked out early in the morning by fire from a DD tank of the 741st Tank Battalion. The gun was removed and the bunker used as a medical aid station. This photo gives a good impression of the solid wall covering the embrasure from naval gunfire on the left side of the photo.
COL. R. McCORMICK RESEARCH CENTER, 1ST DIVISION MUSEUM AT CANTIGNY

A view of 88mm bunker in WN61 a few days after D-Day with a canvas tarp draped over the embrasure to permit it to be used as a medical aid station. NARA

The 88mm PaK 43/41 gun from the WN61 bunker was later moved to the beach as seen here. The landing craft in the foreground, LCI(L)-416, was sunk off the French coast by a mine on 9 June 1944. NARA

WN61 had a single *Panzer Drehturm* for defense, consisting of a war-booty French APX-R turret with 37mm gun mounted on a concrete Tobruk. It hasn't suffered any apparent battle damage and so it was probably overrun by the 16th Infantry or abandoned.
COL. R. McCORMICK RESEARCH CENTER, 1ST DIVISION MUSEUM AT CANTIGNY

There was a heavy concentration of M4 tanks at the foot of WN62, and the fire from the two Belgian 75mm guns in the bunkers made them an obvious target. These bunkers came under repeated tank fire. One ammunition loader in one of the bunkers recalled: "From the interior of the great bunker, we couldn't see anything of the events outside, but everything trembled and shuddered."

At 0745 hours, *Grenadier-Regiment.726* reported to divisional headquarters that one of gun bunkers in WN62 had suffered a direct hit; the other was out of action by 1000 hours. The upper bunker commanded by Cpl. Heinrich Brinkmeier was hit by at least twenty-seven rounds on D-Day, at least seven of which entered the embrasure and exploded inside. The lower bunker commanded by Cpl. Heinrich Krieftewirth was also hit repeatedly, with one of its four crew killed, the other three wounded.

A pair of M4A1 DD tanks had landed near the foot of WN60 on the far eastern side of the beach and began engaging the German gun positions. Sergeant Sheppard's tank hit both of the Belgian 75mm guns that were in open pits on the hilltop. WN60 was also pummeled by gunfire from the destroyer USS *Doyle*, which made a firing pass along the cliffs, engaging the German defenses.

A stream of craft continued to bring in reinforcements. Three more companies from 1/116th Infantry landed from 0740 to 0800 hours, followed by two more from 3/116th Infantry. By 0800 hours, there were elements of eight infantry companies on Fox Green Beach, mainly concentrated in the area where the gaps had been breached between the E-1 and E-3 draws.

A view of Strongpoint Colleville on the morning of D-Day. WN61 was on the low ground to the left side of the photo and WN62 on the hill on the right side. NARA

On the fifth anniversary of D-Day, S/Sgt. Richard Roberts revisited Omaha Beach. He is standing on the top of the lower of the two R669 gun bunkers at the site. This is the back wall of the bunker, with the rear door and protective wall evident below.

THE GERMAN PERSPECTIVE OF THE FIRST HOURS

There was a steady stream of messages from the forward German defense nests back to the *352. Infanterie-Division* headquarters near Molay-Littry about fifteen kilometers (nine miles) south of Omaha Beach.[15] These messages were usually passed by means of the field telephone network to the main switchboard in the command bunker located on the road outside St. Laurent. This bunker contained the command posts for the five companies of *Grenadier-Regiment.916* and *Grenadier-Regiment.726* in the three strongpoints along Omaha Beach. The assorted field-telephone messages were then forwarded to divisional headquarters by radio or telephone by the communication section of *Grenadier-Regiment.726* in the bunker.

At 0715 hours, the *Grenadier-Regiment.726* command post in St. Laurent reported to divisional headquarters that WN60 was under "especially heavy fire" after its pounding by the destroyer USS *Doyle*. Tank action on the western side of the beach near Strongpoint Vierville prompted *Grenadier-Regiment.916* to radio to divisional headquarters at 0720 hours, which elicited a promise of armor support from the divisional *Panzerjäger*. The headquarters waited until 1030 hours to order *1./Panzerjäger-Abteilung.352*, equipped with fourteen Marder III tank destroyers, to stage an attack. This company was located near Mestry-Briqueville and began moving forward in the late morning.

At 0720 hours, the *Grenadier-Regiment.726* command post sent a long message to divisional headquarters outlining the course of the fighting in Strongpoint Colleville. They estimated that the Americans were present in company strength

Another VK.3001 had arrived at Omaha Beach and was supposed to be placed on this combination bunker in WN66 on 5 June. The turret mounting can be seen in front on the lower right, while behind it and to the left is an incomplete R612 intended for another 50mm pedestal gun. This photo was taken in August 1944, after the beach had been substantially cleaned up. NARA

between WN61 and WN62 and that their positions were under artillery fire. The 88mm gun in WN61 was knocked out. The troops in the strongpoint wanted to know when the division would stage a counterattack to drive out the American troops.

The local commanders began to realize their defenses were slowly crumbling. So far, no decision had been made about counterattacks because

of a shortage of resources and a lack of clarity about the progress of the Allied landings. At 0730 hours, *Artillerie-Regiment.352* reported that "landing craft between WN61 and WN62 are being met with as much fire as we can give." At 0745 hours, the *Grenadier-Regiment.726* command post reported that the upper 75mm gun bunker in WN62 had been knocked out.

This 50mm pedestal gun was located in a camouflaged earth pit on the lower eastern corner of WN62, overlooking the E-3 Colleville draw and covering the western side of the antitank ditch. The gun was commanded by Cpl. Siegfried Kuska, who was wounded on D-Day and taken prisoner. This gun was responsible for disabling a number of tanks of the 741st Tank Battalion on D-Day. NARA

After the fighting, one of the 75mm FK 235(b) field guns was removed from its bunker on the crest of the hill at WN62. As can be seen, the gun took a direct hit to its gunshield, probably from tanks of the 741st Tank Battalion. NARA

THE SITUATION AT 0800 HOURS

The successes of the tanks in silencing many of the gun positions on the eastern side of Strongpoint Colleville helped to reduce the casualties among the next landing wave that was coming ashore in the larger landing craft, infantry (LCI). These craft were substantially larger than the LCA, LCVP, and LCM used to land the previous waves of infantry and so were significantly more visible and vulnerable to German heavy weapons. The landing plan had assumed that by 0730, an hour after the first landings, the German resistance would have been overcome and the troops already moving off the beach through the draws. This wave of nine LCIs mainly contained engineers and medical troops, as well as headquarters elements, and the LCIs were sitting ducks for surviving German guns. Lt. W. L. Wade, who led LCI Group 38, recalled the intensity of the German artillery fire on the beach: "Enemy fire on the beaches was terrific—105mm, 88mm, 40mm, mortars, machine guns, mines—everything apparently."

The LCIs that landed in front of Strongpoint Colleville and Strongpoint St. Laurent were subjected

A view inside one of the mortar pits in WN73 overlooking the Vierville draw. This is an 81mm *Granatwerfer* 278(f), the standard war-booty French Stokes-Brandt 81mm mle. 27/31 widely used by the *Wehrmacht*. A number of mortar bombs can be seen in the ammunition racks to the right. COL. R. McCORMICK RESEARCH CENTER, 1ST DIVISION MUSEUM AT CANTIGNY

to machine-gun fire and mortars but were largely spared the direct gunfire that had ravaged the craft during the earlier waves, since most of the guns had been knocked out. This was not the case on the western side, where several LCI were heading for Dog White Beach near Hamel-au-Prêtre. The 88mm bunker and its supporting 50mm bunker in WN71 were still intact, and they had a clear line of sight toward the westernmost LCIs. The guns began firing at the craft, and LCI-91 was struck by an 88mm round in the well deck that exploded the fuel tanks below. LCI-92 was hit in the forward hold, causing a massive explosion and killing forty-one troops. LCI-94 nearby was hit with a volley of shots—probably from the 50mm gun bunker—which struck the pilot house, killing much of the senior Coast Guard personnel. The western side of the beach near Strongpoint Vierville continued to be its most dangerous corner for landing craft.

High tide arrived at 0800 hours, covering the obstacles. The Devil's Garden along the shore became much more difficult to navigate since it was not apparent where the gaps in the obstacle belt had been breached. As a result of the wrecked and damaged craft from the first hours of the landing, the landing area also had become badly congested. At 0830 hours, the navy beachmaster decided it had become imprudent to permit any further craft to land at Omaha Beach and declared the beach closed for the moment. It would be up to the two trapped regiments, the 16th Infantry and the 116th Infantry, to fight their way off the beach until reinforcements began to arrive again after 1015 hours. The Devil's Garden had done its job of confounding the initial U.S. landing and, just as importantly, had stopped the timely reinforcement of the beleaguered troops on the beach for two critical hours.

The U.S. Navy, especially the destroyer crews, knew the army troops ashore were in a dire predicament. One by one, the destroyers began to approach the beach to ranges that were not prudent because of the shallow waters. If there is one cardinal sin for navy skippers, it is grounding their ship, but the young officers ignored this risk and headed into shallow water. Around 0830 hours, the destroyer USS *McCook* arrived off Vierville and began firing at the pillboxes in the D-1 Vierville draw, then turned its fire on the neighboring WN73 strongpoint on the hill. It spotted one of the gun positions in a cave on the cliffs on the Pointe-et-Raz-de-la-Percée and knocked the gun off the cliff onto the beach below. The two gun bunkers in WN72 that had been causing so much devastation were probably knocked out around this time.

There is very little detailed information from the German side about the fate of the bunkers in WN72 because so few of their crews survived. Likewise, information on the U.S. side is contradictory and spotty. A survey team after D-Day was told by some observers that a pair of M4 tanks from the 743rd Tank Battalion charged the WN72 bunkers.[16] One tank was knocked out, but the other managed to fire into the exposed embrasure of the bunker, finally knocking out the 88mm gun. Another observer claimed that a warship knocked out the bunker, presumably the USS *McCook*. Judging from the number of impacts still visible on the bunker, it was obviously hit numerous times by both tank fire and destroyer fire. Likewise, the neighboring 50mm bunker was hit numerous times, and the small tank turret mounted on the roof was blown off by a direct hit. A machine gunner from *3./Grenadier-Regiment.914* in a trench between the 88mm and 50mm bunkers survived the fusillade and withdrew later in the day, but the situation was so chaotic and dangerous that he never realized when the neighboring bunkers were destroyed.

THE GERMAN DEFENSES START TO CRUMBLE

In spite of the heavy losses, both the 16th Infantry and 116th Infantry began to make slow but steady inroads on the Germans defenses in the first hours after the landing. It had become painfully apparent that it was suicidal to try to push through the draws, as originally planned. In contrast, several small formations had learned that the areas between the draws were much more lightly defended, except for the persistent threat of mines. Many units were deterred from advancing off the beach after losing a few soldiers in the minefields that protected the German defense nests. The American advance over the bluffs was entirely opportunistic and random, heavily dependent on the initiative of small groups of soldiers who found gaps in the minefields.

The first penetrations of Strongpoint Colleville began within an hour of the landings. A small number of troops from Companies E and F, 16th Infantry, led by Sgt. Philip Streczyk and Lt. John Spalding, managed to get through the barbed wire and minefields on Easy Red Beach and to start climbing the bluff to the west of the WN62 defense nest, avoiding the dangerous *MF.10* minefield. This eventually became one of the main routes off the beach during the morning since it was shielded from the German strongpoints on either side. Col. George Taylor of the 16th Infantry gathered the battalion and company commanders together and prodded them to get their troops off the beach: "Two kinds of people are staying on the beach, the dead and those who are going to die—now let's get the hell out of here!"

Some squads from Company L, 16th Infantry, made their way into the F-1 Cabourg draw after WN60 had been battered by destroyer fire; they managed to skirt past the defense nest and its numerous minefields and continued moving south. Other troops began a gradual process to reduce the remaining German defenses in the WN60 defense nest. At 0755 hours, the local German commander described the situation in WN60 as "uncertain" because of the intense fighting.

Substantial infiltrations began in the western sector. The 29th Division assistant commander,

Gen. Norman Cota, had arrived with the 116th Infantry staff in the third wave and had begun to reinvigorate the effort on Dog White Beach. A number of Ranger companies that had not been committed to the Pointe-du-Hoc assault were sent into this sector and helped provide additional momentum. At 0750 hours, Cota led a small group of troops from Company C, 116th Infantry, and pushed through tall reeds and marsh grass at the base of the bluffs, then up the bluffs to the plateau east of WN70. Farther east along Dog Red Beach, Colonel Canham led a similar column over the bluffs from Companies F and G, 116th Infantry. The 3/116th RCT landed relatively unscathed in this area, providing the momentum to finally push inland. By 0900 hours, there were portions of three rifle companies over the bluffs between the D-3 and E-1 draws. The neighboring 5th Ranger Battalion made its way to the top of the bluffs by 0900 hours, parallel to Cota's and Canham's growing bands. By late morning, there were about 600 GIs over the bluffs, advancing southward. As the groups reached the crest of the bluff, they began to coalesce and send out patrols toward Vierville around 1000 hours. On the other side of the Vierville draw, Company C, 2nd Rangers, had clawed their way up the cliffs and began probing the defenses of WN73.

All through the morning, the scattered artillery batteries of *Artillerie-Regiment.352* fired on Omaha Beach. Records are too incomplete to detail how much artillery was directed against Omaha Beach, but it was substantial. The commander of the *I./Artillerie-Regiment.352* indicated in an interview that two of his three 105mm batteries took part in the fighting, mainly against the eastern side of Omaha Beach around Colleville and St. Laurent. The third battery was reserved for the defense of Port-en-Bessin, and much to his frustration, Pluskat's requests to use the additional battery were denied most of the day because of concern about the small port. The biggest mystery concerning German artillery at Omaha Beach was the action of the regiment's heavy 150mm battalion,

IV./Artillerie-Regiment.352, which was deployed to the west and southwest of Omaha Beach. It would appear that two, and possibly all three, of the heavy batteries were engaged against the western side of Omaha Beach around Vierville. The firing must have been intense, as around 1000 hours the battalion reported to HQ that its ammunition situation had become critical. This is entirely plausible, since the 150mm sFH 18 heavy field howitzer had a nominal rate of fire of four rounds per minute, and the guns in most cases were firing at pre-registered targets.

The corps ammunition reserve was located at Bully, about ten kilometers (six miles) to the southwest of Caen and more than forty kilometers (twenty-five miles) from Omaha Beach, too distant for quick resupply. Pluskat's *I./Artillerie-Regiment .352* on the eastern side of Omaha Beach began running out of ammunition by early afternoon and was promised a resupply. However, Pluskat was later informed that the ammunition convoy was wiped out in the afternoon when an Allied fighter-bomber patrol switched its attention from a locomotive it was chasing and instead attacked the convoy.

As reports of the American infiltrations over the bluffs began to arrive at the *352.Infanterie-Division* headquarters, General Kraiss faced a difficult predicament regarding any counterattack. In the Omaha Beach sector, *Grenadier-Regiment.916* had only two infantry companies in a second defense line near Formigny and Surrain and had already begun to mobilize these troops for a counterattack. Kraiss's main reserve, *Kampfgruppe Meyer*, had been taken over by the *84.Korps* as its ready-reserve, and parts of the regiment had been sent off in the pre-dawn hours on a wild goose chase to deal with the American paratrooper landings near the Vire River. Through the early morning hours, Kraiss's headquarters had been communicating with the *84.Korps* headquarters in St. Lô to regain control of *Kampfgruppe Meyer* to be used for counterattacks at Omaha Beach and neighboring Gold Beach. During the course of the morning, the three battalions in this battle group were gradually relinquished back to divisional control to take part in counterattacks.

Another dilemma for Kraiss was the question of where the reserves should be committed. His division defended a sector that stretched from the western fringes of Gold Beach all the way to the eastern fringes of Utah Beach. In the early morning, the main threats seemed to be the British breakthrough near Gold Beach and the lingering problems with American paratroopers in the Vire River area. The report from *Grenadier-Regiment.726* at 0725 hours finally forced Kraiss to commit some of his reserve to deal with the threats at Omaha Beach. Since Strongpoints St. Laurent and Vierville seemed to be holding, at 0750 hours he promised to send a battalion from *Kampfgruppe Meyer* to deal with the situation at Strongpoint Colleville between WN61 and WN62. In the meantime, the situation on Gold Beach deteriorated rapidly, with British tanks pushing out of the beachhead around 0830 hours. At 0835 hours, Kraiss was forced to allocate the remaining two battalions of *Kampfgruppe Meyer* to deal with the British threat, leaving only a single battalion, the bicycle infantry of *II./Grenadier-Regiment.915*, to deal with Omaha Beach.

STRONGPOINT COLLEVILLE

At 0905 hours, the *Grenadier-Regiment.726* command post in St. Laurent reported that WN61 was in American hands and that WN62 was still resisting, but was down to a single machine-gun position. It gradually began to emerge that American infantry were bypassing the strongpoints in the draws and advancing through gaps in the German defenses between the strongpoints. At 1114 hours, the *Grenadier-Regiment.726* command post reported that WN60 and WN62 were still resisting, but that the Americans had bypassed them and were already behind the beach in the village of Colleville itself.

By noon, the defense nests in Strongpoint Colleville had been substantially reduced, with WN60 besieged by 3/16th Infantry, WN61 overrun, and WN62 under heavy pressure from the beach area as well as from its western side. The WN62 defense nest had lost its two guns by late morning. Of its original seven machine-gun nests, only the one operated by Cpl. Hein Severloh was still in action. The remaining weapons in WN62 were able to keep American infantry from making a direct assault up from the beach, while the *MF.10* minefield on the northwest shoulder of the position discouraged American attacks from that direction. The crews of the various heavy weapons in the defense nest had gradually slipped away from the site through the morning as they were wounded or ran out of ammunition. The mortar crews reported being out of ammunition at 1426 hours. Severloh fired about 12,000 rounds of ammunition through the course of the day. In the early afternoon around 1400 hours, he had expended all the normal ammunition available from the nearby munitions bunkers and was forced to switch to "night" ammunition, which included tracer rounds. This put an end to his machine-gun position, as the tracers were very apparent to the American troops. A near-miss by tank or destroyer fire disabled his MG 42 machine gun.[*] The nearby observation bunker occupied by

Lieutenant Frerking's forward observer team from *1./Artillerie-Regiment.352* was hit by destroyer or tank fire around the same time. There was a collective decision by the surviving teams to abandon WN62 in the mid-afternoon around 1530 hours.

In the late morning, *II./Grenadier-Regiment.915* arrived in the Colleville sector after having bicycled nearly forty kilometers (twenty-five miles) since the start of the day. The battalion began its counterattack and was quickly engaged with an assortment of troops from the 16th Infantry who had infiltrated past WN60 and WN62 toward Colleville. At 1248 hours, Kraiss was able to report to *84.Korps* headquarters that this counterattack had stopped the American drive on Colleville, but by 1358 hours, the village had been retaken by the Americans. Divisional headquarters ordered *II./Grenadier-Regiment.915* to continue its counterattacks toward Colleville and in a mid-afternoon message instructed that "WN60 and 62 must remain firmly in our hands." There was continual fighting through the afternoon between 3/16th Infantry and other U.S. troops against both the remnants of WN60 and the *II./Grenadier-Regiment. 915*. However, at 1725 hours, the *352.Infanterie-Division* reported that the Americans had broken through and were pouring south. The neighboring artillery observers reported that *II./Grenadier-Regiment.915* had been surrounded by the Americans.

Resistance in the E-1 St. Laurent draw had largely faded by noon. The 50mm pedestal gun in a *Ringstand* near the beach was too exposed to survive very long and had been knocked out in the early morning. The bunkers near the E-1 draw were not completed, except for a R667 bunker with a 50mm pedestal gun in WN65. This bunker had been hit by tank fire from Company A, 741st Tank Battalion, early in the morning; it then was put permanently out of action when an M15A1 antiaircraft half-track of the 467th AAA Battalion attacked later in the morning, spraying the embrasure with

---

[*]Severloh in his memoirs indicates it was fire from the destroyer USS *Frankford*, but the tanks from Company A, 714st Tank Battalion, were still very active at the base of the hill and were an equally plausible source of the fire.

37mm automatic cannon and .50-cal machine-gun fire. Most of the tanks of Company A, 741st Tank Battalion, were operating on the east side of this draw through the morning, and there was a stream of troops from the 16th Infantry moving up the bluff to the east of the draw. Lieutenant Heller's *6.Kompanie/Grenadier-Regiment.916* had attempted to retake WN65 during the morning, but was hit by naval gunfire in the process and forced to withdraw. By noon, German resistance in WN64 and WN65 had largely evaporated, and 1st Engineer Battalion and 37th Engineers began the process of opening the draw to traffic shortly after noon.

Although the *II./Grenadier-Regiment.915* still held a ragged defense line south of Colleville, Kraiss was well aware it could do little to stem the American advance on its own. During the day, the *352.Infanterie-Division* had been promised by General Marcks's *84.Korps* headquarters in St. Lô that they would be allotted *Schnelle-Brigade.30*. This was a light infantry formation with three bicycle infantry regiments. However, it was some distance from the coast, and the first battalion did not appear in the Omaha Beach sector until late on the evening of D-Day.

Many of the bunkers in WN64 on the eastern side of the E-1 St. Laurent draw were not complete on D-Day. This shows the boarding and rebar for the construction of *Bauwerk* Nr. 486, a R612 gun casemate intended for a 76mm iKH 290(r) infantry gun. This weapon, a captured Soviet 76mm regimental gun, was used in combat on D-Day, but from a nearby earth entrenchment. NARA

A view of the incomplete *Bauwerk* Nr. 486 in WN64 near the E-1 St. Laurent draw in use a few days after D-Day as an improvised shower stall. This photo shows one of the types of construction used in Normandy to speed along the process, starting with an outer shell of pre-cast concrete blocks instead of the usual wood boarding, steel rebar, and finally the poured concrete. NARA

One of the best-known bunkers on Omaha Beach is *Bauwerk* Nr. 243, an R667 gun bunker fitted with a 50mm pedestal gun in WN65 on the western side of the E-1 St. Laurent draw. This bunker and gun still exist today. NARA

The gun casemates on Omaha Beach were designed to provide enfilade fire down along the beach. This is the view from inside the 50mm pedestal gun R667 bunker in WN65 on Easy Red Beach, which covered the western side of the antitank ditch blocking the E-1 St. Laurent draw. This scene was photographed on June 14, a week after the D-Day landings, after the antitank ditch had been plowed flat by bulldozers. A great deal of American equipment is evident. NARA

This is an interior view of the 50mm pedestal gun in the R667 *Bauwerk* Nr. 243 bunker in WN65. As can be seen, the shield took at least one direct hit that almost certainly would have killed the gunner, who sat on the right side of the gun. APGOM

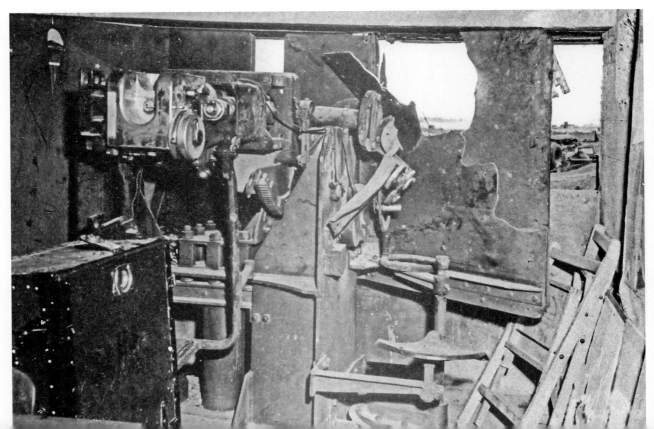

The R667 *Bauwerk* Nr. 243 bunker in WN65 was used almost immediately as a U.S. command post. This is a view of the rear of the bunker with U.S. radio sets set up outside. NARA

The shore area in front of the E-1 St. Laurent draw was covered by this 50mm pedestal gun in a standard *Ringstand*, part of the WN65 defenses. This gun fired extensively at U.S. landing craft, but was eventually overrun by troops from the 16th Infantry.

The WN65 defenses were supposed to include this R667 gun bunker, but it was not completed prior to D-Day. The unfinished section was the seaside wall used to protect the gun embrasure from warship fire. There was another 50mm pedestal gun in the defenses, which was probably intended for this bunker when completed. APG

A view of WN65 on Easy Red Beach a few days after D-Day, immediately to the west of the E-1 St. Laurent draw, showing the incomplete R667 bunker. NARA

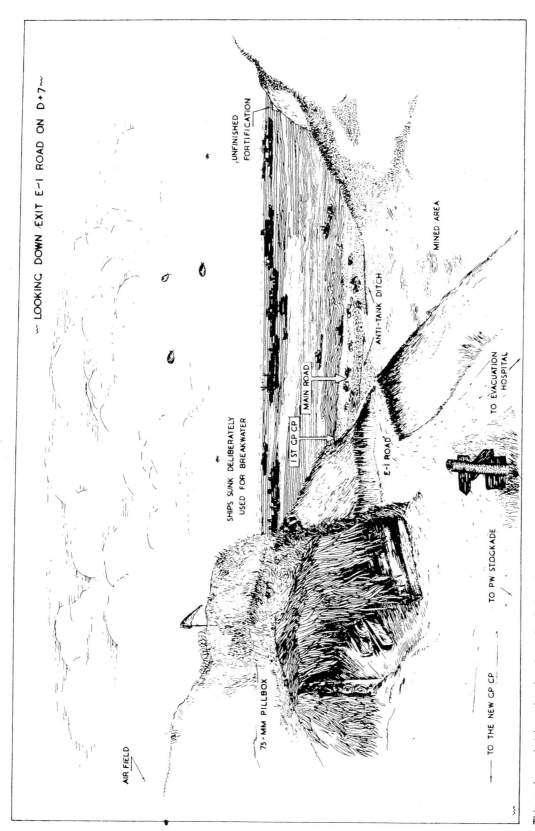

LOOKING DOWN EXIT E-1 ROAD ON D + 7

UNFINISHED FORTIFICATION

MINED AREA

ANTI-TANK DITCH

MAIN ROAD

1ST CP CP

E-1 ROAD

SHIPS SUNK DELIBERATELY
USED FOR BREAKWATER

TO EVACUATION
HOSPITAL

75 - MM PILLBOX

AIR FIELD

— TO THE NEW CP CP   — TO PW STOCKADE

This engineer sketch made a few days after D-Day shows the view inland toward the E-1 St. Laurent draw with the improvised 75mm PaK 40 antitank gun position covering the road on the left side of the draw. MHI

STRONGPOINT ST. LAURENT

The three defense nests in the D-3 Les Moulins draw were the only ones on Omaha Beach to hold out through the afternoon. In the early morning chaos, the *Grenadier-Regiment.916* headquarters at 0915 hours reported that much of Strongpoint St. Laurent had fallen, including WN70 near Hamel-au-Prêtre and WN65 through WN68 in the D-3 Les Moulins draw. WN70 had indeed been overwhelmed by midmorning because of the flow of troops of the 116th Infantry over the bluffs on either side of the defense nest. As a result of this alarming report, at 0930 hours the divisional headquarters committed the *II./Grenadier-Regiment.916* to retake Strongpoint St. Laurent. This was the only divisional reserve in the immediate Omaha Beach area.

In spite of the mistaken report, the three defense nests in the D-3 draw—WN66, WN67, and WN68—were still fighting. Maj. Sidney Bingham had tried rallying the leaderless men of Company F, 16th Infantry, and he led them in the capture of a house in the mouth of the D-3 Les Moulins draw. They attempted to attack the WN67 strongpoint on the eastern shoulder of the draw, but the defenses were too strong and the GIs had to retreat to the protection of the house and neighboring trenches. The counterattack by the *II./Grenadier-Regiment.916* proceeded around 1100 hours, consisting of two companies of infantry—*5.Kompanie*, commanded by Lieutenant Hahn, and *7.Kompanie/ Grenadier-Regiment.916*, commanded by Lieutenant Berthy. The battalion's third company, *6./Grenadier-Regiment.916*, had already been committed to the fighting in the E-1 St. Laurent draw. At 1114 hours, the *Grenadier-Regiment.726* command post in St. Laurent finally corrected the earlier reports and indicated that the three defense nests in the draw were still in German hands. Nevertheless, the counterattack proceeded even though the promised artillery support failed to materialize because of ammunition shortages.

By noontime, the American landings had resumed, and there was a sudden surge of U.S. units in the St. Laurent sector with the arrival of the 115th Infantry, 29th Division, on Easy Red Beach. The 2nd Battalion, 115th Infantry, advanced over the bluffs east of the E-1 St. Laurent draw and made its way toward the village of St. Laurent, bypassing the defense nests in the D-3 Les Moulins draw. They began to push into the eastern side of the village of St. Laurent around 1515 hours. The village had been reinforced as a defense nest (WN69) with a number of entrenchments and small field fortifications. It was manned by infantry platoons of *Grenadier-Regiment.726* and an engineer company of *Landesbau-Pioneer-Bataillon.17*. The St. Laurent defenders were reinforced by Lieutenant Hahn's *5.Kompanie* of *II./Grenadier-Regiment.916*, which had reached the area around 1400 hours. The *5.Kompanie* attempted to push northward from the village to reinforce the defense nest in the draw, but it was ambushed by an American patrol. Lieutenant Hahn was wounded and evacuated.

During the fighting around St. Laurent, the U.S. troops discovered the launch site for the rockets that had been plaguing the beachhead since dawn. The "Screaming Meemies" had been firing from pits to the west of St. Laurent. General Cota's aide later recalled: "Shell fragments of the *Nebelwerfers* resulted in unusually large chunks of shrapnel, the average size being about as large as the blade of an ordinary engineer shovel. One of these large fragments, striking a man in the small of his back, almost completely severed the upper portion of his body from his trunk." The destroyer USS *Thompson* spotted the smoke trails of the rockets around 1155 hours and fired on the target for nearly fifteen minutes, temporarily silencing the rocket launchers. Rocket fire resumed later. Eventually, a patrol led by Lt. Robert Garcia from Company E, 116th Infantry, reached within 800 yards of the launch pits and fired on the site with a .30-cal machine gun, striking some of the rockets—"All of a sudden there was a terrific explosion and a big ball of flame" when some of the incendiary 320mm rockets were struck by the machine-gun fire.

While the 115th Infantry was tangled in combat with the WN69 defenses in St. Laurent, Lieutenant Berthy's *7.Kompanie, II./Grenadier-Regiment.916* had arrived in the area after marching north from

A view from the rear of the VK.3001 *Panzer Drehturm* in WN68. This was located on top of a substantial underground Vf246 bunker, and the camouflaged entrance can be seen in the lower foreground. NARA

This well-known photo has been the subject of controversy for many years, with some accounts attributing it to WN62 on the Colleville draw and others to the Vierville draw. A recently discovered engineer drawing (see p. 211) shows that it was in fact behind the WN65 positions in the E-1 St. Laurent draw covering the road. NARA

This photo of another 75mm PaK 40 position similar to the one in WN65 has recently been discovered. Judging from the surrounding terrain and orientation, it was probably located on the opposite side of the draw. AUTHOR'S COLLECTION

Surrain, about five kilometers (three miles) away. Berthy attempted to skirt around the fighting in St. Laurent by moving cross-country, and so his unit did not reach its jump-off point until 1700 hours. The company advanced to within 100 meters of WN68 and sent out a patrol in the hopes of linking up with the defenders. The patrol discovered that WN68 was occupied by U.S. troops. Berthy was instructed to hold out.*

By early evening, the 2/115th Infantry had secured WN69 and the village of St. Laurent. *Grenadier-Regiment.726* was forced to abandon its command post near St. Laurent, and at 1610 hours, a runner reported that the village of St. Laurent was in American hands. However, WN67 near the beaches continued to hold out until late afternoon and was bombarded again by U.S. Navy destroyers.

With St. Laurent in American hands, many—but not all—of the defenders of WN67 pulled out by early evening. The D-3 Les Moulins draw was the last of the major exits to be cleared on D-Day because of prolonged German resistance in this sector. At 1825 hours, Kraiss ordered Capt. Paul Fritz's pioneer battalion of the *352.Infanterie-Division*, along with the construction troops of Major Riedel's *Landes-Bau-Pioneer-Bataillon.17*, to immediately head for St. Laurent via the *Grenadier-Regiment.916* command post at Trévières. The *Pioneer-Bataillon.352* was stationed about twenty kilometers (twelve miles) southwest of Omaha Beach, so it was unlikely to arrive there until dawn. The division's replacement battalion and march battalion were ordered to Formigny and St. Laurent late in the day to set up a defensive perimeter.

---

*The company remained on the fringe of WN68 until 1100 hours on 7 July, when it was overrun by U.S. forces and much of the company was captured.[17]

There were thirty-eight of these submerged rocket-launch pits near WN69 at the southern end of the D-3 Les Moulins draw. They were armed with the 28/32 s.WG 41, a simple frame launcher for launching 280mm and 320mm artillery rockets.

This is the VK.3001 *Panzer Drehturm* in WN68, armed with a 75mm gun. There was no battle-damage evident on this turret, so it was presumably captured by infantry action or abandoned. NARA

The *352.Infanterie-Division* attempted to stage an armored counterattack against the beachhead in the late morning using the Marder III Auf M 75mm tank destroyers of *1./Panzerjäger-Bataillon.352*. They were spotted by navy observation aircraft and the attack was smashed by naval gunfire near the Bois de Saffrey. MHI

STRONGPOINT VIERVILLE

Strongpoint Vierville was outflanked by the 116th Infantry columns led by General Cota and Colonel Canham, along with the 5th Rangers, who were already approaching the town of Vierville behind the beach by early afternoon. Around 1110 hours, the fortification engineer company stationed in the town was ordered to move to the coast to reinforce the defense nests.* The WN72 strongpoint in the D-1 Vierville draw was pounded mercilessly by the destroyer USS *McCook* through much of the morn-

ing. Between 1200 and 1300 hours, navy shore fire-control parties directed four salvoes from the battleship USS *Texas* against surviving bunkers in the D-1 Vierville draw, including both WN72 and WN73. Stunned by the barrage, about thirty surviving German soldiers exited the defenses and surrendered to a team of beach engineers.

General "Dutch" Cota recognized that the prime tactical objective for the 116th Infantry was to open up the D-1 Vierville draw to permit the exit of

---

Landesbau-Pionier-Bataillon.17 had been deployed to Omaha Beach in March 1944 with one company in Colleville and the other, along with the battalion staff, in St. Laurent. There were also efforts made to round up other construction units in this sector for the counterattacks, including Major Nolte's *Festung-Pionier-Bataillon.11* based in Isigny.

Two R667 gun bunkers were under construction in WN67 on the eastern side of the D-3 Les Moulins draw. This one faced west toward Vierville. NARA

This is a view of the D-1 Vierville draw around noontime from on board the battleship USS *Texas* after it had pounded the German defenses in the ravine. NARA

This is a photo of the H677 88mm gun bunker in the D-1 Vierville draw shortly after the D-Day fighting. The bunker is still in considerable disarray after the intensive navy shelling. This also provides a view of the remnants of the antitank wall on the left side of the photo that was blown up on General Cota's instructions to gain access to the Vierville road. NARA

This photo shows the Vierville H677 bunker a few days after D-Day, with the "D-1 Draw" sign down. This provides an interesting view of the false front porch on the bunker intended to camouflage the bunker as a civilian building. NARA

The 88mm bunker in the Vierville draw was so lethal because of the excellent lines of fire it enjoyed over the entire eastern end of Omaha Beach. This photo was taken in September 1944, after the beach had been cleaned up. NARA

tanks and vehicles. While walking back from Vierville toward the beach, he found a team from the 121st Engineer Combat Battalion. They accompanied him down the Vierville road from behind the defenses toward WN72 after noon, as the USS *Texas* was bombarding the area. As the salvo lifted, Cota's team proceeded to the thick antitank wall that projected from the 88mm bunker in WN72. With the German defenses in the area finally suppressed, the engineers from the 29th Division began placing about a half-ton of TNT charges along the 125-foot long wall. The wall was poured concrete and did not use steel rebar—when the charges were detonated around 1500 hours, a large section of the wall was blown away, finally freeing up the road toward Vierville. By this stage, there were still German defenders in WN73 on the hill overlooking the draw, but the defenses in the Vierville draw, including WN71 and WN72, largely had been overcome. The defenses in WN73 were not cleared out until D+1, when the 29th Division began moving west to link up with the Rangers at Pointe-du-Hoc.

This shows the inside of the Vierville H677 88mm bunker shortly after D-Day, taken by Lt. Brandel's navy survey team. The interior suffered extensive damage from repeated hits by tanks and naval gunfire, though there are no apparent penetrations on the gun shield.
COL. R. McCORMICK RESEARCH CENTER, 1ST DIVISION MUSEUM AT CANTIGNY

The 88mm PaK 43/41 gun is still inside the Vierville bunker, though pushed back into the casemate. This photo taken a few years ago shows the extensive damage caused by gunfire inside the bunker, especially noticeable to the left of the gun.
AUTHOR

This shows the Vierville 88mm bunker in September 1944, after it had been substantially cleaned up. The concrete anti-blast apron in front of the bunker is evident, as is the large-caliber strike on the bunker face above the embrasure, probably from one of the battleships. NARA

This is a view a few weeks after D-Day from the 50mm bunker in the Vierville WN72 looking eastward along Omaha Beach. The large 88mm H677 bunker can be seen on the right, and this view clearly shows the false front porch added on the front to camouflage the building. NARA

This is the double-embrasure 50mm gun bunker in WN72 in the D-1 Vierville draw shortly after the D-Day fighting. This bunker was one of the major causes of the extensive landing craft casualties suffered by the 116th Infantry on D-Day. NARA

A close-up of the embrasure on the east side of the 50mm bunker in WN72 near the D-1 Vierville draw, taken by the USAAF survey team in late June 1944. NARA

This is a close-up of the 50mm double-embrasure bunker in WN72 in late summer after the site was cleaned up. It shows the extensive damage caused to the bunker by tank and naval gunfire. The embrasure shield wall to the right of the embrasure was demolished by U.S. engineers as part of the road-building effort and is not combat damage. The object resting on top of the bunker is a barrage balloon. NARA

This is a view from the D-1 Vierville draw looking westward toward the cliffs of the Pointe-et-Raz-de-la-Percée in the background. The WN73 defenses were located in the center where the various structures can be seen. The cave-like bunker that housed the 75mm PaK 97/38 can be seen below these. Goranson's company from the 2nd Rangers climbed the cliffs in the center of the photo to attack WN73. NARA

STRONGPOINT POINTE-DU-HOC

When the Rangers landed at Pointe-du-Hoc on D-Day, there were very few German troops on the heights above. A section of fifteen troops from *Werfer-Regiment.84* had been transferred to Pointe-du-Hoc on 23 May 1944 and were deployed as machine-gun teams in foxholes dug above the cliffs on both the eastern and western sides of the promontory as a token gesture to move more of the defenses directly up to the coast. The battery officers thought this was a waste of resources since they felt the cliffs offered an impregnable defense. Most of the battery's defenses were oriented southward, expecting that any attempt to take the strongpoint would come from the land side. Many of these troops were hit by the morning bombardment. The other major cluster of German troops was the forward observer team from *2./HKAR.1260* in the fire-control bunker at the front of the promontory.

As the LCA landing craft arrived at the foot of the cliffs, they came under sporadic fire from the scattered machine-gun nests of the *Werfer-Regiment.84* troops. By the time the first wave of Rangers reached the top of the cliffs, casualties on the shore below amounted to about fifteen wounded. The German garrison on the top of the cliffs had been decimated by the pre-dawn bomber attacks and subsequent naval bombardment. The Rangers advancing through the lunar landscape of massive craters discovered that none of the guns was present. Against little German opposition, teams fanned out to find the guns. The five surviving guns were located about two kilometers (one mile) from WN75, pointing westward toward the Vire River estuary and Utah Beach. The guns were not defended, and there was little evidence of their crews.

The Rangers were surprised to find no guns in the Pointe-du-Hoc battery site, but they discovered the five remaining 155mm GPF guns over a mile away, camouflaged in a tree line. The guns were disabled by placing demolition charges in the breech.

COL. R. McCORMICK RESEARCH CENTER, 1ST DIVISION MUSEUM AT CANTIGNY

The Rangers quickly pushed the Germans off the Pointe-du-Hoc promontory, and the main source of resistance through most of the day came from a flak position located to the west. This is the 37mm flak gun that was so instrumental in resisting the Ranger advance on D-Day. COL. R. McCORMICK RESEARCH CENTER, 1ST DIVISION MUSEUM AT CANTIGNY

The *352.Infanterie-Division* was informed of the Ranger landing the moment it occurred by the observation bunker; about an hour later, at 0815, came the ominous news "no messages from Pointe-du-Hoc" after the Rangers knocked off the bunker's radio antennas. The stiffest German resistance in the morning came from the area to the west of Pointe-du-Hoc, where a 37mm flak bunker had escaped the morning's bombardment. German troops around this defense point fired on the Rangers for most of the day. The machine-gun nests from *Werfer Regiment.84* were abandoned in late morning after the regiment ordered its troops to withdraw.

While the Rangers were attempting to secure Pointe-du-Hoc, the *Wehrmacht* was planning to counterattack. The *9.Kompanie/Grenadier-Regiment.726 (9./Grenadier-Regiment.726)* was thinly spread out in defensive positions along several miles of coastline and kept an "assault platoon" of about thirty-five men as a company reserve in St. Pierre-du-Mont. At 0705 hours, this platoon was

given the task of retaking Pointe-du-Hoc from what was originally believed to be a weak Commando force. By 1000 hours, the German headquarters realized that the Pointe-du-Hoc attack was not a small-scale Commando raid but rather a larger raid, assessed to consist of two companies. The platoon from *9./Grenadier-Regiment.726* was clearly inadequate for the task, and *III./Grenadier-Regiment.726* was ordered to send as many troops as possible to continue the counterattacks against Pointe-du-Hoc. In reality, this didn't amount to much as the battalion had only two companies in this sector, the 9th and the 12th (heavy-weapons companies), both of which were thinly spread out in the coastal defense bunkers from the Vire estuary to Omaha Beach. *Grenadier-Regiment.726* eventually contacted the three batteries of *II./Artillerie-Regiment.352* located southwest of Maisy and requested artillery fire on Pointe-du-Hoc, which began later in the morning.

The first major German attack of the day took place in the early afternoon when *9./Grenadier-Regiment.726* finally advanced from St. Pierre-du-

Mont toward the eastern flank of the Ranger positions. There was scattered fighting throughout the day all along the Ranger defensive perimeter, in some cases local efforts by the remnants of the original Pointe-du-Hoc garrison, and in other cases scattered patrols by elements of *Grenadier-Regiment.726.* Since *Grenadier-Regiment.916* had its hands full trying the resist the main U.S. landings on Omaha Beach, in the late morning the division headquarters shifted the regimental boundaries eastward, turning this sector over to Lt. Col. Ernst Heyna's *Grenadier-Regiment.914* in the Grandcamp-Carentan area. Heyna was instructed to deploy two companies of *I./Grenadier-Regiment .914),* headquartered at Osmanville, against Pointe-du-Hoc, a distance of about ten kilometers (six miles). However, the battalion had been skirmishing since the early morning hours with scattered U.S. paratroop groups around Isigny, and it took time to collect elements of the battalion's scattered 3rd and 4th Companies and move them to the northeast. The mission against Pointe-du-Hoc came under question in the afternoon when *Grenadier-Regiment.916* asked the divisional headquarters to send this battalion farther east to assist in counterattacks against the main American landing at Omaha Beach. Colonel Heyna discouraged this, pointing out that the battalion would have to march to Omaha Beach in daylight hours and would be decimated by naval gunfire and air attack. As a result, its mission against Pointe-du-Hoc was reaffirmed. The presence of the Ranger force at Pointe-du-Hoc played a role in weakening the German counterattacks against the exposed 116th Infantry positions in Vierville on the western side of Omaha Beach.

The first platoons to arrive from the *12./Grenadier-Regiment.726* and *3./Grenadier-Regiment.914* launched an attack around 1600 hours from the western side of Pointe-du-Hoc, anchored on the western flak bunker. The German counterattack was repeatedly stymied during evening hours by naval bombardment from the destroyers offshore. At 1950 hours, the Rangers requested the USS *Thompson* to deal with the concentration of troops from the *3./Grenadier-Regiment.914* around the Chateau de M. la Baron near where the battery guns had been found in the morning. The first salvo was a direct hit on the buildings, and so the company waited until dark to stage their attack. The *3./Grenadier-Regiment.914* began its attack against the Ranger advance detachment near the Grandcamp road shortly after nightfall, around 2330 hours. After the first attack was rebuffed, the German company struck again at 0100 hours and pushed through some of the Ranger defenses before being halted. The third attack at 0300 hours succeeded in overrunning several of the Ranger defensive positions and capturing many Rangers. By daylight on D+1, the Ranger force had fallen from the original 200 Rangers to about ninety men able to bear arms. German casualties in the fighting were not recorded. The German counterattack against Pointe-du-Hoc ground to a halt around daylight once it was subjected to naval gunfire.

Skirmishing continued through D+1, and both sides set up defensive positions along the perimeter and harassed each other with machine-gun fire and mortars. The last German position within the Pointe-du-Hoc perimeter, the observation bunker, was finally overcome when its armored door was blasted open with explosives. The eight surviving Germans from the battery command post and fire-control team emerged and surrendered. The Ranger force was gradually reinforced on D+1, but was not relieved until 1135 hours on D+2. By this stage, *Grenadier-Regiment.914* was retreating westward over the Vire River to set up new defensive positions.

THE GERMAN PERSPECTIVE AT THE END OF D-DAY

At midnight on D-Day, Kraiss reported to the higher commands: "The losses in men and weapons in the defense nests has been total. . . . The troops in the defense nests have fought heroically." The division did not have precise details of losses, but the divisional history indicates that there were about 200 killed, 500 wounded, and 500 missing. These figures probably do not include casualties among *Grenadier-Regiment.726*, the construction troops, or other units involved in the fighting. The heaviest losses were suffered by *Kampfgruppe Meyer*, which was crushed in its attempts to staunch the British breakthrough out of Gold Beach. Meyer himself was killed, and his replacement captured almost immediately. Captain Gerth, who commanded *Füsilier-Bataillon.352*, was also killed. By the end of the day, there were only forty-five men left in the *Füsilier-Bataillon* and only about fifty from *II./ Grenadier-Regiment.915* from an original strength of more than a thousand men.

Kraiss claimed that his troops still held WN70 and WN68 at the end of the day, though the German troops near those strongpoints would have found his claims a bit surprising. He reported that his division was fighting against five Allied divisions: the U.S. 1st and 29th Infantry Divisions in the St. Laurent sector; the British 50th Infantry Division and 79th Armored Division around Arromanches; and the American 101st Airborne Division along the Vire River. Kraiss pleaded for additional reinforcements, but little was immediately available beyond the bicycle troops of *Schnelle-Brigade.30*. Even if his division had failed to stop the Allies on the beaches, he could take grim satisfaction in the casualties inflicted on the invaders. The division estimated it had destroyed thirty American tanks, sixty trucks and vehicles, and fifty landing craft during the day's fighting.[18]

CHAPTER 10

D-Day Postmortem

BY D+1, 7 JUNE 1944, IT WAS EVIDENT that Rommel's defense of Fortress Europe had failed. The Allied forces were moving off the beaches and would soon have a solid foothold in France. Omaha Beach was the only one of the landing beaches at which there was any question about the outcome, but by early afternoon, the tide had turned in favor of the Americans. Rommel's innovations in defensive tactics had undoubtedly contributed to the high casualty rate on Omaha Beach but the question remains—why were the casualties here so much higher than on the other beaches?

One bit of data is especially illuminating. Table 17 on the next page compares the casualties of the first landing waves to arrive at dawn— the 16th and 116th Infantry Regiments—against the second wave, which arrived starting in the late morning after 1030 hours. As can be seen, the first two regiments to arrive suffered more than six times the casualties of the following wave. The first wave of troops suffered the brunt of the German defenses when they were delayed in the killing zone on the beach for more than three hours on D-Day morning, at the mercy of German machine guns, mortars, direct-fire guns, and field artillery. The success of the Devil's Garden in delaying their exit out of the German killing zone and the high density of German fire-power were the main causes of this debacle. Both of these causes can be traced back to Rommel's tactical innovations in the months before D-Day.

In order to further examine the reasons for these high casualties, it is useful to go back to the AORG study first discussed earlier in this book. A re-examination of the questions based on new historical research will help to explain why Omaha Beach was so "bloody."

TABLE 17: COMPARISON OF CASUALTIES ON D-DAY			
1st Wave	**16th Infantry**	**116th Infantry**	**Total**
	971	1,007	1,978
2nd Wave	**18th Infantry**	**115th Infantry**	
	204	103	307

There were a number of gun positions in WN74 on the cliffs of the Pointe-et-Raz-de-la-Percée, including this field entrenchment for a 76.5mm *Feldkanone* 17(t), a World War I field gun manufactured by Skoda for the Austro-Hungarian army and, after the war, as an export weapon for Yugoslavia. NARA

WEIGHT OF FIRE PREPARATION

The AORG study concluded that there had not been a great deal of difference in the volume of fire delivered by warships against the five D-Day beaches in the preliminary bombardment. This quantitative assessment overlooked the qualitative issue. A third of the Omaha Beach naval bombardment was directed against the rubble on Pointe-du-Hoc, not the beach defenses. Furthermore, the rocket bombardment, which provided the bulk of the bombardment directed against key targets such as the Colleville and Vierville draws, was completely ineffective. As already mentioned, the air bombardment completely missed the Omaha Beach defenses. The plans had called for the Omaha defenses to be hit by about 1,745 tons of aircraft bombs and naval projectiles prior to the landings. Because of the failure of the bombers and rocket craft, only about 205 tons were delivered—an enormous shortfall. While the volume of fire directed against Omaha Beach may have been similar in quantity to the other beaches, it was conspicuously poor in its targeting and accuracy. Had the naval and air bombardment been successful, German defenses might have been undermined. This was certainly the case on Utah Beach, where the preliminary bombardment severely impacted the defenses, according to German survivors.

An impromptu memorial to the D-Day casualties, erected by the Rangers on Pointe-du-Hoc. NARA

Omaha Beach is littered with the shattered remains of men and machines after D-Day. NARA

STRENGTH OF BEACH OBSTACLES

The AORG study found that the density of beach obstacles was similar among the five beaches. This quantitative assessment was correct, but it failed to recognize the profoundly different results of the obstacle belt at Omaha Beach versus the others. The heavier firepower available to the Omaha Beach defenders had a synergistic effect with the beach obstacles and the natural defensive advantages of the Omaha Beach topography. To begin with, the Gap Assault Teams were decimated by the German beach defenses, especially the direct-fire guns in the strongpoints protecting the three key draws. With the breaching teams ineffective, the obstacles became a major hazard later in the morning after 0830 hours when the tide had risen. With the obstacles no longer visible, the beachmasters were obliged to shut down further landing craft traffic to the beach. This left the two decimated infantry regiments exposed in the kill zone on the beaches without reinforcements. The results are very obvious in the chart (on p. 230), which shows the difference in the casualty rates between the first two infantry regiments, which arrived early in the morning, and the two follow-on regiments, which arrived later in the morning after the German strongpoints had been substantially weakened. Omaha Beach was a classic demonstration of the role of obstacles combined with small-arms and machine-gun fire in order to fix the opposing infantry in a kill box and then destroy them with mortar and artillery fire. This combination of entrapment and bombardment did not occur to anywhere near the same degree on any of the other beaches.

Many of the GIs were killed before even reaching the beach, often near the German obstacles, which offered only the illusion of protection.

German artillery was a major cause of equipment losses on D-Day, such as these M15A1 and M16 antiaircraft half-tracks burned out on Omaha Beach. NARA

The German survivors of Strongpoint Colleville are escorted to the beach near WN65 from the E-1 St. Laurent draw, carrying their wounded. NARA

There were no prisoner-of-war stockades at Omaha Beach, so for several days German POWs were immediately sent to Great Britain aboard whatever ship was available. This *Landser* was from the units fighting around Pointe-du-Hoc and is seen after arriving on the USS *Texas* on 7 June 1944.
NARA

STRENGTH OF BEACH DEFENSES

The AORG study concluded that the beach defenses at Omaha Beach were more substantial than at other landing beaches in terms of firepower. However, there were two critical omissions in the study: firepower concentration and the role of field artillery.

There was not only a greater density of crew-served weapons, mortars, and guns on Omaha Beach than on the other beaches, but also a geographical concentration of these weapons in the kill-boxes at the draws. The misfortune of the original landing waves was that they followed the original plans and attempted to exit the beach through the draws, where German firepower was the most intense. They were not able to exit the beach until units began moving over the bluffs between the German strongpoints. On the other beaches, the German defenses could not be so densely concentrated because there was no similar funneling effect imposed by the terrain. The firepower on the other beaches was not only lower than on Omaha Beach, but also much more dispersed.

Field artillery also played a critical role in the high casualty rates at Omaha Beach, as described before. Indeed, the semi-official *352.Infanterie-Division* history concluded that if *Artillerie-Regiment.352* had a more ample supply of ammunition on D-Day, the defense of Omaha would have been more effective.[1]

On the British and Canadian beaches east of Omaha, there was very little field artillery behind the beaches. The field artillery batteries of the *716.Infanterie-Division* were located near the beaches, in some instances in casemates. In addition, there were two coastal artillery batteries in this sector, along with several other coastal batteries to the east of the Orne River. These positions were well known to Allied intelligence, and the coastal artillery batteries in particular were subjected to both air attacks and pre-landing naval bombardments.[2] Some of the batteries deemed most dangerous, such as the Merville battery and the artillery concentration around Riva-Bella on Sword Beach, were the target of British airborne and Commando raids.

The only significant artillery formation other than these was *schwere-Artillerie-Abteilung.989* with three batteries of four 122mm sFH 386 (r) (Soviet M-30 122mm howitzer). At least two of the three batteries of this unit were identified prior to D-Day.[3] These were in range of Juno, Gold, and Sword Beaches and were bombarded by cruisers of the Royal Navy's Eastern Task Force on D-Day.[*] German artillery dispositions on the D-Day Beaches are detailed in Appendix 3.

The only beach comparable to Omaha in terms of field artillery was Utah. Utah Beach was within range of a significant number of batteries to the north and south. However, the heavy concentration of artillery in the Strongpoint Group Vire on the east side of the Vire River had been configured mainly to deal with landings in the Vire estuary. The aim points (*Zielpunkte*) for the batteries were mostly along the east side of the Vire River estuary. The coastal batteries north of Utah Beach were intended mainly to deal with naval targets. The *II./Artillerie-Regiment.352* on the eastern side of the Vire was ordered at 1000 hours to concentrate its fire against WN3 to WN5, the site of the Utah Beach landings. But by this stage, the U.S. landings already had a firm foothold and were pushing inland, and U.S. Navy counterbattery fire against Strongpoint Group Vire helped to suppress these batteries. As a result, German field artillery was ineffective in stopping the U.S. 4th Infantry Division on Utah Beach on D-Day.

---

*The fate of these batteries on D-Day is a bit obscure as the battalion was largely destroyed in the following weeks during the fighting around Caen.

The initial cemetery at Omaha Beach was located on the low ground west of the D-3 Les Moulins draw on the approaches to the villages of Hamel-au-Prêtre and can be seen here on the left. NARA

This is a recent view of WN62 on the western side of the E-3 Colleville draw. Toward the top of the image is Lieutenant Frerking's observation bunker, while below is one of the gun bunkers for the Belgian 75mm TR field guns. AUTHOR

The upper 75mm gun bunker in WN62 has been used as the base for a memorial to the 5th Engineer Special Brigade, which lost so many of its men on the beach below. AUTHOR

The H677 bunker in WN72 in the D-1 Vierville draw has been heavily reconstructed over the years and forms the base for the U.S. National Guard monument. Although not readily apparent, the 88mm PaK 43/41 gun that wreaked so much havoc on D-Day is still inside the bunker but hidden from public view by a grating over the embrasure. AUTHOR

WN75 at Pointe-du-Hoc remains a frequent tourist destination in Normandy because of its impressive locale and the legendary Ranger attack. The Rangers climbed the cliffs on the opposite side of the promontory. This photo was taken from near the German 37mm gun bunker, which was the main center of German resistance against the Rangers on D-Day. AUTHOR

USE OF TANKS

The AORG study also concluded that differences in tank support could be a possible explanation for the casualty gap. The study had reasonably accurate figures for the British beaches, but lacked accurate figures for Omaha Beach. The study concluded that the U.S. landed twenty-six tanks on D-Day out of fifty-three launched. As a result, the study concluded that the tank shortage was one plausible explanation for the Omaha Beach casualties. The report noted: "Conditions on Omaha resemble in some respects those at Dieppe during the Canadian raid of Aug. 19, 1942. In both cases, troops on the beach were enfiladed by fire from strong natural positions, and in both cases, there were few tanks available to support the infantry in the early stages of the assault."

However, these numbers were considerably mistaken since they failed to consider the deep-wading tanks used on the U.S. beaches. Unlike the British and Canadian units, the U.S. tank battalions had only two of three companies equipped with DD swimming tanks, but used tanks with deep-wading equipment in the other companies. These added another twenty-one tanks on D-Day morning, as Table 18 indicates.

The implication that the lack of tank support was a causative factor in the casualty gap also can be questioned if the numbers are examined more closely. The DD tank losses fell most heavily on the 741st Tank Battalion supporting the 16th Infantry—only sixteen of its original fifty-six tanks were successfully landed on D-Day. In contrast, the 743rd Tank Battalion supporting the 116th Infantry landed thirty-eight of its fifty-six tanks. If tank support contributed to the casualty gap, we would expect that the 16th Infantry suffered heavier casualties than the 116th Infantry, which had more than twice as many tanks. In fact, the 16th Infantry had 971 casualties versus 1,007 for the 116th Infantry, suggesting that the quantity of tanks was not a direct factor in explaining the casualty gap.

A more plausible explanation was that the topography and defenses of Omaha Beach constrained tank support. Aside from the density of German antitank weapons, the singular problem was the lack of mobility caused by the terrain and exacerbated by the presence of antitank ditches and antitank walls that prevented the tanks from exiting the beach. Although some of the other beaches had exit problems, none suffered from the same funnel-

				Lost, Other	Swam to	Landed	Deep-Wading	M4 Tanks
Beach	DD Tanks	Launched	Sank	Causes	Shore	on Shore	M4 Tanks	on Beach
Utah	32	28	0	5	27	0	14	41
Omaha	64	29	21	10	2	31	21	54
Gold	76		3	3	7	63	52	122
Juno	78	29	4	3	22	49	52	123
Sword	38	32	3		29		26	55
Total	288	11	31	21	87	143	165	395

TABLE 18: AMPHIBIOUS SHERMAN TANKS LANDED ON D-DAY MORNING

ing effect caused by the geography on Omaha Beach. The geographic layout of Omaha Beach made the antitank obstacles a much more potent force on Omaha Beach than elsewhere. During the course of the fighting through the afternoon, only a single tank got off the beach to assist the infantry in the fighting around St. Laurent.

These obstacles might have been overcome with more engineer tanks, especially more dozer tanks. A total of sixteen dozer tanks were scheduled to land, but in the end only a handful were operational after the first hour of fighting and were mostly used for obstacle removal rather than breaching the anti-tank ditches. A key reason for the heavy loss of dozer tanks was the decision to place the dozer tanks in the rear of the LCT, with two wading tanks in front. Often, the two gun tanks were able to exit the LCT before the dozer tank; in the meantime, the German guns in the strongpoints were able to bring the LCT under fire in the short interlude between

beaching to delivering the tanks. In numerous cases, the dozer tanks were damaged while still on the LCT or as soon as they exited the LCT or were never delivered because of damage to the LCT during the landing process.

Had there been more dozer tanks available to deal with the antitank ditches, the tanks might have escaped the beach to support the infantry.[4] However, it is by no means clear that this would have been a complete solution since the steep bluffs provided a physical barrier to tank exit as well, and there were substantial minefields in the draws and on the neighboring hills. Until the draws were cleared of mines and obstructions, the tanks were trapped in the beach area. The U.S. Army had request fifty Sherman Flail anti-mine tanks from Britain for the D-Day operation, along with other specialized armored engineer equipment such as flamethrower tanks, but none were delivered prior to D-Day because of British shortages for their own units.[5]

QUALITY AND NUMBER OF DEFENDING TROOPS

The AORG study did not find a strong correlation between German troop strength and the high casualties at Omaha Beach. Although Omaha was on the high side as far as the German garrison was concerned, other beaches, such as Sword Beach, were judged to have as many or more troops. Does newly available data challenge this assessment?

German data on troop strength in the coastal strongpoints is lacking for 1944. The closest date available is for June 1943, a year before the landing. That data was covered in more detail in Chapter 4. Table 19 estimates the strength on D-Day, with troop density indicating the number of troops per thousand yards.

The gun tube of one of the 155mm GPF guns is still preserved at the Pointe-du-Hoc memorial site. NARA

TABLE 19: GERMAN STRONGPOINT STRENGTH

	Utah	Omaha	Gold	Juno	Sword
Beach length (yards)	1,000	7,500	6,000	6,200	5,500
Troops, June 1943	90	243	174	305	370
Troops, D-Day*	90	850	175	305	370
Troop density, D-Day	90	113	29	49	68

*Estimate.

Of the five beaches at the end of 1943, Sword Beach had by far the heaviest concentration of troops, as well as a significant arsenal. However, Sword did not see a major reinforcement between December 1943 and June 1944 and indeed may have lost troops during the late 1943 combings of the *716.Infanterie-Division*. Omaha Beach saw a significant increase in forces in the immediate beach area, with the addition of three infantry companies—each about 180 men strong—and two fortification engineer companies, plus two additional infantry companies within a short walking distance of the beach. As can be seen, the balance of troop strength and quality between Omaha Beach and the other D-Day beaches was probably not great enough to explain the casualty disparity, though it was a contributing factor. The beach that suffered the next highest casualties, Juno, had a relatively low density of troops. This suggests that troop density alone has a low predictive correlation with the number of casualties inflicted.

The *Kriegsmarine*'s *4./HKAR.1260* gun battery in WN48 at Longues-sur-Mer remains a popular destination on tours of the Omaha Beach area because it is one of the few coastal batteries to have retained its guns. The battery's four R272 gun bunkers housed 150mm TbK.C/36 destroyer gun turrets. Even after the tremendous pounding by bombers and naval gunfire, the battery managed to fire 115 rounds on D-Day. AUTHOR

WHY SO BLOODY?

The landings on Omaha Beach suffered disproportionate casualties compared to the other D-Day beaches for three interrelated reasons: geography, the Devil's Garden, and German firepower advantages. The geographic configuration of Omaha Beach not only facilitated German defensive measures because of the funneling effect of the draws, but also provided an ideal firing platform for German crew-served weapons. For example, WN62 was able to prevent an American frontal attack because the steep hill and open fields of fire made any such attack directly up the bluff almost suicidal. The Devil's Garden worked in concert with the geographic problems and kept the 16th and 116th Infantry regiments trapped in the beach kill zones for a prolonged period of time.

The firepower advantages resulting from Rommel's forward deployment of the *352.Infanterie-Division* provided the means to decimate the forces trapped in the kill zones along the beach in the first five to six hours of the operation. This was not simply because of the addition of several infantry companies to the beach defenses, but rather because of the addition of four or more artillery batteries and a rocket artillery unit. The battle for Omaha Beach had more in common with the trench battles fought on the Western Front in 1915–16 during World War I than with the more typical battles in the European theater in 1944–45: it consisted of a direct frontal assault against a prepared defensive position without adequate preliminary bombardment.

This massive R262 command bunker on the cliff overlooks the sea at Longues-sur-Mer. This bunker has seen several cinematic impressions, serving among others as the site of Major Pluskat's D-Day observation bunker, which was in fact a far smaller and more modest structure. AUTHOR

Rommel's innovations in anti-invasion tactics were a significant factor in the debacle on Omaha Beach. His efforts to stop the invasion on the beach inspired his efforts on the Devil's Garden and the forward deployment of troops in the coastal strongpoints. Omaha was the only D-Day beach where Rommel's schemes came close to succeeding because it was the only beach with enough fortification, manpower, and firepower. Ultimately, the emaciated state of the *Wehrmacht* in the summer of 1944 undermined its chances to stop the invasion, whether through Rommel's beach defense or through Schweppenburg's *panzer* counterattack.

Would Schweppenburg's counterattack have succeeded as an alternative to Rommel's tactics? The answer has been suggested by the historical record. The *21.Panzer-Division* was the only German tank division near the beaches, and it did intervene on D-Day with negligible results. The *12.SS-Panzer-Division* was the next to be committed around Caen. As Rommel had argued, the movement of the reserve *panzer* divisions from deeper in France was significantly delayed by Allied airpower. German *panzer* formations did attempt to stem the tide of the Allied invasion in the weeks after the invasion, primarily in the better tank country around Caen, rather than in the hedgerow country near Omaha Beach. Although the *panzer* divisions stymied the British advance on Caen for several weeks, they never seriously threatened to throw the Allies into the sea. The essential problem was not the tactical controversies between Rommel and Schweppenburg, but rather the threadbare state of the *Wehrmacht* in the summer of 1944.

The Normandy American Cemetery and Memorial is located on the plateau between WN62 and WN64 near Colleville-sur-Mer.
AUTHOR

The German Normandy cemetery is some distance away from Omaha Beach at Le Cambe and contains the war graves of more than twenty thousand German soldiers who died in the Normandy campaign in the summer of 1944. WIKIMEDIA COMMONS

Armament of the 716.*Infanterie-Division* in Normandy

DIVISIONAL ARSENAL, 1 DECEMBER 1943		
German Designation	**Quantity**	**Original Designation, Foreign Weapons**
Rifles	6,068	
Pistols	1,078	
MP 38/40 submachine guns	444	
7.92mm MG 34 light machine gun	343	
7.92mm leMG 08/15 light machine gun	3	
7.5mm leMG 116 (f) light machine gun	11	French FM mle 1924/29
MG 34 heavy machine gun	6	
sMG 08 heavy machine gun	13	
50mm Pak 38 antitank gun	6	
75mm PaK 97/38 antitank gun	6	French 75mm M1897 barrel on PaK 38 carriage
75mm PaK 40 Sfl self-propelled tank destroyer	10	
88mm Pak 43/41 antitank gun	2	
20mm Flak 38 anti-aircraft cannon	3	
50mm GrW 36 mortar	31	
81mm GrW 34 mortar	36	
81mm GrW 278 (f) mortar	5	French Brandt mle 1927/31
75mm FK 16 (n.A.) field gun	8	
105mm FK 17 (t) field gun	12	Czech-manufactured Krupp gun from former Austro-Hungarian army

STATIC ARSENAL, 1 DECEMBER 1943

German Designation	Quantity	Original Designation, Foreign Weapons
7.5mm leMG 116(f) light machine gun	61	French FM mle 1924/29
7.5mm leMG 311(f) light machine gun	28	French mle 1929 tank MG
7.9mm leMG 28(p) light machine gun	32	Polish Browning automatic rifle
leMG 08/15 light machine gun	4	
sMG 14(p) heavy machine gun	20	Polish Hotchkiss mle 1914
sMG 30(p) heavy machine gun	11	Polish Colt/Browning CMK wz. 30
8mm sMG 257(f) heavy machine gun	21	French Hotchkiss mle 1914
7.92mm Granat-Büchs 39 antitank rifle	15	
50mm GrW 201(b) mortar	9	Belgian DBT light mortar
50mm GrW 203(f) mortar	9	French mle 37 mortar
Fest.GrW 278 (f) fortification mortar	8	French Brandt mle 27/31: fortification mount
81mm GrW 278(f) mortar	49	French Brandt mle 1927/31
14mm PzBü 782 (e) antitank rifle	12	British Boys antitank rifle
25mm PaK 113(f) antitank gun	6	French SA-L mle 1934
37mm PaK antitank gun	6	
47mm PaK(t) antitank gun	8	Czech vz.37
47mm PaK (f) antitank gun	2	French mle 37
50mm PaK 38 antitank gun	21	
75mm Pak 40 antitank gun	2	
75mm PaK 97/38 antitank gun	3	
88mm PaK 43/41 antitank gun	8	
MG 311(f) PzDrT	5	French FT tank turret with machine gun
37mm KwK 144(f) m/MG311(f) PzDrT	3	French APX-R tank turret with 37mm gun
47mm Kas PaK 36(t) mit MG 37(t)	7	Czech 47mm casemate gun
50mm KwK L/42	35	Pedestal gun
50mm KwK L/60	15	Pedestal gun
75mm FK 231 (f) field gun	4	French M1897
75mm FK 235(b) field gun	10	Belgian TR
75mm FK38 field gun	4	
75mm FK 16 (nA) field gun	3	
75mm IKH 290(r) infantry gun	1	Soviet 76mm regimental gun
100mm leFH 14/19(t) howitzer	16	Czech vz 14/19
150mm sFH 13 SF self-propelled howitzer	3	German howitzer on French Lorraine chassis

Omaha Beach Naval Bombardment

Warship	Target designation	Target (German designation)	Assigned Ammunition
USS *Texas*	T1, T85	Pointe-du-Hoc	250 x 14"
USS *Texas*	T88, T89	WN76, WN77	12 x 14" + 100 x 5"
HMS *Glasgow*	T59, T61	WN66	400 x 6"
USS *Satterlee*	T75, T76	WN74	300 x 5"
USS *McCook*	T71	WN71	300 x 5"
USS *Carmick*	T66, T67, T68	WN70	250 x 5"
HMS *Talybont*	T77, T76, T82, T83	StP Le Guay	600 x 4"
USS *Arkansas*	T60, T63, T65	WN66, WN68	385 x 12"
USS *Arkansas*	T166	Trévières	50 x 12"
USS *Arkansas*	T43	WN62	250 x 5"
Montcalm	T22-T29	WN 59, Port-en-Bessin	300 x 6"
LCG(L)-424	64829187	WN73	120 x 4.7"
LCG(L)-426	64589190	WN73	120 x 4.7"
LCG(L)-449	64479200	WN73	120 x 4.7"
LCG(L)-487	T43	WN62	120 x 4.7"
LCG(L)-811	T54	WN65	120 x 4.7"
LCT(R)-366	T40	WN60	5" rockets
LCT(R)-450	T43	WN62	5" rockets
LCT(R)-482	T47	WN62	5" rockets
LCT(R)-447	T53	WN65	5" rockets

(continued)

Warship	Target designation	Target (German designation)	Assigned Ammunition
LCT(R)-473	T59	WN66	5" rockets
LCT(R)-483	T65	WN70	5" rockets
LCT(R)-423	T66-67	WN70	5" rockets
LCT(R)-464	T72	Vierville	5" rockets
LCT(R)-452	T74-75	WN74	5" rockets

The targets in the U.S. Navy Operations Orders are presented as Lambert Grid numbers with a short description of the target appended. This table was prepared by plotting the targets using the 1943 edition of the GSGS Map 6E/6 (Isigny) and the assault maps of the U.S. 1st Infantry Division. The target list can be found in Operation Order No. 3-44, 25 May 1944, and the assignment of targets can be found in the Annexes of Operation Plan No. 2-44, 21 April 1944, and in Appendix Three to Annex E of Operation Order BB-44: Schedule of Fires, 20 May 1944 (NARA: RG38 Records of the Office of the Chief of Naval Operations, Box 112, Plans, Orders & Related Documents, TF 122, May 1944).

German Artillery Batteries in Vicinity of D-Day Beaches 6 June 1944

Unit	Strongpoint	Location	Weapons
MKB St.Marcouf		Saint Marcouf	4 x 210mm K39/41
3./HKAR.1261		Fontenay-sur-Mer	6 x 155mm K417(f)
2./HKAR.1261	Stp 133	Azeville	4 x 105mm K331(f)
3./AA.191		Le Holdy	4 x 105mm lFH 18/40
6./AA.191		Brecourt	4 x 105mm lFH 18/40
1./sSWR.101		Brucheville	werfer
1./HKAR.1261	WN108	St. Martin de Varreville	4 x 122mm K390/2(r)
8./AR.1716	WN84	Maisy-la-Martinière	4 x 100mm lFH 14/19(t)
9./AR.1716	WN83	Maisy-la-Perruque	6 x 155mm sFH414 (f)
2./HKAA.1260	WN76	Pointe-du-Hoc	4 x 155mm K420(f)
2./AR.352		Formigny	4 x 105mm lFH 18/40
3./AR.352		Colleville	4 x 105mm lFH 18/40
1./AR.352		Houteville	4 x 105mm lFH 18/40
Werfer-Regt. 84	WN67	St. Laurent-sur-Mer	38 x 320mm werfer
1x./AR.352		Asnières-en-Bessin	4 x 150mm sFH 18
11./AR.352		Ecrammeville	4 x 150mm sFH 18

(continued)

Unit	Strongpoint	Location	Weapons
1x./AR.352		Longueville	4 x 150mm sFH 18
2./AR.352		Montigny	4 x 105mm IFH 18/40
3./AR.352		Hill 63	4 x 105mm IFH 18/40
1./AR.352		Houtteville	4 x 105mm IFH 18/40
6./AR.352		Vaux-sur-Aure	4 x 105mm IFH 18/40
5./AR.352		Ferme Tringale	4 x 105mm IFH 18/40
4./AR.352		Lieu-dit-Pierre	4 x 105mm IFH 18/40
4./HKAA.1260	WN48	Longues-sur-Mer	4 x 150mm TbtsK C/36
3./HKAA.1260	WN35a	Mont Fleury	4 x 122mm K390/1(r)
5./AR.1716	WN35b	Hable de Heurlot	4 x 100mm IFH 14/19(t)
3./sAA.989		Creully	4 x 122mm sFH 386 (r)
2./sAA.989		Amblie	4 x 122mm sFH 386 (r)
1./sAA.989		Basly	4 x 122mm sFH 386 (r)
6./AR.1716	WN32	Ver-sur-Mer	4 x 100mm IFH 14/19(t)
7./AR.1716	WN28a	Beny-sur-Mer	4 x 100mm IFH 14/19(t)
1./HKAA.1260	StP Caen 08	Riva Bella	6 x 155mm K420(f)
2./AR.1716	WN16	Colleville	4 x 100mm IFH 14/19(t)
3./AR.1716		Bréville	4 x 75mm FK 16 nA
4./AR.1716	WN12	Ouistreham	4 x 155mm FH414 (f)
1./AR.1716	WN01	Merville	4 x 100mm IFH 14/19(t)
3./HKAA.1255	StP Vill 033	Houlgate	6 x 155mm K420(f)
2./HKAA.1255	WN Vill 013	Mount Canisy	6 x 155mm K420(f)
4./HKAA.1255	WN Trou 032	Trouville/Hennequeville	4 x 105mm K331(f)
1./HKAA.1255	WN Trou 012	Villerville/Bruyères	6 x 155mm K420(f)

Glossary

AOK	*Armeeoberkommando*: field army high command, often used as shorthand for army (e.g., *AOK.7*)
Bauform	Construction plan
Festung	Fortress
FH	*Feldhaubitze*: field howitzer
FK	*Feldkanone*: field gun
GR	*Grenadier-Regiment*
GrW	*Granatwerfer*: mortar
HKAA	*Heeres-küsten-artillerie-abteilung*: army coastal artillery battalion
HKAR	*Heeres-küsten-artillerie-regiment*: army coastal artillery regiment
HMG	Heavy machine gun
Kompanie	Company; in *352.Infanterie-Division*, usually about 180 men; in *716.Infanterie-Division*, usually about 160 men
KVA	*Küsten Verteidigung Abschnitt*: divisional coast defense sector
KVG	*Küsten Verteidigung Gruppe*: regimental coast defense group
KWK	*Kampfwagen Kanone*: tank gun
LAC	Library and Archives Canada (Ottawa, Ontario)
LCVP	Landing craft, vehicles and personnel
LCI	Landing craft, infantry
LCT	Landing craft, tank
LMG	Light machine gun
LST	Landing ship, tank
MAA	*Marine-artillerie-abteilung*: Navy artillery battalion
MF	*Minenfeld*: minefield
MG	*Maschinengewehr*: machine gun
MHI	Military History Institute, Army Historical Education Center (Carlisle Barracks, PA)
NARA	National Archives and Records Administration (College Park, MD)
NCO	Non-commissioned officer, typically a sergeant
OB-West	*Oberbefehlshaber-West*: Supreme Command-West; Rundstedt's HQ
OKH	*Oberkommando Heeres*: Army High Command
OKW	*Oberkommando Wehrmacht*: Armed Forces High Command
PaK	*Panzerabwehr Kanone*: antitank gun
PzDrT	*Panzer Drehturm*: tank turret pillbox
Regelbau	Construction standard
SMG	Sub-machine gun
StP	*Stützpunkt*: strongpoint (company-size defense position)
Tobruk	Class of small bunkers with circular openings for a crew-served weapon
tonne	Metric ton (2,205 pounds)
Vf	*Verstarkfeldmässig*: reinforced field position, such as a Tobruk
Westwall	German fortifications created in the late 1930s on the French-German border; also known as Siegfried Line
WBN	*Wehrmacht Befehlshaber Niederland*: Armed Forces Command-Netherlands
WN	*Widerstandsnest*: defense nest (platoon-size defense position)

Notes

CHAPTER 1: THE CONTROVERSY

1. Helmut Konrad von Keusgen, *Omaha Beach: La tragédie du 6 juin 1944* (Bayeux: Heimdal, 2007): 33.

2. Many of the official U.S. Army histories of World War II prepared by the Center of Military History in the Green Book series had parallel studies of the German role in the battles prepared under the Foreign Military Studies (FMS) program in the R-xxx series. These German studies, often by the historians Magna Bauer and Lucian Heichler, are not well known since they were never published but used instead as background research for the main published study. They are available at NARA II in Record Group 319. So, for example, the Green Book study of Operation Husky, the amphibious assault on Sicily in July 1943, was accompanied by eighteen detailed reports on German and Italian preparations and operations, totaling over a thousand pages. One reason that the German role in the D-Day fighting remains murky is that there was no detailed U.S. Army study of German forces on D-Day undertaken as part of this effort.

3. I would recommend Joseph Balkoski's *Omaha Beach* (Mechanicsburg, PA: Stackpole, 2004) as the gold standard of contemporary accounts of Omaha Beach. The official U.S. Army accounts, the 1946 *Omaha Beach* monograph from the American Forces in Action series and the later Green Book study *Cross-Channel Attack* are also essential, though perhaps a bit harder for the average reader to locate.

4. Steven Zaloga, *US Amphibious Tanks of World War II*. New Vanguard, 192. (Oxford, UK: Osprey, 2012).

5. The official V Corps history put D-Day casualties at 2,476, including 725 killed, 1,399 wounded, and 352 missing in action. The V Corps tally included only casualties within the 1st, 2nd, and 29th Divisions and V Corps troops. N.a., *History of the V Corps* (G-3 Historical Sub-Section: V Corps, 1946): 64. Details of U.S. casualties on D-Day were so confusing and so poorly documented that a researcher for the U.S. Army Office of the Chief of Military History, Royce Thompson, prepared a special memorandum for Gordon Harrison, who was working on the official U.S. Army history of D-Day (*Cross-Channel Attack*) that cataloged the available data. Royce Thompson, *Report on Invasion Casualties* (CMH: 27 May 1948). A more recent assessment in Joseph Balkoski's book puts casualties at 4,720, and includes Coast Guard, Navy, and Army Air Force casualties. Besides broadening the coverage, Balkoski also reassesses the accounting of casualties; for example, he attributes 1,346 casualties to the 1st Infantry Division, while the V Corps assesses casualties as 1,190. The greatest discrepancy is in the calculations for non-divisional army troops, which the V Corps history lists at 441 casualties; Balkoski expands the

255

coverage from V Corps to all First U.S. Army casualties at Omaha Beach, including Ranger, engineer, anti-aircraft, tank, and other arms, which increases the total to 1,568. Joseph Balkoski, *Omaha Beach: D-Day June 6, 1944* (Mechanicsburg, PA: Stackpole, 2004).

6. Col. O. M. Solandt, *Comparison of British and American Areas in Normandy in Terms of Fire Support and its Effects* (AORG Report No. 292, 14 August 1945), U.S. Army copy at MHI.

7. There are a number of studies of U.S. naval fire support at Omaha Beach, but the studies are mainly descriptive and lack analytic content. Barbara Brooks Tomblin, "Naval Gunfire Support in Operation Neptune: A Reexamination," in *The United States and the Second World War: New Perspectives on Diplomacy, War, and the Home Front*. Edited by G. Kurt Piehler and Sidney Pash (New York: Fordham University, 2010); William Kirkland Jr., *Destroyers at Normandy: Naval Gunfire Support at Omaha Beach* (Washington, D.C.: Naval Historical Foundation, 1994); Christopher Yung, *Gators of Neptune: Naval Amphibious Planning for the Normandy Invasion* (Annapolis, MD: Naval Institute, 2006).

CHAPTER 2: THE IRON COAST

1. *Generalleutnant* Max Pemsel, *Report of the Chief of Staff, Seventh Army, June 1942–6 June 1944* (Foreign Military Studies B-234).

2. "Gesamt-ubersicht über den feldmässigen Ausbasustand im Bereich der 7.Armee: Stand vom 1.1.44," Annex 1 from the *AOK.7 Kriegstagebuch* (KTB: war diary), (NARA: RG242, T312, R1563, F199).

3. Michael Howard, *Strategic Deception in the Second World War* (London: HMSO, 1990); Joshua Levine, *Operation Fortitude: The Story of the Spies and the Spy Operation That Saved D-Day* (Guilford, CT: Lyons Press, 2011); Mary Barbier, *D-Day Deception: Operation Fortitude and the Normandy Invasion* (Westport, CT: Praeger Security International, 2007); Thaddeus Holt, *The Deceivers: Allied Military Deception in the Second World War* (New York: Scribner, 2004).

4. *The German Defences in the Courselles-St. Aubin Area of the Normandy Coast* Report No. 41 (Historical Section [GS]: Canadian Army Headquarters, 20 July 1951): 8.

5. The most thorough account of German intelligence assessments of the Allied invasion is Hans Wegmüller, *Die Abwehr der Invasion: Die Konzeption des Oberbefehlshabers West 1940–1944* (Freiburg, Germany: Rombach Verlag, 1986).

6. Steven Zaloga, *German V-Weapon Sites* Fortress, 72. (Oxford: Osprey, 2008).

7. See, for example, the 4 February 1944 note in the Annex to the *7.Armee* war diary: NARA: RG242, T312, R1565, F031.

CHAPTER 3: THE ROMMEL FACTOR

1. For a recent German revisionist approach to Rommel, see: Ralf Georg Reuth, *Rommel: The End of a Legend* (London: Haus Books, 2005).

2. Janusz Piekalkiewicz, *Rommel and the Secret War in North Africa, 1941–1943* (West Chester, PA: Schiffer Pub., c.1992).

3. The most detailed account of Rommel's inspection tour is the Dutch account: Hans Sakkers, *Generalfeldmarschall Rommel: Opperbevelhebber van Heeresgruppe B bij de voorbereiding van de verdediging van West-Europa, 5 november 1943 tot 6 juni 1944* (Brouwer, 1993). A more personal account that includes discussions of Rommel's tactical thinking can be found in the reminiscences of his naval aide: Friedrich Ruge, *Rommel in Normandy* (San Rafael, CA: Presidio, 1979).

4. Alexandre Thers, "Les Troupes de l'Est en Normandie," *Batailles* 8 (July–August 2005): 24–31.

5. Steven Zaloga, *Anzio 1944: The Beleaguered Beachhead*. Campaign, 155 (Oxford: Osprey, 2005).

6. Matthias Strohn, *The German Army and the Defence of the Reich: Military Doctrine and the Conduct of the Defensive Battle, 1918–1939* (Cambridge: Cambridge University Press, 2011).

7. Yves Buffetaut, "Rommel contre les généraux de l'Est," *Batailles* 37 (Nov.–Dec. 2009): 66–73.

8. Rommel's debates with various commands are detailed in the Ruge memoir, as well as in various publications by the Army Group B chief of staff, *Generalleutnant* Hans Speidel. Hans Speidel, *Invasion 1944: A First-hand Account of Rommel's Normandy Campaign* (Washington, D.C.: Regnery, 1950); Hans Speidel, *Ideas and Views of Genfldm Rommel, Commander of Army Group B, on Defense and Operations in the West in 1944* (Foreign Military Studies B-720, 1946).

9. This is based on an interview conducted by the author Cornelius Ryan with Pluskat for his book *The Longest Day*. Cornelius Ryan Collection, Ohio University Archives, Box 27, No. 4.

10. This is especially clear from the memoirs of senior *7.Armee* commanders who were bitter at Rommel's continued favoritism towards the *15.Armee* and the Pas-de-Calais. See, for example, Max Pemsel's recollections (*Report of the Chief Staff*, FMS B-234). For another view of the interaction of Dollmann and Rommel in changing the center of gravity of the *7.Armee* in Normandy, see: Yves Buffetaut, "Le Plan Secret de Rommel," *Batailles* 8 (Jul–Aug 2005): 14–23.

CHAPTER 4: OPPOSING FORCES

1. Yves Buffetaut, "Une division statique: La 716.Infanterie-Division," *Batailles* 1 (Apr–May 2004): 60–65.

2. Although focused on the *716.Infanterie-Division* in the Juno Beach area, this Canadian study provides an overview of the divisional defense plans: *The German Defences in the Courselles-St. Aubin Area of the Normandy Coast*, Report No. 41. (Historical Section [GS]: Canadian Army Headquarters, 20 July 1951).

3. Details of the strength of *716.Infanterie-Division* can be found in the form of the periodic *Gliederung* (organization charts) that were prepared for higher commands. They can be found in the captured German documents in the microfilm of Record Group 242 at NARA II: 1 Aug 1943 (T315, R2260, F432); 1 Dec 1943 (T315, R2260, F479); 1 Jan 1944 (T314, R1604, F1357); 1 May 1944 (T312, R1565, F215).

4. CSDIC(UK) SIT 332, KP/1124.

5. Details of the deployment are contained in the *KTB AOK.7 Anlagen* (NARA: RG242, T312, R1565, various frames).

6. See also: Stéphane Jacquest, "6 juin 1944: des soldats coréens sur Utah Beach," *39-45* 305 (Nov. 2012): 42–44.

7. This table is based on two tables dated 15 June 1943: *Besatzung und Waffen in den Stützpunkten und WN der KVGr Caen* and *Besatzung und Waffen in den Stützpunkten und WN der KVGr Bayeux* (NARA II: RG242, T315, R2260, F364–365).

8. Yves Buffetaut, "La 352.Infanterie Division à Omaha Beach," *Batailles* 34 (May–June 2009): 14–25.

9. *Oberstleutnant* Fritz Ziegelmann, *The 352nd Infantry Division (5 Dec 1943–6 June 1944)* (Foreign Military Studies B-432): 5.

10. NARA: RG242, T314, R1604, F1354.

11. "Erhöhte Verteidigungsbereitschaft," 6 Feb 1944 (NARA: RG242, T312, R1565, F041).

12. This is mentioned in the *AOK.7 Kriestagbuch* entry for 26 January 1944. Details of the 15 February 1944 transfer can be found in the *KTB AOK.7* (NARA II: (RG242, T312, R1565, F-114, -115).

13. Friedrich Ruge, *Rommel in Normandy: Reminiscences* (San Rafael, CA: Presidio Press, 1979): 96.

14. *KTB AOK.7 Anlagen* 34, 9 March 1944 (NARA: RG242, T312, R1565, F238).

15. Fritz Ziegelmann, *The 352nd Infantry Division, 5 Dec 1943–6 Jun 1944* (Foreign Military Studies B-432): 6.

16. NARA: RG242, T312, R1566, F216.

17. Lagenkarte Gen. Kdo. LXXXIV A.K.: Stand 6.12.43, Annex of the *LXXXIV.AK* War Diary. (NARA: RG242, T314, R1604).

18. An account by Grenadier Karl Wegner of *3./Grenadier-Regiment.914* can be found on

the Vierville town website: http://oma-habeach.vierville.free.fr.

19. *KTB AOK.7 Anlagen*, 16–18 Mar 1944 (NARA I: RG242 T312, R1565, F294, F301).

CHAPTER 5: FIRE AND BRIMSTONE

1. The U.S. Army Medical Department's Office of Medical History has an extensive selection of documents dealing with medical issues on D-Day, conveniently located on their website: http://history.amedd.army.mil/booksdocs/wwii/Normandy.

2. J.B.A. Bailey, *Field Artillery and Firepower* (London: Taylor & Francis, 1989).

3. *Breaching the Siegfried Line*, XIX Corps (U.S. Army: 2 October 1944): 48.

4. Major James Beyer, ed., *Wound Ballistics* (Office of the Surgeon General, Department of the Army, 1962).

5. These details can be found in the divisional records at NARA: RG242, T315, R2260.

6. The weapons tables are based on "*Gliederung 716.Infanterie Division*: Stand 1.12.43" (NARA: RG242, T315, R2260, F479). No detailed breakdown of the standard/stationary arsenal closer in date to D-Day has been found. A less detailed summary is available for 1 March 1944 and indicates that the holdings were similar, though not identical, to the earlier tabulation, in most cases with small additional quantities of weapons available. In all likelihood, the stationary arsenal was somewhat higher on D-Day. In the case of certain prominent weapons, such as the 88mm PaK 43/41, it is certain that the division had more on D-Day than indicated on the December 1943 table.

7. The quartermaster of OB-West conducted a detailed survey of the holdings of foreign and German weapons, along with an assessment of ammunition holdings and production capacities. This is too detailed to list here, but can be found in NARA: RG242, T311, R1, F455, et passim.

8. *AOK.7* Quartermaster report, 16 March 1944, in *AOK.7* war diary, Appendix 12 (NARA: RG242, T312, R1570, f 1066).

9. Marcin Bryja, "Artyleria niemiecka w Normandii (cz.1)," *Poligon* 3 (May–Jun 2012): 43.

10. The basic requirements can be found in various quartermaster records such as NARA: RG242, T311 R1, F447.

11. "Bericht über die Reise des Heern Oberbefehlshabers am 17. un 18.5.44." This was a report prepared after Rommel's visit, along with Vice Admiral Ruge and Gen. Lt. Doctor Meise, to Normandy and Brittany on 17–18 May 1944, preserved in the *AOK.7* War Diary (NARA: RG242, T312, R1565, F716).

12. Harry Lippmann, *Die 5 cm Kwk im Atlantikwall* (Cologne: DAWA, 2003).

13. Their actual identity is confirmed in a number of unit documents; see, for example: NARA: RG242, T315, R2260, F883.

14. The earlier movements of this battalion are covered in the *Anlagen* (Appendices) of the *AOK.7* war diary, but there were no updates immediately prior to D-Day. This is not unusual, as the same was the case for many of the other batteries in the regiment.

15. This is confirmed in Cornelius Ryan's interview with the *I./Artillerie-Regiment.352* commander after the war, who indicated that the batteries had over 2,000 rounds. Werner Pluskat interview, Cornelius Ryan Collection (Ohio University Archives, Box 27, No. 4): 10.

16. The Pluskat interview indicates that the battery was located at Criqueville. However, prisoner interrogations on D-Day indicated that it was located in the woods near Asnières with the headquarters nearby in Crauville. Neither source identifies the battery number. G-2 Periodic Report No. 1, 7 June 1944, Headquarters, V Corps. (NARA: RG407).

17. *G-2 Journal*, V Corps, 8 June 1944.

18. "Ferngesprach Feldmarschall Rommel mit Chef H.G.," *KTB AOK.7 Anlagen* 16 May 1944 (NARA: RG242, T312, R1565, F712).

19. These twenty-one launchers are listed in the *Bodenständig* entry on the division's 1 May 1944 *Gleiderung*.

20. Although the rockets were usually launched from the frame, individual rockets could be

launched from the transport/launch pallet, a tactic sometimes used by German troops in urban fighting. Further details of these weapons can be found in: T. J. Gander, *Field Rocket Equipment of the German Army 1939–1945* (London: Almark Publishing, 1972).

CHAPTER 6: THE DEVIL'S GARDEN

1. "Rommel's Defenses of Stabilized Position at El Alamein," *Tactical and Technical Trends* 32 (26 August 1943).

2. "Minenverlegung durch Kustenvorfeld und hindernisse gessperrte Strecke im Bereich des OB West," OB-West Quartermaster records in Appendix 4 and 5 of the OB-West War Diary (NARA: RG242, T311, R5).

3. The mine maps can be found in the *KTB AOK.7* (NARA: RG242, T312, R1569).

CHAPTER 7: DEADLY GEOGRAPHY

1. Maj. Robert Schmidt, *ASF Report No. 33-Beach Obstacles and Defenses at St. Malo, Dinard, Mont St. Michel, and Cabourg, France* (Chief of Engineers, U.S. Army, 30 October 1944).

2. An interview with Heinze appears on the Vierville town website as "Un officier Allemand à Formigny le Jour J."

3. "Besatzung und Waffen in den Stützpunkten. und W.N. der K.V.Gr. Caen: Stand 15.6.44," from divisional records of the *716.Infanterie-Division.* (NARA: RG242, T315, R2260, F364).

4. The *7.Armee* war diary reported the slow pace of construction in their 3 May 1944 day report, though the designations for the defense nests in the report are mistaken. (NARA: RG242, T312, R1565, F681).

5. Alain Chazette, et al., *Atlantikwall Südwall Spécial Typologie: Le canon de 5cm KwK et ses casemates et Les Tobruk pour tourelles de char, canons, mitrailleuses, mortiers, lance-flammes* (Paris: Histoire & Fortifications, 2012).

6. For a survey of this type of bunker in Normandy, see: Georges Bernage, "H677: de redoutable 88 sur la côte normande,"*39-45* 292 (Sep. 2011): 58–60.

CHAPTER 8: THE PIGEON PATROL

1. Paul Carell, *Invasion!: They're Coming!* (Bantam Book, 1964): 1–2.

2. Rivalry between the various police units was most intense in Berlin, but with greater cooperation at lower levels. The problems grew more intense in the final year of the war. Lt. Col. Andrew Berdin, "Dissension in German Intelligence Services," (Office of Strategic Service: Mission for Germany, 7 July 1945).

3. Wilhelm Krichbaum, *The Secret Field Police* (Foreign Military Studies C-029, 1947).

4. The classic account of British special operations in France is M.R.D. Foot, *SOE in France* (London: HMSO, 1966).

5. Jean-Louis Perquin, *Resistance: The Clandestine Radio Operators* (Paris: Histoire et Collections, 2011): 56.

6. There is a splendid little account of the British employment of pigeons during the war, published to honor their service: W. H. Osman, *Pigeons in World War II* (London: The Racing Pigeon Publishing Co., 1950).

7. *Special Questions for 352.Infanterie Division Chief-of-Staff Fritz Ziegelmann* (Foreign Military Studies B-021): 2.

8. Cassel Bryan-Low, "UK Code-Crackers Stumped," *Wall Street Journal* (24–25 November 2012): A9; *Reuters*, "Enigmatic code found on WWII pigeon," *Washington Post* (24 November 2012): A9.

9. A survey of Resistance actions in Normandy can be found in Raymond Ruffin, *La résistance normande face à la Gestapo* (Paris: Presses de la Cité, 1977).

10. Gilles Perrault, *The Secret of D-Day*, translated by Len Ortzen. (Boston: Little, Brown, 1965): 37.

11. A description of the wartime actions of the resistance in Vierville can be found on the town's website: http://vierville.free.fr/811-ResistanceVierville.htm.

12. The French role in the construction of the Atlantic Wall has been the source of some controversy. See, for example: Jérôme Prieur, *Le Mur de l'Atlantique: Monument de la Collaboration* (Paris: Denoël, 2010).

13. Perrault, *Secret of D-Day*, 85. Giskes wrote an account of German counterintelligence activities after the war, but it focuses mainly on the Netherlands. H. J. Giskes, *London Calling North Pole* (New York: Bantam Books, 1982).

14. The U.S. collection of the "Martian Reports," kept by the G-2 Intelligence Division of Eisenhower's SHAEF headquarters, can be found at the U.S. National Archives in Record Group 331, Entry 13, along with related collections of later reports, such as the "Neptune Argus" series.

15. *Interpretation Report No.SA.1517: Attack on Coastal Gun Positions at Point du Hoc on 25.4.44* (National Archives [UK] AIR 34/371).

16. Further details of the pre-invasion Allied bombing of Pointe-du-Hoc can be found in Steven Zaloga, *Rangers Lead the Way: Pointe-du-Hoc D-Day 1944*. Raid, 1. Oxford: Osprey Pub., 2009).

17. For an overview of the construction and fate of the battery, see: Dominique Forget, "La batterie allemande de Longues-sur-Mer, *39–45* 252 (January 2008): 30–35.

18. See, for example, the recollections of Lt. Hans Heinze, who served on the staff of *2./Grenadier-Regiment.916*, on the Vierville town website: http://omahabeach.vierville.free .fr/index.htm.

19. This lingering mystery is discussed in an inconclusive fashion in a footnote in the official U.S. Army history of D-Day: Gordon Harrison, *Cross-Channel Attack* (Center of Military History, 1989): 319. The original U.S. Army history provides a very confused description of German deployments: *Omaha Beachhead (6 June–13 June 1944)* (Historical Division, War Department, 1945): 110.

20. A typical example is the V Corps assessment, which can be found in their postwar account, *Intelligence Operations ETO V Corps* (NARA II: RG407): 11.

21. The original messages sent by officers of the V Corps G-2 (intelligence) can be found in the corps G-2 records (NARA II: RG407). A typical message, time-stamped 0900AM on 6 June reads: "Elements 726 Regt identified along entire line. 914 Regt identified on our right. 915 Regt in center vicinity Formigny. 916 Regt on our left."

22. Jock Haswell, *D-Day: Intelligence and Deception* (New York: Times Books, 1979): 145.

23. The myth that the *352.Infanterie-Division* arrived a short time before D-Day for tactical exercises has been repeated in numerous accounts, most surprisingly in the recent German semi-official history: Hirst Boog, et al. *Germany and the Second World War, Vol. VII: The Strategic Air War in Europe and the War in the West and East Asia 1943–1944/45.* Translated by Derry Cook-Radmore. (Oxford: Clarendon Press, 2006): 590.

24. The standard U.S. Army intelligence manual on German coastal defenses presented an excellent overview of the defenses encountered in the Mediterranean theater, but was not up-to-date on the Atlantic Wall defenses since this type of strongpoint had never been encountered. *German Coastal Defense*. Special Series No. 15. (U.S. War Department Military Intelligence Service, 15 June 1943).

25. The controversy over Pacific tactics versus European tactics is examined in Williamson Murray, "Needless D-Day Slaughter," *Military History Quarterly* (Spring 2003): 26–31.

26. Charles Corlett, *Cowboy Pete: The Autobiography of Maj. Gen. Charles H. Corlett* (Santa Fe: Sleeping Fox, 1974).

CHAPTER 9: DAY OF RECKONING

1. Rudy De Saedeleir, "Affligemse club: bunker Pluskat," *De Standaard* (17 August 2009).

2. Heinze interview, the Vierville town website.

3. Hein Severloh, *WN62: A German Soldier's Memories of the Defence of Omaha Beach, Normandy, June 6, 1944* (Garbsen, Germany: HEK Creative Verlag, 2011): 53. Severloh was the orderly to Lt. Bernhard Frerking, the battery commander of *1./Artillerie-Regiment.1352*. On D-Day, he was assigned to guard Frerking's observation bunker at WN62 and was located in a trench a short distance away, armed with an MG 42 light machine gun.

4. Franz Gockel, "Invasion 1944 an der Kuste der Normandie in Colleville sur mer." Typed memoirs in the Robert A. Rowe Collection (U.S. Army Military History Institute: Carlisle Barracks, PA). A fuller set of memoirs was later published by Gockel in German as *Das Tor zue Hölle* and in French as *La Porte de l'Enfer* (Strasbourg: Éditions Hirlé, 2004). Gockel served in *3./Grenadier-Regiment.726*.

5. Alain Chazette, *Mur de l'Atlantique: Les batteries de côte en Normandie* (Paris: Histoire & Fortifications, 2007): 127–134.

6. "Summary of present situation of Batteries which might affect the NEPTUNE beaches on their approaches—31 May 44 (amended 1000 hours 1 June)." National Archives (Kew) WO205/172.

7. Gockel memoir, Rowe collection, MHI.

8. Commander, U.S. Naval Forces in Europe, "Operation Neptune-Report of Naval Commander Western Task Force, Annex 1, Naval Gunfire" (16 August 1944): 6.

9. There were at least two surveys of Omaha Beach made to determine the level of damage from naval gunfire and aerial bombardment. Both surveys were complicated by the fact that the bunkers were heavily damaged by destroyer and tank fire later in the morning, and it was difficult to distinguish between the preliminary bombardment and later combat action. Lt. (j.g.) Stuart Brandel, a naval gunfire liaison officer attached to the 16th Regimental Combat Team on D-Day, conducted a tour some days after the fighting. His report provides the most detailed photographic record of the German defenses on Omaha Beach, but there is no known written assessment surviving. His report can be found at the Robert McCormick Research Center at the 1st Division Museum at Cantigny, and some of his photos have been reproduced here. The U.S. Army Air Force's USSTAF sent a team headed by Col. C. P. Gilger to Normandy on 20 June 1944, and their 7 July 1944 report, "Survey of Effectiveness of Bombing of Invasion Coast defenses," deals more with the naval bombardment than the air attacks since there was so little evidence of bombing attacks except for Pointe-du-Hoc and Longues-sur-Mer. Neither report presents much evidence of extensive damage on Omaha Beach.

10. This chart was calculated using the data presented in the Appendix 2 chart, combined with projectile data from John Campbell, *Naval Weapons of World War II* (Annapolis, MD: Naval Institute, 1985).

11. *Provisional Engineer Special Brigade Group, Neptune Operation Report—Omaha Beach* (History Section, ETOUSA, 1944): 84.

12. Helmut Konrad von Keusgen, *Point d'appui WN62: Omaha Beach* (Bayeux: Heimdal, 2004): 88.

13. Keusgen, *Point d'appui WN62*: 95.

14. Gockel memoir, Rowe collection, MHI.

15. A partial telephone log of the *352.Infanterie-Division* is in Foreign Military Study B-388, and reprinted in Guenther Blumentritt, et al., *Fighting the Invasion: The German Army at D-Day*. Edited by David Isby. (London: Greenhill, 2000): 204–20.

16. "Survey of Effectiveness of Bombing of Invasion Coast Defenses" (USSTAF, July 1944). It's worth noting that the after-action report of the 743rd Tank Battalion does not mention this action.

17. An interview with Lieutenant Berthy can be found in Allied POW interviews (CSDIIS [UK] SIR 363, KP/4599[H].

18. *Die Geschichte der 352.Infanterie-Division* (Kameradschaft, n.d.): 26.

CHAPTER 10: D-DAY POSTMORTEM

1. *Die Geschichte der 352.Infanterie-Division*: 25.

2. See for example: "Summary of present situation of Batteries which might affect the NEPTUNE beaches on their approaches—31 May 1944" (National Archives [Kew], WO 205/172).

3. These were identified on Allied planning documents as No. 21 and 22, *Moulineaux* and *Moulineaux II*, corresponding to the *2./s.Art.Abt.989* and the *1./s.Art.Abt.989*.

4. The reasons for the relatively small number of engineer tanks on Omaha Beach was in part because of the recent production of the new dozer tanks, but also because of the shortage of LCT space. This issue is dealt with in more detail in Appendix C of Rich Anderson's book on engineer tanks, *Cracking Hitler's Atlantic Wall: The 1st Assault Brigade Royal Engineers on D-Day* (Mechanicsburg, PA: Stackpole, 2010).

5. The list of armored engineer equipment requested by the U.S. Army for Overlord on 16 February 1944, entitled "US Requirements for British Devices—Overlord," from Montgomery's 21st Army Group headquarters to the War Office, can be found at NARA in RG331, Entry 30C, SHAEF Records (G-3) Boxes 180–183, Decimal 470.8.

Bibliography

PUBLISHED ACCOUNTS of the German perspective of Omaha Beach are far less extensive than those from the American side. The best accounts are by Helmut Konrad von Keugsen. Over the years, he has conducted numerous tours of Omaha Beach with German veterans and has collected many accounts from the dwindling number of survivors. Most of his books are not available in English, though there are both German and French editions. Two of the veterans have written book-length memoirs—Franz Gockel, a young machine-gunner with *3./Grenadier-Regiment.726*; and Hein Severloh, Lieutenant Frerking's orderly from the *1./Artillerie-Regiment.352*. Gockel's account is available in German and French, while Severloh's account is also available in English.

The most extensive collection of German records in English consists of those prepared by captured German officers for the U.S. Army Center of Military History for their Foreign Military Studies (FMS) program. Some of the most relevant are listed below. These can be found at the U.S. National Archives and Records Administration II in College Park, Maryland, and the U.S. Army Military History Institute (MHI) at the Army Heritage and Education Center at Carlisle Barracks, Pennsylvania. David Isby's books contain excerpts from some of them, and digital versions can be found on the Internet at the Fold3 website.

As mentioned earlier, surviving records from the *352.Infanterie-Division* in early 1944 are scant. They are somewhat better for the *716.Infanterie-Division*, but tend to be more complete for late 1943 than early 1944. I used the microfilm records in Record Group 242 at NARA II. Fortunately, some of the higher levels of command have records relating to Omaha Beach, and I went through the chain of command including *84.Korps*, *7.Armee*, Army Group B, and OB-West. The *Kriegstagebuch* (War Diary) of *AOK.7* is especially useful, particularly the *Anlagen* (Appendices), while other collections, such as Army Group B, are largely missing. An extremely useful published collection of German documents dealing with D-Day was prepared by Hans Sakkers and is listed below. He also wrote an extremely detailed account of Rommel's tours of the Normandy Front prior to the invasion, which is also listed below.

Allied intelligence reports are also a valuable resource, with the obvious caveat that they are often incomplete and frequently misleading because of the spotty nature of intelligence collection. The Martian Reports provide an interesting insight into Allied knowledge of the Atlantic Wall but are rather thin on detail about Omaha Beach. They can be found at NARA II in Record Group 331, Entry 13. The G-2 sections of First U.S. Army, V Corps, 1st Division, and 29th Division all contain interesting material, including a handful of prisoner-of-war interrogations from German troops captured at Omaha Beach. They are in Record Group 407 at NARA II. The MHI has a great deal of material on D-Day. The Robert Rowe collection also is especially worth mentioning. Rowe, a retired Navy officer, planned to publish a book about D-Day—he conducted thousands of interviews and collected a vast trove of official reports and documents, but his book was never finished. Although thin on German material, this collection has a wealth of textual material on Omaha Beach.

I have not listed the many documents and books I used on the American perspective about Omaha Beach. That is not the focus of this book, and there are simply too many sources to fit here. Over the years, I have gone through most of the U.S. Army After-Action Reports for D-Day, including the V Corps, 1st Division, 29th Division, and the supporting tank and engineer battalions. These are available in Record Group 407 at NARA.

German-language accounts of Omaha Beach are fairly slim, but French historical accounts dealing with the *Wehrmacht* are far more ample. This is especially true for the Atlantic Wall, which the French regard as a part of their historical patrimony since so much of it still survives on French soil. Alain Chazette and his colleagues have produced numerous in-depth studies of the Atlantic Wall, many of which have very useful sections on the D-Day beaches. George Bernage and the Bayeux-based publisher Heimdal also have numerous publications dealing with D-Day, and they have been one of the prime promoters of von Keugsen's works outside Germany. The Paris-based publisher Armes & Collections has a number of WWII-oriented magazines that have published a great many articles on German forces in Normandy; some of these are listed in the Notes.

Since this book is heavily illustrated, a few words would be appropriate about photo sources. My main source has been the Still Photos Collection at NARA II in College Park, and I have gone through the various official collections of the U.S. Army Signal Corps, U.S. Navy, U.S. Coast Guard, and U.S. Army Air Force, as well as some of the smaller collections. Likewise, MHI at Carlisle Barracks has a variety of unique material, often in the personal collections. A few collections are especially worth mentioning. The Colonel Robert McCormick Research Center at the 1st Infantry Division Museum at Cantigny outside Chicago has a great deal of D-Day material, and a collection donated by Thomas Lane includes the photographs

of Omaha Beach taken by Lt. (j.g.) Stuart Brandel, who served as a navy gunfire liaison officer with the 16th Infantry Regiment on D-Day. Although there are hardly any photographs of Omaha Beach from the German side, the Library of Congress in Washington D.C. has a captured collection of photos commissioned by the *OKH Pionierstab* in Berlin. Their staff photographer, Cpl. W. Neuser, was sent to Normandy and Brittany in February 1944 to photograph the progress of Atlantic Wall construction work. While he did not photograph Omaha Beach, he did take extensive photos in other parts of the *716.Infanterie-Division* sector, mainly near the Orne River estuary (Sword Beach). Some of these are reproduced here.

I have found other German photos from the D-Day period in various locations. A young U.S. Army officer of Russian extraction, Lt. K. Solovieff, was serving with the U.S. 4th Infantry Division in World War II and was stationed in Berlin in May 1945. Since he spoke Russian, he was tasked by divisional G-2 to go into the Russian sector where a *Luftwaffe* photo archive was located. The USAAF was looking for photos of U.S. aircrews shot down over Germany to help determine their fates. While going through the photo files, he stumbled on a number of photos of German troops in Normandy in June 1944, which interested him since he had landed on Utah Beach on D-Day. He later donated them to the MHI, and some are reproduced here.

Many of the contemporary photos here are from my own collection, from my various visits to Omaha Beach since the 1980s. I have also expanded the coverage by preparing maps and computer illustrations to help cover gaps in the photo coverage or to better explain some technical details, such as bunker construction and layout. The maps are based on both German and Allied records. German maps can be found in the RG 242 microfilm records group at NARA II. There is also a small collection of original German paper maps captured by the 26th Infantry, 1st Division, in 1944 in the Map collection on the 4th Floor at NARA II. I also have collected a sizeable collection of Allied maps of Omaha Beach over the years from many sources in NARA II, MHI, and elsewhere.

UNPUBLISHED GOVERNMENT REPORTS

Amphibious Operations: Invasion of Northern France-Western Task Force June 1944 (U.S. Fleet, HQ of CinC, Cominch P-006)

Comparison of British and American Areas in Normandy in terms of Fire Support and its Effects ([British] Army Operational Research Group Report 292, 1945)

The German Defences in the Courselles-St. Aubin Area of the Normandy Coast, Report No. 41 (Historical Section [GS], Canadian Army Headquarters, 20 July 1951)

German Permanent Fortifications (U.S. War Department Intelligence Division, 1945)

German Seacoast Defenses-European Theater (7 volumes, Seacoast Artillery Evaluation Board, U.S. Forces, ETO, 1945)

History of the V Corps (G-3 Historical Sub-Section, V Corps: 1946)

Liberation Campaign: Northwest Europe 1944–45, Overlord, D-Day 6 June 1944, Book 3: The American Beaches Omaha and Utah (British War Office: 1945)

Operation Report Neptune: Omaha Beach Provisional Special Brigade Group (History Section, ETOUSA: 1944)

Report on German Concrete Fortifications (Chief Engineer, HQ, U.S. Army-ETO, 1944)

Royce Thompson, *Report on Invasion Casualties* (CMH: 27 May 1948)

GERMAN MICROFILM UNIT RECORDS AT NARA II (RG242)

OB-West T311, Rolls 1–5

Heeresgruppe B, T312, Rolls 276–278

7.Armee (AOK.7), T313, Rolls 1552–1571

84.Korps (LXXXIV.AK), T314, Rolls 1603–1604

352.Infanterie-Division, T315, Roll 1566, 2148

716.Infanterie-Division, T315, Rolls 1566, 2260–2261

U.S. ARMY FOREIGN MILITARY STUDIES SERIES

Blumentritt, Gunther, Gen. der Inf. *Evaluation of German Command and Troops: OB-West*. B-283.

Criegern, Friedrich von, Lt. Gen. *LXXXIV Corps (Jan–17 Jun 1944)*. B-784.

Dosch, Xaver. *Organization Todt: Operations in the West*. B-671.

Gersdorff, Gen. Maj. von. *A Critique of the Defense against the Invasion*. A-895.

Goettke, Ernst, Gen. Lt. *Preparations for the Defense of the Coast*. B-663.

Krancke, Adm. *Defensive Measures Against Invasion taken by Naval and Army Group HQ-West*. B-169.

Pemsel, Max, Lt. Gen. *Construction of the Atlantic Wall Part III: The preparations in the Invasion Area 'til the end of January 1944* . B-668.

Pemsel, Max, Lt. Gen. *Report of the Chief of Staff, Seventh Army, June 1942–6 June 1944*. Foreign Military Studies B-234.

Pickert, Wolfgang, Gen. der Flak. *III Flak Corps: Orders for the Initial Commitment in Normandy*. B-597.

Richter, Wilhelm, Lt. Gen.*The Battle of the 716th Infantry Division in Normandy, 6 June to 23 June 1944*. B-621.

Schmester, Rudolf, Gen. Lt. *Construction of the Atlantic Wall Part IV: The Effect of Bombs and Heavy Naval Guns on the Fortified Defense System of the Atlantic Wall*. B-669.

Schramm, Percy, Maj. *OB-West War Diary*. B-034.

Speidel, Hans, Gen. Lt. *Ideas and Views of Genfldm Rommel on Defense and Operations in the West in 1944*. B-720.

Schweppenburg , Leo Freiherr Geyr von, Gen. der PzTr. *Panzer Group West (Mid 1943–5 July 1944)*. B-466.

Triepel, Gen. Maj. *Coastal Artillery Sector 1-Contentin from 6 June until 18 June 1944*. B-260.

Weissmann, Eugene, Gen. *Flak in Coastal and Air Defense: the Atlantic Wall*. D-179.

Ziegelmann, Fritz, Lt. Col. *The 352nd Infantry Division (5 Dec 1943–6 June 1944)*. B-432.

Ziegelmann, Fritz, Lt. Col. *352nd Infantry Division (6 June 1944)*. B-388.

Ziegelmann, Fritz, Lt. Col. *Special Questions for 352.Infanterie-Division Chief-of-Staff Fritz Ziegelmann*. B-021.

Zimmermann, Bodo, Lt. Gen. *OB-West: Atlantic Wall to Siegfried Line, Chapter 2: Preparation of Coastal Defenses Against Invasion*. B-308.

BOOKS

Ambrose, Stephen. *D-Day, June 6, 1944: The Climactic Battle of World War II.* New York: Simon & Schuster, 1994.

Anderson, Richard. *Cracking Hitler's Atlantic Wall: The 1st Assault Brigade Royal Engineers on D-Day.* Mechanicsburg, PA: Stackpole Books, 2010.

Balkoski, Joseph. *Beyond the Beachhead: The 29th Infantry Division in Normandy.* Harrisburg, PA: Stackpole Books, 1989.

———. *Omaha Beach: D-Day, June 6, 1944.* Mechanicsburg, PA: Stackpole Books, 2004.

Barbier, Mary. *D-Day Deception: Operation Fortitude and the Normandy Invasion.* Westport, CT: Praeger Security International, 2007.

Baumgartner, Lt. John, et al. *The 16th Infantry Regiment 1861–1946.* Du Quoin, IL: Cricket Press, 1999.

Berger, Sid. *Breaching Fortress Europe.* Society of American Military Engineers, 1994.

Bernage, Georges. *Omaha Beach.* Bayeux: Heimdal, 2002.

———. *Gold, Juno, Sword.* Bayeux: Heimdal, 2003.

Bernage, Georges, and Dominique Francois. *Utah Beach: Sainte-Mère-Église.* Bayeux: Heimdal, 2004.

Blumentritt, Guenther, et al. *Fighting the Invasion: The German Army at D-Day.* Edited by David Isby. London: Greenhill, 2000.

Boog, Hirst, et al. *Germany and the Second World War, Vol. VII: The Strategic Air War in Europe and the War in the West and East Asia 1943–1944/45.* Translated by Derry Cook-Radmore. Oxford: Clarendon Press, 2006.

Carell, Paul. *Invasion!: They're Coming!.* Bantam Book, 1964.

Chazette, Alain. *Artillerie Côtière: Atlantikwall et Südwall en France.* Vertou, France: Fortifications & Patrimonie, 1999.

———. *Le Mur de l'Atlantique en Normandie.* Bayeux: Heimdal, 2000.

———. *Atlantic Wall-Südwall.* Paris: Histoire et Fortifications, 2004.

———. *Les Batteries Côtières en France Vol. 1: Les batteries lourdes de Marine.* Paris: Histoire et Fortifications, 2004.

———. *Tobrouks Typologie: Atlantic Wall-Südwall.* Paris: Histoire et Fortifications, 2011.

———. *Mur de l'Atlantique: Les batteries de côte en Normandie.* Paris: Histoire et Fortifications, 2007.

———, et al. *Atlantikwall Südwall Spécial Typologie: Le canon de 5cm KwK et ses casemates et Les Tobruk pour tourelles de char, canons, mitrailleuses, mortiers, lance-flammes.* Paris: Histoire & Fortifications, 2012.

David, Patrick. *La fortresse impossible: Réflexions sur les constructions et les aménagements consécutifs à l'occupation allemande puis à ceux de la libération dans le Bessin de 1940 à 1945.* Maison du Guetteur, 2004.

Desquesnes, Rémy. *Le Mur de l'Atlantique: Normandie 1944.* Cully, France: OREP Editions, 2008.

———. *Omaha: La Pointe du Hoc-Colleville.* Cully, France: OREP Editions, 2008.

———. *Le Mur de l'Atlantique: Les Batteries d'Artillerie.* Rennes: Éditions Ouest-France, 2012.

Ewing, Joseph. *29 Let's Go!: A History of the 29th Division in World War II.* Nashville: Battery Press, 1979.

Gawne, Jonathan. *Spearheading D-Day: American Special Units of the Normandy Invasion.* Paris: Histoire & Collections, 1998.

Gockel, Franz. *La Porte de L'Enfer: Omaha Beach 6 Juin 1944.* Strasbourg: Éditions Hirlé, 2004.

Harrison, Gordon. *Cross-Channel Attack.* Washington, D.C.: U.S. Army CMH, 1951.

Haswell, Jock. *D-Day: Intelligence and Deception.* New York: Times Books, 1979.

Holt, Thaddeus. *The Deceivers: Allied Military Deception in the Second World War.* New York: Scribner, 2004.

Howard, Michael. *Strategic Deception in the Second World War.* London: HMSO, 1990.

Kaufmann, J.E., and H.W. Kaufmann. *Fortress Third Reich: German Fortifications and Defense Systems in World War II.* Cambridge, MA: Da Capo, 2003.

Keusgen, Helmut Konrad von. 2004. *Point d'appui WN62: Omaha Beach.* Bayeux: Heimdal.

———. *Pointe du Hoc: Énigme autour d'un point d'appui allemand.* Bayeux: Heimdal, 2006.

———. *Omaha Beach: La tragédie du 6 juin 1944.* Bayeux: Heimdal, 2007.

Kilvert-Jones, Tim. *Omaha Beach: V Corps Battle for the Beachhead* . Barnsley, South Yorkshire: Leo Cooper, 1999.

Kirkland Jr., William. *Destroyers at Normandy: Naval Gunfire Support at Omaha Beach*. Washington, D.C.: Naval Historical Foundation, 1994.

Knickerbocker, H.R., et al. *Danger Forward: The Story of the First Division in World War II*. Nashville: Battery Press, 2002.

Lewis, Adrian. *Omaha Beach: A Flawed Victory*. Chapel Hill: University of North Carolina Press, 2001.

Levine, Joshua. *Operation Fortitude: The Story of the Spies and the Spy Operation That Saved D-Day*. Guilford, CT: Lyons Press, 2011.

Lippmann, Harry. *Die Regelbauten des Heeres im Atlantic Wall*. Cologne: DAWA, 1986.

———. *Heeres-Regelbauten: Bildband*. Cologne: DAWA, 1995.

———. *Die 5cm Kwk in Atlantikwall*. Cologne: DAWA, 2003.

Milano, Vince, and Bruce Conner. *Normandiefront: D-Day to Saint-Lô through German Eyes*. Stroud, Gloucestershire: Spellmount, 2012.

Morison, Samuel E. *The Invasion of France and Germany 1944–1945*. Boston: Little, Brown and Company, 1957.

Perrault, Gilles. *The Secret of D-Day: Where and When?* Translated by Len Ortzen. Boston: Little, Brown, 1965.

Prieur, Jérôme. *Le Mur de l'Atlantique: Monument de la Collaboration*. Paris: Denoël, 2010.

Ramsey, Winston. *D-Day Then and Now, Volume 2*. Essex: After the Battle, 1995.

Reardon, Mark, ed. *Defending Fortress Europe: The War Diary of the German 7th Army in Normandy 6 June to 26 July 1944*. Bedford, PA: Aberjona Press, 2012.

Reuth, Ralf George. *Rommel: The End of a Legend*. Translated by Debra S. Marmor and Herbert A. Danner. London: Haus Books, 2005.

Rose, Yannick. *L'Artillerie Côtière de l'Est Cotentin HKAR 1261*. Alençon: A.C.R.E.Di.C, 1994.

Ruffin, Raymond. *La Résistance normande face à la Gestapo*. Paris: Presses de la Cité, 1977.

———. *La Résistance dans l'Opération Overlord*. Paris: France-Empire, 2004.

Ruge, Friedrich. *Rommel in Normandy: Reminiscences*. San Rafael, CA: Presidio Press, 1979.

Sakkers, Hans. *Generalfeldmarschall Rommel: Opperbevelhebber van Heeresgruppe B bij de voorbereiding van de verdediging van West-Europa, 5 november 1943 tot 6 juni 1944*. Brouwer, 1993.

Sakkers, Hans. *Normandie 6.Juni 1944 im Spiegel der deutschen Kriegstagebücher*. Osnabrück: Biblio Verlag, 1998.

Saunders, Anthony. *Hitler's Atlantic Wall*. London: Sutton, 2001.

Severloh, Hein. *WN62: A German Soldier's Memories of the Defence of Omaha Beach, Normandy, June 6, 1944*. Garbsen, Germany: HEK Creativ Verlag, 2011.

Speidel, Hans. *Invasion 1944: A First-hand Account of Rommel's Normandy Campaign*. Washington, D.C.: Regnery, 1950.

Stillwell, Paul, ed. *Assault on Normandy: First-Person Accounts from the Sea Services*. Annapolis, MD: Naval Institute Press, 1994.

Vernier, Franck. *Le premier "Mur de l'Atlantique" 1914–1918: Les batteries allemandes au littoral Belge*. Verviers, Belgium: Éditions du Patrimonie Militaire, 2012.

Wegmüller, Hans. *Die Abwehr der Invasion: Die Konzeption des Oberbefehlshabers West 1940–1944*. Freiburg, Germany: Rombach Verlag, 1986.

Whitlock, Flint. *The Fighting First: The Untold Story of the Big Red One on D-Day*. Boulder, CO: Westview Press, 2004.

Wilt, Alan. *The Atlantic Wall*. New York: Enigma, 2004.

Wood, James, ed. *Army of the West: The Weekly Reports of the German Army Group B from Normandy to the West Wall*. Mechanicsburg, PA: Stackpole Books, 2007.

Yung, Christopher. *Gators of Neptune: Naval Amphibious Planning for the Normandy Invasion*. Annapolis, MD: Naval Institute, 2006.

Zaloga, Steven. *D-Day 1944 (1): Omaha Beach*. Campaign, 100. Oxford: Osprey, 2003.

———. *D-Day Fortifications in Normandy*. Fortress, 37. Oxford: Osprey, 2005.

———. *The Atlantic Wall (1): France*. Fortress, 63. Oxford: Osprey, 2007.

————. *Rangers Lead the Way: Pointe-du-Hoc D-Day, 1944*. Raid, 1. Oxford: Osprey, 2009.

————. *US Amphibious Tanks of World War II*. New Vanguard, 192. Oxford: Osprey, 2012.

Zetterling, Niklas. *Normandy 1944: German Military Organization, Combat Power and Organizational Effectiveness*. Winnipeg, Manitoba: Fedorowicz, 2000.

N.a. *Die Geschichte der 352.Infanterie-Division*. Kameradschaft, n.d.

N.a. *Omaha Beachhead (6 June-13 June 1944)*. American Forces in Action. Washington, D.C.: U.S. War Department, Historical Division, 1945.

Index

Afrika Korps, 37, 38
   surrender, 41
amtrac amphibious tractors, 183
Anderson, Richard, 12
AORG study, 229
   Omaha Beach casualties analysis, 12–17
   quality and number of defending troops, 242–43
   strength of beach defenses, 236
   strength of beach obstacles, 233
   use of tanks, 240–41
Artillerie-Regiment.352, 87, 181–83, 203–4
Artillerie-Regiment.1716, 86
artillery
   28/32 sWG 41 rocket launchers, 93
   50mm pedestal mounted tank guns, 79–81
   75mm FK 235(b) field guns, 81
   ammunition holdings, 77–78
   basic, 75–78
   biggest mystery concerning, 203–4
   field, 86–92
   increase of, on Omaha Beach, 96
   lack of standardization of, 77
   rocket launchers, 93–94
   static arsenal, 76–77
   statistics concerning, 73–74
Atlantic Wall, 19, 21
   completion, 30
   construction of, 23–24
   fortifications, 35
   major planning meeting for, 23
   mine deployment pattern on, 107
   See also batteries; bunkers; Devil's Garden;
     Tobruks

batteries
   Longues-sur-Mer, 177–78, 187
   Pointe-du-Hoc, 170–77, 187, 224–26
   See also bunkers
Bingham, Sidney, 212

Block, Paul, 186
Bongard, Heinz, 191
British Army Operation Research Group study.
   See AORG study
Bryant, C. F., 187
bunkers
   gun emplacement, 130, 132
   ringstand, 132
   See also batteries; Tobruks

Coast Defense Sectors, 26
Colleville-sur-Mer, strongpoint, 147–55
   attack on, 193–94
   on D-Day, 205–11
   penetration of, 203
Collins, J. Lawton, 183
Corlett, Charles, 183
Cota, Norman, 203
Couliboeuf, Marcel, 163

D-Day, 185–86
   assault, 190–98
   casualties, 227
   defenses start to crumble on, 203–4
   end of, 227
   first attacks near Omaha Beach on, 187
   first hours of fighting on, 199–200
   initial fighting on, 193
   Landing Craft, Infantry (LCI), landing, 201–2
   naval bombardment, 188–89
   Strongpoint Colleville-sur-Mer on, 205–11
   Strongpoint Pointe-du-Hoc on, 224–26
   Strongpoint St. Laurent-sur-Mer on, 212–16
   Strongpoint Vierville-sur-Mer on, 217–23
   view of landings on, 186–87
De Cointet, Leon, 113
Devil's Garden, 101–23, 102
   anti-craft stakes, 110
   anti-glider program, 115

antitank obstacles, 115
  Belgian Gates, 113
  Czech hedgehogs, 114
  flamethrowers, 121
  flooding program, 115
  Goliath remote-control demolition vehicles, 121
  landmines, 107–8
  mines, 104–6
  ramps, 113
  Rommel's "Asparagus," 109–20
  tetrahedrons, 114
  unit responsible for erecting, 123
Dieppe raid, 23
Directive No. 51, 31, 42
Dog Red Beach, 203
Dollmann, Friedrich, 33

Festung Pioneer Stab.11, 123
5th Ranger Battalion, 203, 217
1st Infantry Division, 5. *See also individual regiments*
Flak-Regiment.32, 95
French Resistance, 159–65, 180
  in Lower Normandy, 162–65
  use of homing pigeons, 160–61
Fritz, Paul, 214

Gap Assault Teams, casualties, 8, 191–93
Garcia, Robert, 212
Geddes, Sergeant, 194
Giskes, H. J., 165
Gockel, Franz, 193
Gold Beach, 204
  topography of, 125
Götsch, Hermann, 193
Grenadier-Regiment.726, 66, 68, 212, 214, 225–26
Grenadier-Regiment.914, 66, 68, 226
Grenadier-Regiment.915, 206
  bicycle infantry of, 204
  counterattack, 205
Grenadier-Regiment.916, 66, 68, 85, 212–14, 226

Hamel-au-Pretré, 129
Heinze, Hans, 129, 187
Hitler, Adolf
  Atlantic Wall fortification program, 21
  Directive No. 51, 31, 42
  missile launch sites plan, 35
  Westwall fortification program, 21–22

intelligence, Allied
  British Special Operations Executive (SOE), 159
  failure to identify transfer of German troops,
    179–80
  French Resistance, 159–65
  HUMINT (human), 158
  Martian Reports, 166–69

Operation Columba, 161
  photographic, 158
  on Pointe-du-Hoc battery, 170–77
  ramifications of failure of, 181–83
  SIGINT (signal), 158
  Ultra secret, 157–58
  use of pigeons, 157–61
intelligence, German, 32–35
  aerial reconnaissance program, 32–33
  military, 159
  Secret Field Police (GFP), 159
  shortcomings of, 33–35
  state police, 159
  types of, 32
Iron Coast, 24, 43
Italy, Axis withdrawal, 53–54

Juno Beach, topography of, 125

Kampfgruppe Meyer, 70, 186
Kraiss, Dietrich, 62
Kriegsmarine, 19, 24
Kyoungjong, Yang, 60

Landesbau-Pioneer-Bataillon.17, 68
Landing Craft, Infantry (LCI), 201–2
Le Guay, strongpoint, 133
Lemière, Desiré, 163
Longues-sur-Mer battery, 177–78
  attacks on, 187
Loustaunau-Lacau, Georges, 162–65
Luftwaffe
  aerial reconnaissance program, 32–33
  Flak-Regiment.32, 95

Marshall, George C., 183
Martian Reports, 166–69
Mercader, Guillaume, 163
Meyer, Karl, 65
mines, 104–6
  floating wooden, 105
  improvised, 108
  KMA, 104
  land, 107–8
  Nutcracker, 105
  pole, 105

National Pigeon Service, 160

Omaha Beach
  amphibious assault on, 190
  arsenals, 75–78
  buildings on, 129
  casualties, ix, 2, 12–17, 96, 191–93, 229, 244–45
  Coastal Defense Sector H, 66
  D-Day fighting on, 2

D-Day landings on, 4–9
defense of, 66
defenses start to crumble on, 203–4
destroyers approaching, 202
draws, 128
firepower on, 14–15
first attacks near, 187
first hours of fighting on, 199–200
first waves of infantry on, 191
garrison, 68–70
increase in artillery firepower on, 96
initial fighting on, 193
initial garrisons at, 56–60
Landing Craft, Infantry (LCI), landing on, 201–2
naval bombardment on, 188–89
obstacles, 101–23
records of German actions at, 2–3
Rommel's tactics factor in debacle on, 245
Strongpoint Colleville-sur-Mer, 147–55, 193–94,
    203, 205–11
Strongpoint Le Guay, 133
Strongpoint St. Laurent-sur-Mer, 142–46, 189,
    205–6, 212–16
Strongpoint Vierville-sur-Mer, 133–41, 217–23
terrain, 128–31
352.Infanterie-Division arsenals, 85
topography of, 125
troop density on, 16
visual record of, ix
weight of naval fire on strongpoints at, 189
116th Infantry Regiment, 5, 217
    casualties, 8
    Company A casualties, 191
    Company C, 203
    Company E, 212
    Company F, 203
    Company G, 203
121st Engineer Combat Battalion, 220
Operation Doublecross, 32
Operation Fortitude, 32, 33
Operation Neptune, 170
Organisation Todt, 23
*Ost-Bataillon*s
    Asian volunteers from Turkmenistan in, 60
    personnel recruited Soviet army prisoners of war, 58

panzer divisions, 47
    deployment of, 49
Pas-de-Calais, 24
    defenses denser on, 50
    Iron Coast, 43
pigeons, 157–61
    homing, 160–61
Pioneer-Bataillon.352, 214
Plage d'Or. *See* Omaha Beach
Pluskat, Werner, 51, 87, 182, 186

Pointe-du-Hoc battery, 170–77
    attacks on, 187
    on D-Day, 224–26
    Ranger raid on, 174–77
prisoners of war, Russian, 58

Reagan, Ronald, 174
Regimental Combat Teams, landing the first, 8–9
Roger, Jean, 162–63
Rommel, Erwin, 35, 37–44
    actions shaped defenses at Omaha Beach, ix
    Afrika Korps, 37, 38, 41
    and Allied invasion locations, 50–51
    appointed to lead Army Group B in Italy, 41–42
    "Asparagus," 109–20
    Atlantic Wall tours, 43, 43
    British admiration for, 37
    in command of *7.Panzer-Division*, 38
    demands for mines, 107
    elevated to rank of field marshal, 38
    experience with Devil's Garden in North Africa,
        101
    learning about new Allied amphibious landing
        tactics, 42
    on location for Allied landing, 63–64
    with Mercedes staff car, 47
    Normandy coast tour, 1
    outstanding leadership in France, 38
    personal association with Hitler, 38
    plan to place firepower on beaches, 48
    string of defeats, 40
    success in halting British drive in North Africa, 38
    on tactical doctrine, 45
    tactics of desperation, 45–49
    tactics factor in debacle on Omaha Beach, 245
    transfer to northern France, 42–44
    transfer to *352.Infanterie-Division*, 51
Ruge, Friedrich, on Rommel's obsessive demands for
    mines, 107
Rundstedt, Gerd von, 30, 48, 49
    central problem faced by, 32–35
    main mission of, 31

St. Laurent-sur-Mer, strongpoint, 142–46
    on D-Day, 212–16
    naval gunfire on, 189
    resistance, 205–6
Salmuth, Hans von, 48
    on state of Atlantic Wall, 44
Saving Private Ryan film, 2, 191
Schmetzer, Rudolf, 34
Schnelle-Brigade.30, 70, 206
Schweppenburg, Geyr von, 23, 49
seawalls, 125–27
2nd Ranger Battalion, Company C, 203
Selbach, Hans, 193

716.Infanterie-Division, 56–60
    ammunition holdings, 77–78
    field artillery batteries of, 89
    Omaha Beach arsenals, 75–78
    supply of rocket launchers, 93
    Volksdeutsch personnel, 58
741st Tank Battalion, 5
743rd Tank Battalion, 5
Severloh, Hein, 205
16th Infantry Regiment, 5
    2nd Battalion, 191
    3rd Battalion, 191
    casualties, 8
    Company F, 212
    Company L, 203
Soviet volunteer units, 43
Spalding, John, 203
Streczyk, Philip, 203
Strojny, Frank, 194
Sword Beach, topography of, 125

tactical doctrine, German, 45, 46–49
    advent of *panzer* forces, 47
Taylor, George, 203
323.Infanterie-Division, 56
352.Infanterie-Division, 61–65, 214, 225
    arsenals, 85
    field artillery batteries, 86–88
    Kampfgruppe Meyer, 70, 186
    move to Normandy, 181–83
    rated at Combat Value One, 62
    retaining in France, 64
    transfer to Normandy coast, 179–80
    troops on Omaha Beach on D-Day, 70

Tobruks, 28, 132
29th Infantry Division, 5. *See also individual regiments*
299th Engineer Combat Battalion, LCM landings, 193

U.S. National Guard monument, 238
USS *McCook*, 202, 217
USS *Texas*, 217, 220
USS *Thompson*, 212, 226
Utah Beach, 204
    topography of, 127

Vierville-sur-Mer, strongpoint, 133–41
    on D-Day, 217–23
    defense nests, 133–40
    draw, 223
Volksdeutsch, 58

Wade, W. L., 201
weapons. *See* artillery
Wehrmacht
    blitzkrieg tactic, 46
    categorizing divisions on sliding scale, 56
    deployed in three major formations in France, 26–27
    impression of, 53
    personnel problems within the, 53
    primary method of communication, 158
    reinforcement of anti-invasion front, 48
    See also individual battalions, brigades, divisions, and regiments
Werfer-Regiment.84, 224, 225
Westwall, 21–22
Williams, E. T., 180
Witte, Günter, 157